Counselling
Christian Women

on how to deal with domestic violence

Dr Lynne M. Baker

www.
AUSTRALIANACADEMIC**PRESS**
.com.au

First published in 2010
Australian Academic Press
32 Jeays Street
Bowen Hills Qld 4006
Australia
www.australianacademicpress.com.au

Reproduction and communication for educational purposes:

Reproduction and communication for other purposes:

National Library of Australia cataloguing-in-publication entry:

Author:	Baker, Lynne M.
Title:	Counselling Christian women on how to deal with domestic violence / Lynne M. Baker.
ISBN:	9781921513503 (pbk.)
Notes:	Includes bibliographical references.
Subjects:	Abused wives--Counseling of.
	Church work with abused women.
	Marital violence.
	Spousal abuse.
	Wife abuse.
Dewey No:	362.829286

Contents

Preface

This publication is an outcome of an investigation into the experiences, and in particular the coping strategies, of Christian women who identify themselves as victims of domestic abuse. In this setting, Christian women are viewed as a unique group who, while remaining part of society as a whole, are not only confronted with what might be considered the usual issues surrounding domestic abuse but also faced with the potential complication of these issues as a result of their belief system. Each chapter progressively builds an image of the difficulties confronting Christian women who are victims of domestic abuse, and provides an accurate coverage of their stories in relation to both secular and religious experiences. Excerpts from the interview transcripts are utilised throughout to highlight the significance of particular issues in the lives of the women.

Domestic abuse is identified as a multifaceted issue that has the potential to permeate every aspect of the life of the victim as well as the members of her family. Not only has domestic abuse permeated secular society, it is also found within the Christian church, where it presents substantial difficulty for women who desire to practise their faith but find conflict between the teachings of their church and the need to protect themselves and their children, physically and/or emotionally, from the damaging effects of domestic abuse. This book identifies power and control as key elements of domestic abuse, particularly when set within a patriarchal societal structure that fosters the subjugation of women.

Each of the 20 women who chose to share their stories has been allocated a pseudonym, and is introduced according to her age, profession, denomination, current family, the length of her marriage and her current marital status. The women come from diverse back-grounds, both professional and religious, vary in age from 26 to 70 years, and report a variety of experiences within their respective denominations (chapter 2).

The experiences of the women include the forms of abuse they suffered and some of the obstacles with which they were forced to deal, sometimes on a daily basis. Forms of abuse experienced include physical, verbal, emotional, sexual, social, financial, spiritual, property and child abuse. The ongoing nature of domestic abuse, combined with the effect of the cycle of violence, often results in extreme con-fusion for the victim, who frequently endeavours to pacify the perpetrator and maintain a harmonious balance within the house-hold. The image of perpetrators presented by the women highlights the issues of power, domination and control, together with the intimi-dating and manipulative means by which perpetrators choose to maintain their power base (chapters 3 and 4).

The key theological issues pertaining to Christian women who are victims of domestic abuse are presented in a sequence of three chapters that focus individually on the Scriptural principles of for-giveness (chapter 5), marriage as a sacred union (chapter 6), and female submission to male headship (chapter 7). The foundational principles of specific Scriptures are discussed with regard to issues of context, setting and culture, with particular consideration being given to their operation and relevance in the light of domestic abuse situa-tions. Such Scriptures, if misused, have the potential to create extreme difficulty for Christian women who are victims of domestic abuse. It has been indicated, however, that the scriptural principles in question in no way support domestic abuse in any form, nor do they condemn a victim who chooses to remove herself from an abusive relationship.

The specific coping strategies employed by Christian women who are victims of domestic abuse are expounded. A variety of strate-gies emerged, both religious and nonreligious, in addition to a blend of both problem-focused and emotion-focused approaches. Their Christian faith proved to be extremely important, and also effective, in the lives of the women represented. The choice of religious coping strategies included maintaining a relationship with God, praying, and drawing encouragement from Scripture and from scriptural song. Nonreligious strategies included focusing on the children, turning to activities, reading as a source of learning and encouragement, and planning a specific course of action (chapter 8).

As a final gesture, the women offer advice, based upon their own experiences, to both victims of domestic abuse and to members of the clergy who desire to support and encourage those women seeking their assistance. Victims of domestic abuse are advised to maintain their faith in God, not to accept abuse, and to constantly seek assistance, because domestic abuse is not their fault. Separation (and subsequent divorce) is presented as a viable option, with the choice of action remaining with the individual woman. Members of the clergy are advised by the women to listen attentively and believe the victim, while demonstrating unconditional love and respect and refraining from judgment. Additionally, they are encouraged to ensure that they become informed on matters of domestic abuse, avoid issues that can potentially inflame the situation (such as theological understandings of female submission to male headship), and exhibit a willingness to confront the perpetrator regarding his behaviour. Ultimately, it is recommended that the church as a whole, adopt a proactive approach to domestic abuse. This includes denouncing injustice, developing relevant policies, and networking with churches and professional organisations within the greater community (chapter 9).

This publication highlights the ongoing need for the Christian church as whole to remain relevant to current society by continuing to offer practical and meaningful assistance to those in need. While this particular book relates specifically to the requirements of Christian women and their experiences of domestic abuse, the universal maxim of listening to the voice of experience can be aptly applied.

How to Use This Book

It is important for counsellors to have some knowledge of the benefits, but also some of the difficulties, that can arise for those who belong to a religious community. This book aims to assist counsellors, and other interested parties, to develop an understanding of the situation in which Christian women find themselves when they are faced with domestic abuse. Such insight has potential benefits in:

- increasing client understanding of domestic abuse and how it has been manifested in her life
- addressing possible feelings of guilt and/or condemnation
- supporting the decision-making process regarding whether to remain in a relationship or choose to leave
- fostering emotional release for the client and thus the freedom to move forward.

Throughout this book, the words of individual women have been frequently used in an effort to clearly illustrate their plight; increase the reality of the material presented; and also increase the reader's connection with the thoughts, feelings and experiences of those women who have lived in a domestic abuse situation. Counsellors may use the book as a whole, or draw on specific chapters as the need arises. Likewise, individuals may choose to read the book for themselves or perhaps focus on key sections as part of the counselling process.

Chapters 2 to 9 each conclude with a set of questions for reflection or discussion. Some thoughts are directed solely to the counsellor, but the majority of questions are designed to help the client explore and gradually work through some of the issues that have been raised throughout each chapter. The questions provided serve as a guide for the counsellor and client working together, and may be extended or omitted depending on their suitability or relevance to each particular case. It is important to note that the issues arising from some chapters, and the associated questions or reflections, may take some time to work through, according to the needs of each client. Sessions should be paced accordingly. Questions may also prove useful in a small group setting should a few women choose to discuss their situations together, with the counsellor acting in the role of facilitator.

Abbreviations

DVPC   Domestic Violence Prevention Centre
DVRC   Domestic Violence Resource Centre
JCDVPP   Joint Churches Domestic Violence Prevention Program

Books of the Bible

(in alphabetical order)

Chronicles	Kings
Colossians	Leviticus
Corinthians	Luke
Deuteronomy	Malachi
Ephesians	Mark
Exodus	Matthew
Ezekiel	Numbers
Galatians	Peter
Genesis	Philippians
Habakkuk	Proverbs
Hebrews	Psalms
Isaiah	Romans
James	Ruth
Jeremiah	Samuel
John	Song of Songs (Solomon)
Joshua	Timothy

All Scripture quotations contained within this book are from the King James Version of the Bible, unless otherwise stated. The above list includes only those books of the Bible referred to in this publication.

Set Me Free

by *Anna*

'Where did I go wrong?
It has to be ME,
I've been told so often,
You're selfish, insensitive, can't you see!
Look at yourself, why can't you change?
You need treatment with the 'psych' again!'

Lord of all love, hear my plea
Hold me firm, set me free.

Children exclaim 'Why did you stay?
You married the man and
We had to pay!
All that anger, abuse and pain
Regular Church attendance
What did it gain?'

Lord of all love, hear my plea
Hold me firm, set me free.

'Why are you late, who did you see?
Where have you been and didn't tell me?
It's only polite, do you hear, I'm the *MAN*
To tell all your movements to ... understand?'

Lord of all love, hear my plea
Hold me firm, set me free.

Dinner for friends, such a happy night,
     Front door closed, another fight,
'Don't embarrass me!' I'm told,
     The evening's warmth goes dangerously cold.

Lord of all love, hear my plea
Hold me firm, set me free.

'How can I please him? Make him a cake?
     He likes the fruit ones, it will maybe *placate*',
Walking on eggshells is a daily routine,
     Keeping the pretence up, his anger's *not* seen.

Lord of all love, hear my plea
Hold me firm, set me free.

'Dad's hurting Mum!' was the urgent cry
     on the phone to the clergy —
But he just passed it by
     With 'Are you alright?' and never came,
Never responded to the child's pain.

Lord of all love, hear my plea
Hold me firm, set me free.

With no cracked bones, but a broken heart,
     Years of pretence have pulled me apart …
         Into someone *UNREAL*, 'Who am I?' I cry
'Who would believe me, what if I die?'

Lord of all love, hear my plea
Hold me firm, set me free.

The years of abuse have taken their toll,
    Thirty-nine years is a long time to roll
In waves of anxiety, grief and fear,
    And sadly the clergy did not want to hear.

Lord of all love, hear my plea
Hold me firm, set me free.

Into my path through God's love, a gift came,
    A new found friend shared my pain
Saw clearly the signals of my futile position
    Gave me the impetus to change my direction.

Lord of all love, hear my plea
Hold me firm, set me free.

After I left, hurt, rejection and grief
    Followed me daily, there was little relief
Till the message of *HOPE, LOVE, TRUST, and PRAYER*
    Lifted me in the arms of *THE ONE WHO CARES!*

Lord of all love
  you have heard my plea
  you have held me firm
and set me free!

CHAPTER 1

Behind the Scenes

> Speak up for those who cannot speak for themselves;
> Ensure justice for those who are perishing.
>
> (Proverbs 31:8)

These were the words that strengthened Dietrich Bonhoeffer, a German theologian who eventually became a martyr as he fought the tyranny of the Nazi regime that threatened the well-being of the Christian church in Germany during World War II (Baker, 1998; Cairns, 1996; Kalland, L.A., 1992; McGrath, 1995). While the Christian church may be considered alive and well today, another form of tyranny still remains. It is domestic abuse. Behind closed doors and often silenced (Abrahams, 2007; Cooper & Vetere, 2005; Hague & Marlos, 2005), the victim quails before the perpetrator, powerless, voiceless and often without recourse. 'Speak up for those who cannot speak for themselves; Ensure justice for those who are perishing.' Surely this is a mandate for all those who seek to abolish this form of tyranny.

This chapter presents an initial overview of the subject of domestic abuse, its pervasive and destructive nature, and its prevalence within both secular and church communities. It further highlights the vast impact of domestic abuse on a significant proportion of community resources — including government, police, and legal, education and health systems — and supports the need for a strong and unified stand against all forms of domestic abuse.

This chapter introduces the issues of power and control, and includes a brief outline of the different forms of abuse that are often used by the perpetrator to control and manipulate the victim. (These issues are addressed more fully in chapters 3 and 4.) This section also indicates the manner in which domestic abuse has the potential to affect all members of the household, physically, psychologically and emotionally, regardless of whether or not the abuse is actually witnessed first hand.

The Origin of this Book

This book has evolved as a result of the author's increased awareness of the pervading presence of domestic abuse — not only in the community but also in families that call themselves Christian and are often actively involved in their faith. The plight of women who have become victims of domestic abuse is significant, to say the least. However, the situation for Christian women is considerably more complex, often as a direct result of their faith. This book highlights the experiences of Christian women who identify as victims of domestic abuse, and also the manner in which they have dealt with the difficulties confronting them. It further explores the significance of their faith as a part of the coping process.

Behavioural Attributes of the Christian

Christians are expected to be identified by their behaviour. This is clearly stated in the Book of Matthew (7:16–19), which uses the illustration of a fruit tree, saying that 'every good tree bringeth forth good fruit; but a corrupt tree bringeth forth evil fruit' (Vs. 17). This is paralleled to a later comment in Matthew (12:35) that explains, 'A good man out of the good treasure of his heart bringeth forth good things: and an evil man out of the evil treasure bringeth forth evil things'. These Scriptures are, in effect, adopting the position that a Christian can be identified by his or her behaviour; and although one may be able to imitate such behaviour for a time, the true nature of the individual will ultimately become evident (Carson, 1984; Earle, 1964).

Terminology

For the purpose of this book, I have chosen to use the term *domestic abuse* to describe any and all aspects of domestic abuse in relation to the women represented. While I am aware that *domestic violence* is perhaps the more widely used term, my choice was made initially in relation to the invitation for women to share their stories. This decision was made in an effort to encourage the participation of individuals who had experienced any form of abuse, and to not exclude those who had not specifically experienced physical violence. The choice was further solidified as the women involved indicated their lack of comfort with the term domestic violence, because even those who had experienced a single incident of physical violence did not necessarily classify themselves as having experienced domestic violence. Hence, from this point, I will use the term domestic abuse to include all forms of what might otherwise be referred to as domestic violence.

To be a victim of abuse is terrifying, but to be made a constant target of abuse over a lengthy period of time by a member of your own household is debilitating. Yllo (1999) puts it best when she says:

> When you are raped by a stranger, you live with a frightening memory, but when you are raped by your husband, you live with your rapist. (p. 1060)

Domestic abuse can take many forms. It is not restricted to physical violence, but includes verbal, psychological, emotional, sexual, social, financial, spiritual and property abuse (Hague & Marlos, 2005; VicHealth, 2004). While all forms of abuse might not be contained within the one relationship, it is common to experience clusters of behaviour that work together to assist the perpetrator to maintain power and control over the victim (Abrahams, 2007).

Nature of Domestic Abuse

Domestic abuse is a multifaceted issue, its outworking persistently permeating almost every part of society. The influences of what has been referred to as a *hidden crime* are indeed far reaching, initially affecting the individual lives of family members but ultimately extending to the community as a whole (Commonwealth of Australia, 2004; Queensland Police Service, 2008a, 2008b). The lifestyle of the family may be described as intolerable, or even as a war zone, as members are never really aware of what forms of abuse are likely to occur on a daily basis; for even when physical abuse is absent, psychological and emotional abuse are surely present as fear of an incident looms heavily on the horizon (Bagshaw & Chung, 2000). The cycle of violence continues, with victims not only suffering greatly but also endeavouring to make sense of seemingly senseless and volatile outbursts of anger, intermingled with somewhat unstable and tense periods of calm (Walker, 1979). The situation may be likened to living on the edge of a volcano. While the volcano may lie dormant for a time, it remains active and unpredictable, its destructive capabilities reinforced by intermittent rumblings that may appear in the form of an angry look, a quiet word, simple body language, or even silence (Barnett & LaViolette, 1993). These are hidden messages that pass a silent but definite warning from the perpetrator to the victim, yet often go unnoticed by outsiders.

While there are many factors contributing to domestic abuse, issues relating to power and control would appear to be a central feature (Dutton, 1995; Lemon, 1996; Miles 2000). The overwhelming need of the perpetrator to control the life, actions and even thoughts of the victim (Domestic Violence Prevention Centre [DVPC], 2008a; Tifft, 1993) is often a significant factor underlying a large amount of domestic abuse. According to Adams (1994), the choice to abuse is just that — a choice. It is a choice to control. This concept is reflected in the fact that the abusive person frequently restricts their negative behaviour to include only specific individuals (Tifft). Sometimes the need to control may be explained in terms of low self-esteem, insecure attachment, social learning or personal development (Baumeister, 1997; Browne, 1987; Dutton, 1995). Regardless of these issues, the perpetrator should never be excused, and must at all times be held accountable for actions taken and the subsequent consequences of those actions, as innocent lives are not only marred but even shattered and destroyed for decades.

The victims number approximately one in three women, with 90% of children in a household prone to domestic abuse being aware of the behaviour of the perpetrator even if they do not witness the abuse first hand (Adams, 1994; Amnesty International, 2005a, 2005b). The most unfortunate state of the situation is described in practical terms by Jaffe, Lemon, Sandler, and Wolfe (1996) when they suggest that 'a woman is more likely to be victimized in her own home by someone she knows and trusts than in a parking lot at the mall' (p. 11).

Often the victims are a long way from receiving any true assistance as shame, degradation and fear — not to mention the continuing intimidation, domination and control exerted by the perpetrator — confine them to a physical, psychological, emotional and often financial prison (Gregory, 2004; Kirkwood, 1995; Queensland Government, 2008a; Walker, 1979).

Despite any existing code of silence, the complexities of domestic abuse do not remain solely in the home but branch out into other areas. These include: education, with regard to behaviour and counselling issues, low self-esteem, and restricted academic and personal development (Blanchard, 1999; Mills, 2008); the workplace, where employers are forced to address issues of employability, absenteeism, loss of productivity, staff replacement, and even security considerations should the perpetrator endeavour to gain access to the offices (Berry, 1998; CEO Challenge, 2000a; 2000b); and the legal system, which is already significantly overtaxed in relation to police time and the resources available for the criminal court, the family court and legal aid (Scutt, 1990). Further inspection of the nature of domestic abuse indicates an ongoing effect on: government, including policy formation, legislation, welfare and financial input (Hopkins & McGregor, 1991; Queensland Government, 2008b); the health industry, in both the provision and cost of hospitalisation, medication and counselling; and the wider community, which incorporates a variety of welfare and support agencies (Abrahams, 2007; Education Queensland, 2000).

A report commissioned by VicHealth (2004) maintains that 'intimate partner violence is responsible for more ill-health and premature death in Victorian women under the age of 45 than any other of the well-known risk factors, including high blood pressure, obesity and smoking' (p. 8). In a brief summary provided by the former Australian prime minister during the time of his office,

Mr Howard stated succinctly that 'violence against women is unacceptable. It diminishes the lives of all those it affects and it tarnishes any community that tolerates it' (Commonwealth of Australia, 2004, p. 1).

Historical Perspective

Over the centuries, domestic abuse has existed in its many forms, particularly in societies that operate through a strong patriarchal system and consider women to be substantially inferior to men (Feder, 1999a; McCue, 2008; Wilson, 1997). Such an attitude is reflected in the words of John Knox, a Scottish reformer (Reid, 1992), when he stated: 'Woman in her greatest perfection was made to serve and obey man' (Grady, 2000, p. 18). An even less complimentary comment appears in the form of an ancient proverb by Confucius (551–479 BC), which states: 'One hundred women are not worth a single testicle' (Centre for Transformational Psychotherapy, 2005).

Gradual developments occurred during the 18th to 20th centuries, often as a result of actions taken by the feminist movement of the time, as individuals such as Mary Wollstonecraft and Frances Power Cobb agitated for equality between men and women. Positive results included: the provision for legal separation; financial support by the husband for his former wife and their children; and the introduction of refuges where women and their children could obtain food and experience some measure of safety (Murray, 2002; Wilson, 1997). Before the more public recognition of this overwhelming need — and the modifications undertaken to the existing legal system together with the introduction of the support described above — abused women often had no means of support and nowhere to find shelter, and were thus forced to remain with their abusers (Pizzey, 1974) or perhaps risk losing their children if the matter was reported to local welfare agencies. In short, even during the 1950s and 1960s, virtually no provision of housing, finance, employment or counselling was made by welfare agencies for women who were victims of domestic abuse (Hague & Wilson, 2000).

Since domestic abuse has been named, conceptualised and considered a legitimate issue of public policy, numerous individual and government research studies have been conducted. This has led to an increase in the number of organisations available to assist victims of abuse (Finn, 2000). Developments have addressed the concept of the cycle of violence, introduced by Walker during the 1970s (Walker, 1979), and provided insight into the relevance of the power and control issues surrounding domestic abuse, as represented in the 'power and control' wheel presented by the Domestic Abuse Intervention Project based in Duluth, Minnesota (Joint Churches Domestic Violence Prevention Project [JCDVPP], 2002). The power and control wheel highlights a number of strategies used by perpetrators of abuse in an effort to exert power and control over their female victims. Strategies listed include coercion, threats, intimidation and the use of male privilege. During the late 1980s and the 1990s, as concerns continued to be raised, the establishment of taskforces and committees at both state and national levels led to an increased focus on domestic abuse, particularly the issue of abuse against women as a gender group (Murray, 2002; Scutt, 1991). During 2004, government undertakings focused on issues surrounding health cost to victims of abuse (VicHealth, 2004) as well as a national awareness campaign aimed at increasing community awareness of not only the prevalence of domestic abuse within society but also the symptoms that can indicate the presence of abuse within an intimate relationship (Commonwealth of Australia, 2004). The issue of domestic violence continues to be brought to the attention of the general public through the use of television commercials and a variety of brochures and booklets explaining the concept of domestic abuse and highlighting the need for both victims and perpetrators to seek assistance (DVPC, 2008a; Queensland Government, 2008a, 2008c).

Regardless of the vast amount of research that has already been conducted, it is difficult to determine with any degree of accuracy (due to the lack of statistical evidence) the level and frequency of domestic violence incidents over past decades, such is the hidden nature of this form of criminal activity (Hague & Marlos, 2005; Queensland Domestic Violence Task Force, 1988). For many years society has considered marital difficulties to be a private issue, and something to be addressed solely by the couple concerned (Feder, 1999b; Lentz, 1999). Available surveys indicate that approximately

17% of the community at large continues to support this view, while 83% of individuals simply do not wish to become entangled in an intricate web of ongoing complications (Domestic Violence Resource Centre [DVRC], 1998a). Jaffe et al. (1996) further confirm the existence of such perceptions as they describe the plight of injured victims seeking medical assistance who are still too ashamed or afraid to speak openly of their experience:

> Long shrouded in a conspiracy of silence, family violence was the mystery no one talked about. Women badly beaten by their partners, turned up at hospitals and claimed to have fallen down stairs. (p. 10)

Statistics indicate domestic abuse to be an issue affecting 23% of Australian women who have ever been married or in a de facto relationship (Bagshaw & Chung, 2000; DVPC, 2008b; DVRC, 1998a; Mulroney, 2003). This abuse includes not only physical violence but also other actions such as verbal, psychological and emotional abuse that are designed to manipulate, dominate and control the victim (Adams, 1994; Dutton, 1995; DVRC, 1998b; Kirkwood, 1995; Lynch & Graham-Bermann, 2000). In addition to the abuse of the victim, the children of the families involved often suffer psychological and emotional trauma as a result of witnessing or hearing the conflict, even if they are not the direct targets of physical abuse (Cooper & Vetere, 2005; Education Queensland, 2000; Hershorn & Rosenbaum, 1985; Rosenbaum & O'Leary, 1981). Such trauma includes behavioural problems (Jaffe, Wolfe, Wilson, & Zak, 1986; Miller & Knudsen, 2007), anxiety and low self-esteem (Hughes, 1988; Hughes & Barad, 1983), anger (Jenkins, 2000; Mills, 2008), depression (Forsstrom-Cohen & Rosenbaum, 1985), long-term symptoms associated with posttraumatic stress, and impaired social functioning (Feerick & Haugaard, 1999; McCue, 2008).

Domestic Abuse and the Christian Church

It is further recognised that domestic abuse is present within Christian church communities (Buxton, 2000; Leehan, 1992; Miles, 1997, 2000, 2002; Nason-Clark, 1997; Nolan, 1994; Victorian Council of Churches' Commission, 1992). While the nature and depth of domestic abuse can often remain hidden, an Australian study of Anglican, Uniting and Catholic church communities within the Brisbane area revealed that '22% of the perpetrators attended church regularly and a further 14% were involved in church leadership' (JCDVPP, 2002, p. 24). This indicates that a total of 36% of perpetrators were seemingly active within their particular denomination. Further to these figures is the consideration that, while the abovementioned denominations are of considerable size and significance within the community, a number of other denominations (such as Presbyterian, Baptist and some fundamentalist churches) were not included in the study. Similar research relating to the remaining denominations would no doubt provide a fuller picture of the prevalence of domestic abuse within Christian communities, and the subsequent need for continual awareness on the part of both clergy and parishioners. Both Buxton (2000) and Miles (2000) discovered during the course of their work a certain unwillingness among some members of the clergy to either acknowledge or address the presence of domestic abuse within their congregations. Further, members of the clergy can exhibit a reluctance to refer victims of abuse to professionals or other agencies outside the church, fearing the advice or assistance provided may be in conflict with Christian values (Nason-Clark, 1997; Wortmann, 2003). While these factors do not necessarily apply to every clergy person within every denomination, they are worthy of consideration because they have the potential to affect the quality of support made available to individuals experiencing domestic abuse-related difficulties who seek assistance from local churches.

Theological, doctrinal and personal differences across denominations and within churches are considerable, to say the very least. It is therefore necessary to consider the plurality that exists within the Christian church as a whole. There exists a great diversity within the Christian church, and this applies to the beliefs themselves and also to the manner in which those beliefs are held and practised in the lives of individuals who consider themselves members of a particular faith. In many cases, the understanding of Scriptural concepts differs between denominations ranging from the liberal to the conservative, and from the traditional to the fundamentalist positions. Even within denominations, variances occur between churches and also between members of the clergy regarding the interpretation of particular Scriptures.

While not all Christian churches adopt an identical position on given issues, and there remains significant diversity in both the beliefs and also the degree to which those beliefs are held, and indeed practiced, the beliefs of some Christian churches can effectively inhibit total escape, safety or sanctuary for the victim, thus presenting as a distinct disadvantage for women professing and seeking to uphold a Christian faith when faced with domestic abuse. For example, some beliefs regarding forgiveness (Tracy, 1999), the sanctity of marriage, and female submission can be presented in a manner that acts as a stumbling block for Christian women who have become victims of domestic abuse. Depending on the way certain beliefs are interpreted or expressed by an individual member of the clergy or church body, Christian women may feel torn between the need to escape to physical and/or emotional safety and the desire to uphold the values associated with their religious faith (Miles, 2000, 2002). Issues surrounding these three topics will be discussed more fully in chapters 5 to 7.

While still bearing in mind the differing practices within the various denominations of the Christian church, this book considers the coping strategies of Christian women from a number of those denominations, specifically in relation to domestic abuse and the associated issues with which each woman has been forcibly confronted.

Summary

Domestic abuse is a prevalent condition in society, and its far-reaching impact can easily destroy the lives of those who find themselves in its path. The ongoing battle against the criminal nature of violence and the tyranny of abuse requires the committed assistance of a vast number of community and government resources. Such assistance is also required from the Christian church, which is not immune from the presence and effects of repetitive violence and abuse within the walls, and behind the closed doors, of the homes of a number of its members.

Power, control and coercion are all key words in relation to domestic abuse. These words are central to the concept of domestic abuse, regardless of which form/s of abuse may be employed. Even in the absence of physical abuse, other forms of abuse (such as psychological or emotional abuse) can easily be used by the perpetrator to manipulate any or all members of the household, resulting in a tense and perhaps fearful state of domination.

Numerous theories attempt to provide a framework for understanding the dynamics of domestic abuse, and while each has valuable aspects to contribute to the overall description and analysis of domestic abuse, no single theory can stand alone. Each theory tends to differ with regard to the root cause of domestic abuse, and offers explanations centred around psychology, background, circumstance or gender. However, a common denominator between a number of theories appears to be the need for the perpetrator of abuse to maintain power and control.

CHAPTER 2

People Like Us

Throughout this chapter it is my intention to provide an overall summary of the 20 women represented in this volume, and then to introduce each individual by providing the reader with initial background information pertinent to each woman's situation. The following information has been compiled from introductory questionnaires and interview transcripts. Each person has been allocated a pseudonym for the purpose of confidentiality; the use of a name is necessary to maintain continuity within the storytelling process and to foster increased familiarity with the individual voices as they are used to communicate their stories throughout this volume.

Summary of Profiles

The women whose stories have been included in this publication were required to be Christian women — whether married, separated or divorced — who had experienced domestic abuse during their marriages. Those who decided to participate wanted to be heard. They expressed a clear desire to share their stories in a safe setting where they felt respected and accepted. Hannah commented that I was the only person who had expressed any interest in hearing about her situation; others did not want to listen to her. Thus the reality and truth of the experiences of the women were rarely heard or acknowledged, thereby leaving them in a state of exclusion and isolation. Atkinson (2002) maintains that sharing one's own story allows the individual 'to be heard, recognised and acknowledged by others' (p. 125). Such acknowledgment has the potential to serve as a powerful means of validation for those whose stories, and therefore lives, have been treated as insignificant and seemingly relegated to the back shelf of a darkened closet.

It was also important for the women to know that their stories would be used to help others. They came from a variety of denominational backgrounds, including Roman Catholic, Anglican, Uniting, Baptist, Salvation Army, Pentecostal, Seventh Day Adventist, and the Church of Jesus Christ of Latter-day Saints. In some cases, individuals had changed denominations as a result of the abuse, in an effort to find spiritual support; and in three of the cases presented, the women had chosen to no longer attend denominational services because they had lost hope in the ability of the church to meet their needs.

Individual Profiles

Abigail

Abigail is 35 years old and a member of the Worldwide Church of God. While she was raised in this denomination and attended services on a weekly basis, Abigail felt she was unable to attend services during the time of the abuse. Abigail describes the abuse as physical, verbal and emotional, and reports without hesitation that it commenced on her wedding night. Some time after the abuse started, she chose to tell members of her family and also her mother-in-law. While reporting at least partial support from her own family, Abigail recalls very little practical assistance being forthcoming. Abigail explains the devastating effect the abuse had on her, as she speaks of feeling suicidal on a number of occasions. After she left the marriage for a short time three years ago, her husband agreed to attend counselling sessions organised through a domestic violence men's group associated with Centacare. This proved successful, and Abigail openly acknowledges the change that has occurred in her husband's behaviour. She and her husband have two children, and have now been married for 11 years.

Anna

Anna, a former schoolteacher, is now aged 70. For many years she attended the Methodist church and then the Uniting church with her lay preacher husband. During her marriage of 38 years, she raised three children in a very abusive environment. Anna tells of extreme verbal, emotional and psychological abuse as well as physical abuse commencing during the first year of her marriage and continuing throughout her marital life. She also speaks of feeling rejected and completely deserted by her friends, and her church, during the four years of separation from her husband. Anna has not yet filed for divorce, but does not discount the possibility of doing so in the future. Anna did not attending formal denominational services for 15 months. During this time, Anna chose to connect with God through meditation and devotion at a favourite place by the river. Eventually, Anna found sanctuary in the support and care provided by clergy and members of the Catholic church, which she now attends on a regular basis.

Deborah

Deborah, one of 12 children and a member of the Church of Jesus Christ of Latter-day Saints, was raised in a loving and supportive family environment. Thus she had no frame of reference for the more covert forms of domestic abuse that, she now realises, commenced shortly after her honeymoon. She was therefore unable to positively identify her husband's behaviour as abusive. Deborah speaks of extreme financial abuse coupled with calculated emotional and verbal abuse, in addition to one incident of significant physical abuse. Deborah trained as a nurse's aide, but has worked only occasionally (on a casual basis) throughout the last five years of her marriage. Her husband, a professing Christian and a school principal holding a masters degree, fortified his position of power by totally controlling the financial resources of the household, thereby causing Deborah to have to ask for even the smallest and most personal of items. Deborah has been married for 23 years and, at this point, chooses to remain so, although she does admit to having considered separation and perhaps divorce from her husband. Deborah retains her faith in God, attends regular services and enjoys teaching a daily class of religion for 14–17 year olds.

Elizabeth

Elizabeth is a 56-year-old woman, and the mother of three adult children. She was initially trained in secretarial work but, during the course of her 20-year marriage, attended Bible College, trained for the ministry and was an active member of the leadership team at her local church. Elizabeth suffered severe physical abuse at the hands of her husband, who was also in training for the ministry and was later ordained as a minister. Elizabeth and her family attended a Christian

Outreach Centre church. Although very little assistance was provided through the church at the time of the abuse, Elizabeth still chooses to regularly attend the same denomination, although in a significantly different geographical area. Upon reflection, Elizabeth notes that the abuse commenced before she and her husband were married, but she did not recognise it as such. Eleven years ago, Elizabeth's husband left her for another woman and eventually filed for divorce. Elizabeth speaks of the lengthy nature of the healing process in her life, and also refers to both the lack of understanding and the continued judgment she feels is present within the church in relation to domestic abuse and subsequent divorce.

Esther

Esther, aged 42 and the mother of two, worked as a police officer for a number of years. She was married for six years and suffered frequent verbal, emotional and sexual abuse, which she reports commenced on her honeymoon. Ultimately, Esther experienced a nervous breakdown before finally leaving and subsequently divorcing her abusive husband 12 years ago. Esther's situation was further complicated by the fact that her husband was both a professing Christian and the son of a minister. Esther explains that members of the clergy 'wanted to believe me, but didn't know how to believe that this could be happening' when the perpetrator was the son of a minister. As a result, Esther received very little assistance from the local Baptist church she was attending at the time. Eventually, Esther ceased attending denominational services, but she has gradually increased her attendance again over a period of approximately six years. She now attends Assemblies of God services on a regular basis.

Eunice

Eunice is 61 years old, and was initially employed in an office while raising her three daughters. She completed a diploma of teaching in 1983 and went on to follow a career in education, where she continues to work. Eunice speaks of physical, sexual and emotional abuse, and also indicates that her three daughters were witnesses to the ongoing abuse. However, the final decision to leave the marriage of 17 years came when the extreme anger of her alcoholic husband was physically directed at her 12-year-old daughter. Although Eunice left the marriage in 1979, she never attempted to file for divorce. Eunice explains, 'I had all the papers. I was going to get a divorce ... That was when he said, "If you get a divorce, I'll kill you."' Eunice took this threat very seriously and therefore chose to remain separated from, but legally married to, her husband. Eventually, Eunice's husband passed away as a result of his alcoholism. In relation to this event, Eunice further explains, 'I can remember thinking, the day I knew he was dead. I thought, "My goodness. I'm a free woman."' Eunice was raised in the Catholic church and, although she moved to another parish as a result of her family situation, she continues to practise her faith and attend services on a regular basis.

Eve

Eve married at the age of 18 and remained in the marriage for 20 years. Now 47 years old, she speaks of feeling trapped. She refers to the marriage as 'the biggest mistake of my life', explaining that she married only to please her parents. Eve experienced ongoing sexual abuse throughout her marriage, in addition to verbal, emotional and financial abuse. Upon reflection, Eve identifies the abuse as commencing even before she married her husband. Initially, Eve worked as an assistant nurse, but eventually became a stay-at-home mum raising her four children. Eve sought counsel through the minister and those in leadership within her local Assemblies of God church. She describes the counsel provided as extremely negative, and says she received no support from the leadership. Such was the impact of the negative response that Eve, a woman with a strict religious upbringing who attended church most of her life, no longer attends any denominational services. Eve further states: 'I just could never ever get involved ... in church life again'. She has been out of that marital relationship for nine years. Now divorced and remarried, Eve reports her current marriage of six years to be most satisfactory.

Hannah

Hannah is 43 years old. Married at the age of 16, she has now been married for 27 years. She has chosen to remain married to her husband, and explains that there has at least been some improvement in his behaviour over the years. Hannah has three children, who at times witnessed the physical, emotional and verbal abuse she suffered.

After 17 years of marriage, Hannah sought assistance from Lifeline and moved into a refuge with her 9-year-old daughter. After a separation of approximately six weeks, during which Hannah's husband sought counselling through Relationships Australia, Hannah and her husband reunited. Initially, Hannah was raised in the Catholic denomination but, from her late teens, she and her family attended a Pentecostal church, and her children attended a school administered by the church. Hannah no longer attends any denominational services.

Joanna

Joanna grew up in the Anglican church, and attended both Sunday services and midweek meetings at her local Assemblies of God church during the time of her marriage. She is a hairdresser, and has four children ranging in age from 3 to 9 years. Joanna speaks of physical, verbal, sexual and emotional abuse, in addition to living in an environment of constant threat and intimidation during her 11-year marriage. Joanna's husband attended Bible College, and held the position of an elder in the church he and Joanna attended. However, Joanna had 'caught him with pornography' and also knew that he was in some way involved with another woman. Joanna believes the abuse was always present in some form in her relationship with her husband, but she did not always recognise it as such. She has now been separated for seven months and expects to eventually file for divorce. Unfortunately, Joanna was judged quite severely for her decision to separate from her husband. As a result, she is no longer permitted to continue her role in the music ministry of the church. Joanna uses the words 'I'm the baddie' to describe the manner in which she feels she is looked upon by both pastoral staff and congregational members, simply because she left a violent and abusive marriage.

Leah

Leah, a library assistant, grew up in the Baptist church before moving to a Pentecostal church at the age of 22, where she remained throughout her 12-year marriage. Leah speaks of her experiences of abuse — physical, emotional and sexual — and the destruction of some of her personal possessions. In hindsight, Leah is very aware of the presence of emotional abuse in her relationship with her husband prior to their marriage, and recalls physical abuse commencing after approximately 11 months of marriage. Leah explains how she sought ongoing assistance from church leaders, only to be told she should be reading Cleo magazine and treating her husband as the head of the home. After 12 years of searching for answers through counselling and marriage guidance seminars, Leah decided to terminate the relationship and subsequently divorced her husband. After raising her three boys alone for almost five years, Leah now aged 44, is remarried and says she is very happy in her new relationship. She no longer attends denominational services.

Lois

Lois, aged 41, has two children from her first marriage and two from her second marriage. She was married for the second time at the age of 32, and remained married for a period of four years during which time she suffered as a result of the physical, sexual, emotional and financial abuse perpetrated by her husband, who was active in the Salvation Army church. Lois had previously attended the Christian Life church, but moved to the Salvation Army as a result of her marriage. She now attends fortnightly, but chose to withdraw from church involvement for a time as she 'felt disheartened and unsupported'. Lois identifies the abuse as commencing prior to her marriage when, in addition to other issues, her then fiancé exhibited a total disregard for her wishes for abstinence from sexual intimacy before marriage. Suffering from severe depression, Lois sought assistance through counselling outside the denominational structure of the church, and thereby developed an understanding of the issues surrounding domestic abuse. After four years of separation, Lois now feels comfortable in applying for a divorce and no longer views it as a betrayal of her husband or her marriage vows.

Lydia

Lydia is the daughter of a minister. She has acquired university level training, including a bachelor of ministry and an associate diploma as an anaesthetic technician, and is currently employed on a permanent basis at a local city hospital. Lydia was raised in a Christian home as a member of the Baptist denomination but, as a result of her marriage, moved to the Anglican church. She has remained part of the

Anglican church and is now able to regularly attend denominational services in addition to midweek house meetings. Lydia's freedom to attend services was limited during the time of her marriage. She states very precisely that she was married for a period of two years and ten months, and clearly explains that the abuse commenced within the first two weeks of her marriage. Together with financial and social abuse, the verbal and emotional abuse escalated over time and 'culminated in a couple of ... rather nasty physical events'. Lydia tells how her husband struck her with a barbecue skewer and 'pushed me up against the wall and actually held me up by my neck against the wall ... tried to choke me a bit and then threw me into a couple of bookcases'. Now aged 30, she is divorced and has no children from her marriage.

Mary

Mary is a 63-year-old Catholic woman who was raised in a strict Catholic home and attended a traditional Catholic school, where she was instructed by nuns. She was married for 37 years before her homosexual husband divorced her. She has been separated for a period of four years and has three grown children. Before her marriage, Mary had worked in a clerical position. Once married, however, she devoted her time to her children, all of whom were born during the first four years of her marriage. In 1973, Mary was rejected by her husband of 12 years when he chose to announce his homosexual preferences. Although Mary and her husband remained married and even slept in the same bed for a further 25 years, there was no longer any form of intimacy between them. Mary suffered physical, emotional and social abuse, all of which she explains commenced around the time of her husband's shock announcement. Mary remains committed to her faith and attends local church meetings two or three times each week.

Miriam

Miriam, aged 52 and a member of the nursing profession, raised two boys in the midst of a domestic abuse situation. Miriam tells of her experience of systematically yet secretly planning an escape strategy for herself and her children, knowing she would only have one chance for her actions to be effective. She shares how her two sons were not only witnesses to the abuse but also direct victims of it at the hands of her husband. Miriam speaks of a number of forms of abuse, including sexual, verbal and emotional, in addition to property damage. Of particular significance is the fact that her perpetrator husband would calculate his physical attacks using his knowledge of her incapacity as a result of back surgery. Miriam was married for 15 years, and reports that the abuse commenced only four months into the marriage and continued during her pregnancy. Miriam was raised in the Catholic denomination and continued to raise her boys accordingly, even after their flight to freedom and also during a transition period as they settled into their new routines. Miriam reports that, while she had always attended denominational services on a regular basis, she found herself relying more heavily on her faith as a result of the abusive situation in which she found herself. Now divorced, she explains that according to her faith she is entitled to, and has indeed considered, an annulment of her marriage. During the interview, Miriam made a specific point of informing me that she had revealed to me only a very small portion of what had actually happened to her during her marriage.

Naomi

Naomi is a laboratory technician who remained in an abusive marriage for 28 years before separating from her husband almost four years ago. She is now divorced. Naomi was raised in the Seventh Day Adventist faith, and continued to regularly attend meetings throughout her marriage. However, during the final year before the separation, Naomi reports that her husband no longer permitted her to attend services. Naomi is 52 years old, and openly expresses the fear she felt of her husband and his abusive behaviour. Sexual abuse was common in the relationship. One evening when Naomi's husband began burning her belongings and threatening to kill both Naomi and her animals, Naomi hastily seized her phone, her dog and a few personal items, and 'took off ... down the road'. As a result of the separation, Naomi explains that technically she now has less income but, from a practical viewpoint, she also has total control over all available finances.

Rachel

Rachel, aged 46, was raised in an Anglican church but later moved to a strongly patriarchal Baptist church, which she attended throughout her marriage. Rachel raised two sons in the midst of ongoing physical, sexual, emotional and financial abuse. Her older son walked out of the family home and lived on the street when he was only 16, rather than continue to suffer physical abuse from his father. Rachel says:

> We lost track of him for quite a few years. My oldest was nearly 21 before we found him. My youngest and I tracked him for — probably two years, a year and a half it took us to find him, but we did.

Rachel explains that the abuse commenced during the second year of her marriage, initially as verbal abuse but later escalating into severe physical and sexual violence. Like many victims of domestic abuse, she lived in constant fear throughout her 13-year marriage. After leaving her husband eight years ago, Rachel was able to work more frequently as a teacher's aide, but later attended university and now works in the field of human services related to domestic violence. She has changed denominations and now attends a Uniting church that has functional programs in place to assist victims of domestic abuse, providing aid and community support as required.

Rebekah

Rebekah, aged 26, has been married for six years and is the mother of three girls. She became a Christian and joined a Pentecostal denomination a year before her marriage. This event led Rebekah to separate (for six months) from her de facto partner of five years until they could formalise their union through marriage. Rebekah reports that physical, verbal and emotional abuse were all present in the relationship prior to and during the marriage, although she expected significant change to occur as a result of the joint commitment to the Christian faith made by her partner and herself. Rebekah experienced frequent geographical relocation, which made obtaining counselling and any other forms of assistance somewhat difficult. Rebekah says, 'I think moving around so much is what prolonged ever getting help'. To separate herself and her children from her husband and his abusive behaviour, Rebekah would occasionally stay with friends or in a refuge. She finally left the marriage six months ago, but has a view to possible restoration if her husband is willing to receive help and demonstrates an ongoing commitment to change over a substantial period of time. Thus Rebekah does not consider divorce to be an option at this point in time.

Ruth

Ruth is a qualified nurse who has undertaken a substantial amount of professional training, both during her marriage and after her separation. Her university level training includes a bachelor degree, a graduate diploma and a masters degree. Ruth is 56 years old, and was raised as a Seventh Day Adventist. She enjoyed attending her denominational services until her husband forbade her to attend any longer, insisting that she and their five children attend a Pacific Island church that was more in keeping with his culture. During her 20-year marriage, Ruth suffered many forms of abuse — physical, sexual and emotional. A great deal of the abuse commenced within the first year of her marriage. Ruth left the marriage 10 years ago, after she discovered her daughter had been sexually abused several years earlier by her husband's cousin. At the time of the discovery, Ruth's husband 'disowned the child and almost said it was the child's fault that it happened'. Ruth sought assistance from a counsellor, and is now divorced. She has changed denominations and now attends weekly services at a Catholic church.

Sarah

Sarah is a 40-year-old schoolteacher who was raised in the Catholic denomination. She attends services on a monthly basis, and is the single mother of a 2-year-old girl. Sarah's marriage lasted for 23 months, the final five months of which were particularly abusive. Sarah describes the change in her husband's behaviour, and the escalation of abuse from verbal to physical, as 'dramatic' and occurring over the very short timeframe of 'a couple of days'. Only three-and-a-half months after the birth of her daughter, Sarah was geographically relocated from Queensland to Tasmania. As Sarah knew nobody in Tasmania, this move successfully removed all access to any support network available to her. Sarah reports that the abuse commenced approximately 10 weeks after the relocation. She immediately sought assistance from an agency, but received very little satisfaction. Sarah's most effective assistance came through her parish priest, a family friend still based in Queensland. He provided care and understanding, and supported her decision to escape from her situation and move back to the mainland, where she could receive ongoing support and encouragement from family and friends. Sarah is now divorced.

Susanna

Susanna, aged 50, is a mother of five who has been separated from her husband of 28 years for the last four months. She is not yet divorced, but plans to file for divorce once the legally prescribed 12-month period of separation has elapsed. Susanna worked as a secretary before she was married, and later as a childcare worker for seven years. She has recently completed the first year of a human services degree at a local university. Susanna suffered constant rejection from her husband, in addition to a great deal of verbal and emotional abuse. She speaks openly of the extremely stressful conditions under which she lived throughout her marriage. Susanna continues to regularly attend the Church of Jesus Christ of Latter-day Saints, where she found the clergy and congregational members to be quite supportive during her struggles with both domestic abuse and a lengthy period of ill-health as a result of cancer. Although Susanna has been separated from her husband for only four months, she reports experiencing a definite feeling of liberation in her newfound freedom.

Summary

This chapter has provided the reader with a basic guide to the background and some of the life experiences of the women who responded to the invitation to share their stories, thereby laying the foundation for the effective utilisation of the different voices depicted within subsequent chapters. Each of the women presents a story that is in many ways unique to herself, yet many of the stories also have a great deal in common apart from the more obvious themes of domestic abuse and eventual survival. Elements of strength and courage, frustration and confusion, disappointment and determination are all evident in their stories, in most cases intermingled with a continuing religious faith even in the face of great adversity. Each woman speaks of difficulties and challenges, and the dilemma of not knowing what course of action to follow in situations that seem almost entirely beyond her control. The material presented in this chapter aims to provide support for subsequent chapters by providing a foundational context in which each individual voice may be firmly established.

Reflections for the Counsellor

1. Think about the idea of a perpetrator as a professing Christian, perhaps the son of a minister, an elder in a church or a minister in training.
   - What is your immediate reaction to this? How do you feel? How does this sit with you?
   - What are your thoughts in relation to this issue?

2. A victim often does not realise the gravity of a domestic abuse situation or is unable to identify it clearly.
   - How do you see this as being possible?
   - What is your experience?

Client Discussion

1. What do these stories have in common? What do you see?
   - Create a diagram.

2. How would you write your story? Describe your experience.

3. Where are you on your journey?
   - How are you feeling now?
   - How did you feel?
   - How would you like to feel?

4. Which stories stand out most in your mind?
   - Which stories are you most able to relate to? Why?

5. Take time to consider one of the women described in this chapter.
   - What positive qualities do you see in this person?
   - What positive qualities do you see in yourself?

CHAPTER 3

An Unrelenting Cycle

This chapter presents the experiences of the Christian women who offered to share their stories. It defines the concept of victimisation in relation to domestic abuse, and identifies the varying forms of domestic abuse reported by the women. These include physical, verbal, emotional, sexual, social, financial, spiritual, property and child abuse.

This chapter further endeavours to convey the serious nature of the impact that domestic abuse can have on the lives of Christian women from a variety of socioeconomic backgrounds. It outlines the cycle of violence and the contribution that the cycle makes to keeping women in abusive relationships. The chapter then considers two specific issues that can arise from the presence of domestic abuse and the cycle of violence: learned helplessness and learned hopefulness.

Finally, it presents some of the effects of living with ongoing domestic abuse that were specifically reported by the women involved. These include changes in personality, depression, stress-related conditions and physical illness, and the desire to commit suicide.

Victimisation

To be a victim of domestic abuse is to experience, and often to continue to experience, incidents of domestic abuse. Walker (1979) clearly defines a battered woman as 'a woman who is repeatedly subjected to any forceful physical or psychological behavior by a man in order to coerce her to do something he wants her to do without any concern for her rights' (p. xvi). Similarly, Douglas (1987) defines a battered woman as 'any woman who has been the victim of physical, sexual, and/or psychological abuse by her partner' (p. 39).

A victim of domestic abuse is not always easily identifiable and may appear to be an average person in the community. The women whose stories are included in this book come from a wide variety of backgrounds, education and training; they include nurses, teachers and clerical assistants, in addition to store and factory workers. Victims of abuse are not restricted to any specific social or cultural group. Domestic abuse takes many forms and has significantly permeated a great deal of society, occurring in upper, middle and lower socioeconomic sectors, and exhibiting no regard for levels of education, social position, ethnicity or religious standing (Basham & Lisherness, 1997; Department of Communities, 2005a; Dienemann et al., 2000; Ezell, 1998; Miles, 1999; Nelson, 1997; Walker, 1979). Although victims can be physically battered, it is clear from the above definitions that this is not always the case. In many cases, victims can experience a variety of forms of abuse, including verbal, psychological, social and financial abuse (Abrahams, 2007; Kirkwood, 1995; NiCarthy, 1986), and yet continue to function externally without displaying any obvious signs of their victimisation.

Frequently, the incidents of abuse remain hidden within the relationship, sometimes as a result of shame (Education Queensland, 2000; Gregory, 2004; Lynch & Graham-Bermann, 2000), fear (Martin, 1976), or confusion — or even as a result of the woman thinking that perhaps she was guilty of provoking the situation (Bagshaw & Chung, 2000; Browne & Herbert, 1997; King, 1998; Queensland Government, 2008a; Walker, 1994). Additionally, victims of abuse frequently minimise the serious nature of the event in an effort to cope (Kelly, 1988). However, many times silence prevails as a result of the question in the heart of the victim about the response she will receive should she choose to divulge the truth surrounding the difficulties she is facing in her home (Miles, 2000). The concern uppermost in the mind of the victim is often related to whether or not she will be believed (Borkowski, Murch & Walker, 1983; Miles, 1999; Ulrich, 1998).

Becoming a victim of domestic abuse is not planned or expected, and does not always take place quickly or in an obvious fashion. Rather, it progresses gradually over a period of time, with emotional, verbal and psychological abuse paving the way for more aggressive and violent forms of abuse (Hague & Marlos, 2005; Lempert, 1996). The individual is slowly and carefully undermined step by step. Thus, women who have not been accustomed to violent surroundings in their family of origin are far less likely to identify some behaviour as abusive as 'they have no frame of reference' (Barnett & LaViolette, 1993, p. 20). This was indeed the case for 13 of the 20 women interviewed. Anna initially describes the verbal abuse as commencing within the first year of her marriage, but upon reflection states:

> I suppose I was feeling something even before I married him, because I'd had a few operations when I was young. And he wouldn't let me even talk about it when he came to the hospital. And it was the same when I had the babies. I had extremely difficult births and that ... weren't allowed to talk about it. So I sensed something sort of then. I should have been awake up really then. Because I started to feel ... I had to watch my behaviour.

Even after suffering physical, verbal, emotional, sexual, social and financial forms of abuse, Rachel clearly indicates her difficulty in coming to terms with the concept of domestic violence in her marriage of 13 years:

> At the beginning, and even when I had ... when I finally rang the domestic violence telephone service to actually get out, I still didn't have in my mind that it was domestic violence.

Mary explains quite succinctly:

> Well, see, I think I was very naïve. I didn't really know ... I led a very sheltered life. My mother and father were staunch Catholics in the old tradition. Like, I never knew anything. At 15, my mother was still picking suitable books for me to read.

Of the 20 women interviewed, 19 described the abuse as commencing quite early in their marriages. Eight considered the abuse to have commenced before their marriages took place, while a further seven described changes occurring at the start of the marriage. In effect, the marriage became a pivotal point for change. Elizabeth describes her long-term abuse situation:

> The abuse was over 20 years I was married. It actually started before I got married but it was mainly verbal beforehand. But very shortly after I was married, it became physical ... and it was also emotional ... and verbal.

Naomi also describes the manner in which the abuse commenced prior to her marriage, but then escalated:

> Well, before I was married, it was mainly just verbal abuse and control ... 'cause he was very controlling. In the mid-80s it really escalated 'cause he had an alcohol problem. And there was quite a lot of times I was raped. It started off mainly as control, and verbal abuse and just increased from there.

Frequently, the victim is blamed for the unpleasant conduct of the perpetrator, not only by the perpetrator himself (Kirkwood, 1995; McCue, 2008; NiCarthy, 1986), as illustrated in the example of Miriam (below), but sometimes even by misguided and misinformed individuals who see themselves as helping a troubled individual (Hoff, 1990; Scutt, 1990; Seddon, 1993). The victim can therefore devote a great deal of time endeavouring to correct her alleged faults in an effort to avoid further confrontation. While any attempts at correction may appear to work for a time, they eventually emerge as futile because the cycle of violence continues and the victim is left to search in vain for yet another solution to an ever-increasing problem (Barnett & LaViolette, 1993; Magen, 1999), as was the case for Elizabeth (below). This strategy is not effective as it places the responsibility for the behaviour of the perpetrator on the victim rather than declaring it to be solely the responsibility of the individual user of violence and/or abuse (Adams, 1994; Dutton, 1995; Pease, 1996). Such action continues to perpetuate the myth that not only is the victim responsible for the behaviour of the perpetrator but that, as her husband, 'he has the right to chastise' (Bograd, 1988, p. 22) her. Further, Schissel (2000) maintains that in cases where communities exhibit a tendency to blame the victim and thereby hold the victim responsible for the actions of the perpetrator, there is very little support provided for victims of abuse. In doing this, such communities 'foster a patriarchal ideology that privileges men and endangers women' (p. 971).

Miriam explains her experience of being constantly blamed by her husband:

> I was just a scapegoat for anything and everything that went wrong. Everything was my fault all the time, and that's what made me twig that, no, no one is all at fault all the time. I thought no! No one could be totally, 100% wrong every minute of every day.

It took Miriam approximately two years to come to the realisation that she could not possibly be entirely wrong all of the time. This realisation included the fact that her husband was probably never going to accept responsibility for his behaviour. While Miriam was ultimately assisted by members of the clergy, Elizabeth describes herself as being blamed for the problems in her marriage and thus 'revictimised' by her pastors:

> I went repeatedly to them, and the main thing they always said to me was, 'Well, what are you doing? What, what, what are you doing to cause this?' So I would rack my brain. I would repent of whatever it was ... and put that right, believing that everything was going to be OK, but nothing ever changed.

Like Elizabeth, many victims of domestic abuse can turn to individuals they trust to assist them, only to experience further victimisation. Such forms of revictimisation can compound the impact of the trauma, and even inhibit the recovery process (Hattendorf & Tollerud, 1997).

Frequently, the mind of the victim becomes the playing field for the perpetrator as subtle suggestions are made regarding her worth, appearance or capabilities, as indicated in the following example from Esther:

> There was continual ... sort of degrading remarks, and in particular about my body ... about being fat, which I wasn't. And then I ... he might walk into the bedroom when I was getting undressed and he would just sit there and bag my body.

As the campaign continues over time, the victim becomes more likely to begin to doubt her own judgment and even to accept the comments of the accuser (Dutton, Burghardt, Perrin, Chrestman & Halle, 1994; NiCarthy, 1986). Frequently, it is the strengths of the victim that are targeted. In the case of Esther (above), who worked with the police force and attended gym sessions four or five times per week, her husband targeted her body, her weight and thus her self-esteem. Often, it is the areas in which the person is considered, and indeed considers herself, to be capable, effective and even powerful that become the specific target of the perpetrator (Thorne-Finch, 1992). For example, a woman who is extremely popular socially may finally withdraw from the social arena as a result of the continuing negative social behaviour of her partner, or simply from the underlying fear of public humiliation should he react openly either to herself or to those around him. Alternatively, she can attend social engagements alone, only to be confronted with a tirade of verbal and/or physical abuse, or perhaps a number of days of sullen, moody silence upon her return. Thus, the much anticipated social event moves from the position of being classified as a potentially joyous occasion to become instead an effective weapon to be brandished at will (Walker, 1979), as illustrated in the case of Lydia (below). Unfortunately, ultimate withdrawal from social settings only increases the level of control and influence the perpetrator is able to exert, as any level of positive communication and feedback is removed and there remains nothing to oppose the distorted images being continually reinforced by the perpetrator (NiCarthy, 1986). Naomi comments on the fact that she was not permitted to attend church and was often taunted regarding her religion. She then goes on to say:

> It started happening when he wouldn't allow ... if I contacted my family I'd get into ... I'd — after I'd talked to them, then he'd become quite abusive. And then when I'd be going to church ... and I'd come home and he'd be abusive. So in the end it was a lot easier not to go because whenever I went he ... and he actually told me I shouldn't be going.

Lydia found it was often easier not to attend functions than to deal with her husband's negative attitude:

> Pretty much almost any activity that I did — if I went with him he would make it ... it would be such a rigmarole to get out that it would sometimes be easier just to say, 'Oh forget about it'. Other times he'd go to things with me. He'd consent to come out to things with me and then — after, you know, he'd lose interest halfway through. I'd realise he was not keen to be there and ... like, you know, we'd apologise and leave. And then he'd get home and say, 'Oh, I'm sick of going to things like that with you'.

Forms of Abuse

Domestic abuse is not restricted to physical violence. It encompasses a vast range of behaviours that may appear insignificant in and of themselves but, when observed or experienced in a cluster formation, create an atmosphere of fear, control and subjugation (Hague & Marlos, 2005; Randall, 1991; Taylor, 2003). Coercive control manifested in any of its forms — including domination, intimidation, deprivation, physical and sexual abuse, and verbal and emotional abuse — constitutes domestic abuse (Ashur & Witwer, 1993; McCue, 2008). Ward (2000) boldly compares domestic abuse to cultic abuse, highlighting the parallels between the two: environmental control, coercion and threats, blaming the victim, feelings of helplessness, and ongoing residual effects. In an effort to understand the difficulties faced by victims of abuse, it is also important to understand that abuse is ongoing, and continues apart from the specific acts of physical violence (Sullivan, 2003). Covert forms of abuse can prove equally as debilitating and 'dehumanizing' (Gill, 1995, p. 876) as their more obvious overt counterparts, and therefore should not be excluded from consideration when interviewing victims of abuse or evaluating an abusive situation (James, 1999). Even the woman who appears strong and confident within the community may well be suffering silently behind closed doors (Berry, 1998).

In cases where abuse is prevalent within a relationship, the violence does not necessarily commence immediately but, as previously noted, can develop progressively over a period of time (Berry, 1998). Verbal and emotional forms of abuse serve to bring the victim under the control of the abuser by systematically undermining the victim's sense of self-efficacy (Herman, 1997; Kirkwood, 1995). Many times, as the strengths of the victim are targeted for attack, a severe weakening of the super-structure of the individual can occur. Victims begin to question their own

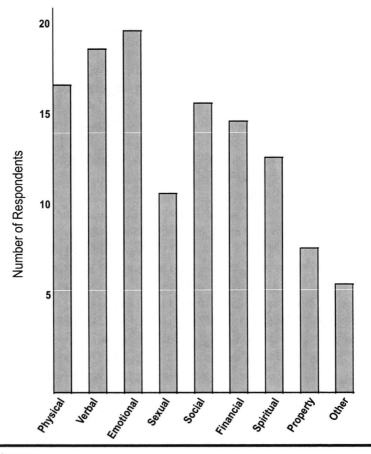

Figure 3.1
Forms of abuse.
Note: (*N* = 20).

actions as they are continually blamed for the actions of the perpetrator. This creates feelings of guilt in the victim, in conjunction with the actual belief that perhaps she has provoked the abuse (Browne & Herbert, 1997; Eisikovits & Buchbinder, 1999; Gregory, 2004).

The following pages outline nine forms of abuse identified by the women as they told their stories. These include: physical, verbal, emotional, sexual, social, financial, spiritual, property and child abuse. All nine forms of abuse have been reported to have a damaging effect on the lives of the individuals in question. Each person reported experiencing at least four of the forms of abuse listed, with two of the women (Naomi, Miriam) reporting an experience of all nine forms of domestic abuse listed. Figure 3.1 provides an outline of the types of abuse reported by the women.

Physical Abuse

Physical violence is perhaps the most obvious form of abuse, and includes a wide variety of destructive physical behaviours such as hitting, punching, kicking, shoving and choking (Basham & Lisherness, 1997; DVPC, 2008a; Ezell, 1998; Lynch & Graham-Bermann, 2000). It may also include sleep deprivation (Biderman & Zimmer, 1961). Injuries sustained as a result of physical abuse can be extensive and require medical attention and possible hospitalisation, leaving the victim in an ongoing state of exhaustion (NiCarthy, 1986). Such injuries include cuts, bruises and broken bones, in addition to various internal injuries that in some cases result in miscarriage (Dobash & Dobash, 1979). The victim experiences not only the physical pain of the abuse but also the psychological and emotional pain associated with it. Physical abuse need only occur once for the threat of repetition to act as a controlling force. Thus the victim is controlled by fear (Barnett & LaViolette, 1993; Herman, 1997; Martin, 1976; Sackett & Saunders, 1999). Such fear is felt not only for their own wellbeing but also that of their children. Shock often accompanies the initial outburst of violence (Hoff, 1990), as it is often unexpected and seemingly out of character for the perpetrator to behave in such a manner.

Elizabeth speaks of a situation that occurred approximately two years into her marriage, when she was suffering from absolute exhaustion as a result of caring for two very young children who rarely slept through the night:

> I became very, very tired and run down. And I just decided one day that I was going to have a sleep. We had a bunga-low up the back, and I just said, 'Look, I'm going to have a sleep. I'm really too tired', and he said, 'No you're not', and I said, 'Oh yes I am', and I decided I was going to. And I'd never tested that out before ... I locked the door and I thought, 'No! I'm doing this. This is what I'm doing. I never do this, but I'm going to today ...'

Elizabeth's husband endeavoured unsuccessfully to break down the door before finally smashing the window to gain access to the room, whereupon:

> He just broke me with his fists. He'd done karate and boxing and ... my face was really mangled and I just ... I was really shocked. Like, it had never got to that stage before ... because I had never said no. There'd never been a test.

Elizabeth clearly identifies this incident as a power issue. She had never previously disobeyed her husband. She had never previously said 'no'. Until this time, she had always played the role of the obedi-ent and compliant wife. The conflict arose as she challenged his authority over something as basic as a much-needed time of rest. This was certainly not the only incident of physical abuse that occurred during Elizabeth's 20-year marriage. In this case, she was taken to hos-pital with a broken nose. Instead of a private interview, which is recommended for women who are suspected of having been abused (Furniss, 1998), and the subsequent gathering of relevant information (Brockmeyer & Sheridan, 1998; Page-Adams & Dersch, 1998; Soeken, McFarlane, Parker & Lominack, 1998), Elizabeth was told by a member of the clergy, 'I could lay charges, but if I did I would ruin him for life'. This same comment was further reinforced by the accompanying police officer. During a later incident, she suffered with broken ribs that were never reported or formally treated, but simply bound by a woman who had some nursing experience. That beating left Elizabeth in a great deal of physical pain, without assis-tance, and ultimately attributing her injuries to a fall on the stairs.

Verbal Abuse

Verbal abuse consists of insults, either private and/or public, designed to belittle and embarrass the victim, thereby leading to submission and ultimate control for the perpetrator (Thorne-Finch, 1992). Verbal abuse may involve shouting; swearing; criticism; subtle (or not so subtle) put-downs relating to appearance, ability or sexuality; or venting anger upon the victim for trivial infractions such as the manner in which household chores are completed (DVPC, 2008a; Hunter, 1998). Verbal abuse can be extremely threatening and intimidating for the victim. Lydia describes her experience this way:

> He was six foot one and I'm — I'm not sure what, but ... he'd stand right up in your face a few centimetres from your face and just roar at you.

In a South Australian report on domestic violence, Bagshaw and Chung (2000) indicate that verbal abuse, in addition to emotional and psychological abuse, in the majority of cases 'occurred daily, and was far more devastating and long lasting in its effect' (p. 9). Further, victims of abuse reflected upon the strong controlling characteristics of the perpetrators, linking to all forms of abuse, and reaching into all aspects of life.

Like all forms of abuse, verbal abuse is closely linked to emotional and psychological abuse, as the wellbeing of the victim is systematically undermined throughout the course of the relationship. Such behaviour is typical of the clustered patterns of abuse that become apparent when the desire of the perpetrator is to dominate and control the victim (Schumacher, Smith Slep & Heyman, 2001). The result is the gradual destruction of the 'psychological identity of the victim as her own person' (Anderson et al., 2003, p. 153). After 11 years of marriage, Joanna came to the point where she felt that she was quite likely to experience a nervous breakdown and become unable to care for her children adequately. She goes on to say:

> And I sort of felt like I was ... you know, I'm no good. He used to tell me that I'm not the person that I am. I'm not the bubbly, happy, friendly person that everyone thinks that I am.

Frequently, throughout the course of a week Joanna would be called names such as 'bitch' or 'bitch face', and arguments were constant. Joanna says, 'Just argument after argument just ... there was no peace at all', and describes the ongoing situation as 'horrendous'.

Emotional Abuse

Emotional abuse is described by Kirkwood (1995) as 'a subtle, nearly invisible, process through which the fundamental components of its impact are ingrained in women' (p. 60). White (1998) refers to emotional abuse as 'the silent killer of Christian marriages' (p. 99). As previously stated, emotional abuse can be closely linked to verbal abuse; it twists at the very heart of the victim, constantly reminding her that she is not good enough, and does not deserve the respect or even the attention of her captor.

Emotional abuse is also closely associated with physical abuse. Both revolve around the desire to control and dominate the victim (Dutton, 1995; White, 1998). Actions such as sulking, ignoring requests, refusing to speak or touch, withholding intimacy either in the form of sex or general affection, and lying about the victim may all be considered forms of emotional abuse (Thorne-Finch, 1992). This is the form of abuse that allows the perpetrator to consume a roast dinner while the victim and her child are permitted only stale bread and butter. The message is clearly one of inferiority: they are beings of lesser status. Emotional abuse does not have to be verbal. Previously spoken messages may be continually reinforced through a myriad of actions, leaving the victim to shelter behind nothing but crumbling walls, which may once have provided a substantial line of defence. This form of abuse can have grave psychological implications for the victim, and eventually contribute significantly to health problems (Marshall, 1996), including depression and eventual withdrawal (Jantz, 2003).

Like other forms of abuse, emotional abuse is not accidental; rather, it is a deliberate attempt to control and subjugate the victim (Jantz, 2003). In some cases, it may be considered 'even more devastating than other forms of abuse' (Lachkar, 2000; Thorne-Finch, 1992, p. 13). However, because of the seemingly invisible nature of emotional abuse, women endeavouring to terminate such a harmful and damaging relationship may receive considerably less social support than women wishing to leave a physically abusive relationship (Langhinrichsen-Rohling, Shlien-Dellinger, Huss, & Kramer, 2004). When recounting their experiences, all 20 women acknowledged the presence of significant levels of emotional abuse within their relationships.

Deborah describes withheld affection as a form of emotional abuse that was very prevalent in her relationship with her husband of 23 years:

> I remember for a long time I was perhaps ... we'd be out somewhere and I'd try and hold [husband]'s hand and he just would push it away. I would try and kiss him on the cheek somewhere, and he's very tall, so I have to kind of ... get it at the right moment anyway. But he would pull away, or push me away. I was very hurt for years. It's only in the last couple of years that I've recognised that now I'm angry about that.

Deborah considers emotional abuse to be the most significant form of abuse for her. She described her life as being 'filled with emotional abuse'. In explaining my own presence in her home to one of her daughters, Deborah relates the following:

> She [daughter] said something, 'Yeah, but he doesn't hit you, Mum', and I said, 'No, but you can't see the scars'. Emotional abuse doesn't leave wounds, it leaves scars, and you can't see the scars.

Emotional abuse reaches into many areas, perhaps none more significant than what might be termed the most intimate of interactions. Emotional abuse has the potential to reach new heights of personal destruction for the victim when such abuse is perpetrated in the form of sexual abuse.

Sexual Abuse

Sexual abuse within marriage cannot be more vividly described than by Yllo (1999) when she states that 'when you are raped by a stranger, you live with a frightening memory, but when you are raped by your husband, you live with your rapist' (p. 1060). Finkelhor and Yllo (1985) further note that 'battered women are at especially high risk of sexual assault' (p. 22) and that as many as half of these women can be victims of repeated sexual assault by their husbands.

Marital rape includes any form of forced sexual activity, regardless of whether or not the couple are living together or separately (Brownmiller, 1975; McCue, 2008). Consent on a previous occasion does not imply ongoing consent to subsequent sexual interaction. Sexual abuse is a degrading and humiliating experience, once again designed to dominate and subjugate the victim (Morrone, 2003). This often results in a diminished trust towards others and the inability of the individual to feel any reasonable level of safety (Walker, 1979). Kernic, Holt, Stoner, Wolf and Rivara (2003) report levels of depression to be substantially higher in those women who report a combination of physical, sexual and psychological abuse compared with those who report only psychological abuse. Dienemann et al. (2000) also report experiences of forced sexual interaction to be strongly linked to depression in victims of domestic abuse.

Naomi describes her experience of sexual abuse:

> There was sexual abuse, and — like keeping me up all through the night and trying to do funny little sexual acts. The sort of things that I didn't want to ... actually do, other than just having sex ... also a couple of times he ... grabbed hold of me and forced me. And also I was raped quite a few times.

Eunice described her husband as being 'very demanding in sexual relations', and then later describes an event that took place after their separation:

> He actually came back and broke into the house through the night when ... we were alone, when we'd separated. Came in and came into my room and technically raped me ... and terrified the kids. You know, they woke up and they could hear ... well, I got a fright, he was there.

In contrast to the more violent and forced forms of sexual abuse, Mary explained a very different form of what she clearly classified as sexual abuse. During the course of their marriage, her husband would often entertain his male partner in the marital home. While Mary was initially unaware of the nature of the relationship, she continued to feel uneasy. Having been married for 11 years and with three children together, Mary's husband withdrew from any intimate interaction, and only after some time told her of his homosexuality. Mary and her husband continued to remain married and to share the marital bed, but without intimacy, for a further 25 years, at which point her husband decided to leave.

Abuse operates in many arenas, each one displaying its own set of characteristics, but equally able to mesh together with other forms of abuse to increase the overall power base of the perpetrator. Social abuse is no exception.

Social Abuse

Social isolation contributes greatly to the power of the perpetrator by preventing the victim from receiving accurate and positive feedback from significant others. It effectively limits access to the support necessary to empower the victim to take decisive action to seek help from friends, neighbours or agencies (Kirkwood, 1995; NiCarthy, 1986; Walker, 1979; Walker & Meloy, 1998). Social isolation may come about in numerous ways. It may be specifically geographical, such as living on a large property in the outback (Fishwick, 1998), or moving to a new area away from family, friends or support networks. Alternatively, social isolation may be influenced by the demands or moods of the perpetrator, or brought about by the attempts of the victim to protect and shield others from the negative actions of the perpetrator (Abrahams, 2007; Martin, 1976). Put simply, the victim may choose to refrain from going out or inviting people to the home because of the moods, behaviour, demands or intimidation of the perpetrator (Riessman, 1989).

Elizabeth speaks of a very pointed geographical isolation where she was deliberately moved away from family and friends at the choice of her husband:

> I had always been a fairly confident, outgoing person ... and willing to give in the marriage and ... and work towards it ... but I got isolated off. That was the big thing [sigh]. Very early in the piece, it was, 'We can't live ... in Sydney, we have to go down to Melbourne', which is where he came from. So I was isolated off from everyone who

> knew me ... and didn't have a circle of friends. I make
> friends easily, but found that I didn't sort of want to,
> because things were difficult. Like it was difficult to ... I
> was covering up a lot.

Likewise, new mother Sarah found herself relocated from Brisbane to Tasmania, leaving behind everyone and everything familiar, at the request of her husband of approximately 12 months. After barely 10 weeks in the new location, verbal abuse commenced and quickly escalated to severe physical abuse, leaving Sarah 'terrified' and without familial support.

Regardless of the reasons for social isolation, a mantle of silence often shrouds the victim as shame and degradation become an all-powerful barrier to freedom (Gregory, 2004; Martin, 1976). No voice is raised in condemnation of the abuse or in support of the victim. As a result of isolation and silence, the victim is again left powerless against the manipulation and control of the perpetrator.

Financial Abuse

Economic abuse may take a number of different forms, but generally results in deprivation for the victim (Abrahams, 2007). Initially, total control of the finances may remain with the perpetrator, thereby forcing the victim to request or beg for any item required, regardless of how small or personal (Fawcett, Featherstone, Hearn & Toft, 1996; Wittwer, 1995), thus enforcing continued dependence upon the perpetrator (DVPC, 2008a; Stotland, 2000). Alternatively, the victim may be constantly humiliated by being required to account for each and every purchase (Conway, 1998). In some cases, the victim may be forced to bear the total financial burden of the household while the perpetrator chooses not to engage in work outside the home (Walker, 1979). Further, the victim may be given no opportunity for input regarding the manner in which family finance is distributed or spent (Heise, 1998). Such deprivation, in whatever form it is expressed, leaves the victim only extremely limited financial resources, thereby governing to a large extent both her freedom and her overall ability to escape the situation.

Deborah clearly defines her situation as one of continued financial abuse:

For years he would do the shopping, so I had no say in the money. I remember that there'd be times in the first 18 … 19 years of our marriage, I would have to every month say, 'Can I have some money to go and get some girlie things from the shop?' So that was really hard. That … he would never give me money to do that. And he would even go to the shop and buy them for me.

Deborah was so humiliated by this process that she took steps to protect her daughters from the same embarrassment and humiliation, by gathering together what little money she could to ensure the regular availability of sanitary protection. Deborah later describes another form of financial abuse. For some months her husband had been giving her $400 per fortnight to feed a family of seven. After one child left home, the amount was significantly reduced:

He gave me $150 a fortnight and would complain when I would go over that. This is now to feed … six people. Anyway, so I had complained about that. So anyway he just told me in the last fortnight that he's stopped putting the $400 into my account, and gave me $100 to do the shopping last week.

Financial abuse commenced very early in Deborah's marriage, although it was not initially identified as such. However, this along with other forms of abuse, has continued throughout the 23-year relationship. At the time of the interview, Deborah was still married to her husband and, while her advice to others is 'you don't have to stay there,' she continues to hope for change in her husband.

Spiritual Abuse

The term *spiritual abuse* may be used to describe a number of circumstances, including criticism of the faith of an individual, or forbidding attendance at religious gatherings (DVPC, 2008a). The term may also be extended to include forced attendance at religious gatherings where an individual does not feel comfortable. Further, biblical principles and Scriptures may be used by the perpetrator as a point of authority to condone his actions, or perhaps to 'prove' to the victim that she is not fulfilling her marital obligations (Education Queensland, 2000; JCDVPP, 2002, p. 29; Wittwer, 1995). This is clearly noted in a narrative study conducted by Reissman (1989). The victim reports that she does not wish to be sexually intimate, but the perpetrator boldly responds, 'No, you're my wife and in the Bible it says you've got to do this' (p. 238). Thus the Bible is used as a control point for the perpetrator to enforce his wishes over those of the victim.

Ruth explains how she and her children were forbidden to attend the church of her choice:

> I had come from church with the children … and he said to me, 'Why isn't the food cooked?' And he said to me, 'That's the last time I want to see you … take the children to church'. And it was a church that he didn't want to be part of. He also wanted to dominate what church we went to and everything.

Ruth's Christian husband enforced his decision in the following manner:

> I have always been passive and never talked back, because I knew the moods could enrage. I possibly did talk back that day, because that was taking my *whole soul* away from me when he told me I could not go to church. He smashed me across the face … and I screamed. Because it was for the first time that I had ever had such physical abuse. Yes, I had had his sexual abuse and things like that … but never such a grotesque physical abuse. So … I complied.

Miriam and her two sons were not stopped from attending their regular Catholic services, but rather were forced by Miriam's husband to attend services at an Assemblies of God church where they felt uncomfortable and did not understand some of the religious practices, such as the concept of 'faith healing'. When Miriam questioned their need to attend the services, she was plainly told, 'You come, or you'll pay for it'.

Unfortunately, spiritual abuse is not limited to the behaviour of the perpetrator. It can easily include well-meaning individuals from a Christian congregation, or even members of the clergy, who minimise the circumstances of the victim — often as a result of disbelief; use Scripture to provide shallow and nonfunctional responses to legitimate and significant problems — such as paralleling domestic abuse to the sufferings of Christ (Graham & Fortune, 1993); or simply fail to take appropriate action to assist or protect the victim (Barnett, 2001; JCDVPP, 2002; McCue, 2008). The classification of spiritual abuse may be justifiably extended to include the defence and protection of perpetrators as a direct result of a general unwillingness on the part of some members of the clergy to hold perpetrators accountable for their actions. Based on findings from his study, Buxton (2000) in his article entitled 'There is an elephant in the sanctuary and no one is talking about it' suggests that 'perhaps it is time for the church to take on a zero tolerance attitude to domestic abuse among its own members' (p. 75).

In the case of Elizabeth, the pastors of her church were well aware of the constant abuse that was taking place within the marriage. The abuse included black eyes, broken ribs and various other injuries sustained as a result of the physical abuse perpetrated against her by her Christian husband. Not only did the pastors avoid any confrontation with the perpetrator, who was holding a leadership position in the church, they actually assisted him in gaining his ministry credentials.

Anna tells of a situation where, on the advice of her doctor, she had removed herself from the family home for a short time. Anna chose to advise her minister of her location, only to have him drive after her and force her to return to her husband. This situation was indicative of the continued lack of support Anna that received from her minister and church. This troubled Anna deeply, and was a constant theme throughout the duration of the interview. Anna's incredulous disbelief is apparent when she says:

> He [the minister] knew all this pain of me and yet … when
> it came to the crunch even of that night of my husband
> trying to choke me, he still did nothing.

On this occasion, Anna's very frightened young daughter had placed an urgent telephone call to the minister, who chose to do nothing other than promise to call around in the morning. That promise was never honoured.

Property Abuse

Property abuse refers to the harm or destruction, or even the threat of harm or destruction, of the property of an individual. Such abuse is used as a form of threat, intimidation or coercive control against the victim (Queensland Government, 2008d). Property abuse may apply to the destruction of material possessions that are especially meaningful or emotionally significant to the victim, such as her great-grandmother's tea set, or perhaps a project that she has been working on that is important to her (Basham & Lisherness, 1997; Miles, 2000). Alternatively, property abuse may simply be aimed at anything that belongs to the victim, such as her clothes or any other personal possession. Hegstrom (2004) maintains that perpetrators who use this form of abuse are very much in control of their behaviour. The property destroyed is always that of the victim, and never that of the perpetrator. Hegstrom further explains that such destructive behaviour can also be extended to the family pet. Pearson (1998) reports that 91.5 % of women in her study were threatened with harm to either their possessions or their pets in an effort by perpetrators to gain compliance.

Hannah tells of her experience of property abuse. She speaks frankly of how household articles, in addition to her own personal ornaments, were destroyed by her husband in a fit of rage:

> He would break my things. He grabbed the TV set one time and just flung it out the front door. One night ... which was in a fit of temper. Just stuff like that he would do all the time. I had some little ornaments and he just smashed them. He was angry and he just grabbed them and smashed them. And he knew they were mine.

Leah used to enjoy making things or working on a variety of projects. However, her hobbies were often destroyed by her husband:

> I had a hobby, wanted to set up the fish tank. Well, he'd drain the water out because ... he ... because it was my idea and ... well I was doing something. But for some reason he didn't like it so he would want to destroy it.

Further, Leah felt she could never show if she was angry or sad as a result of something her husband did, as he would then continue to do those things he knew would cause her pain or distress.

As stated earlier, the definition of property abuse can be extended to include the abuse, or threat thereof, in relation to animals or pets belonging to the women. The abuse of pets may be used by the perpetrator in an effort to highlight his potential for violence, leaving the victim feeling fearful and totally intimidated (Bowker, 1993). Flynn (2000) reports that almost 50% of the women in his study reported either the abuse or threatened abuse of their pets by the perpetrator. He states, 'pets may be targeted for abuse by batterers to inflict emotional abuse or control their female partners' (p. 172). Flynn further suggests that in cases where pets have played a significant role of companionship, and therefore an emotional role in the life of the victim, separation from or even total loss of the pets may result in 'additional trauma' (p. 170). Pearson (1998) indicates that 12.8% of the domestic abuse victims included in her study had their pets killed by the perpetrator.

Unfortunately, victims of domestic abuse are not always able to take their pets with them if they have to leave the marital home. Thus, some women are reluctant to move to a shelter out of fear for the wellbeing of their pets. Naomi tells briefly of the night she left her marital home:

> First there was the sexual abuse. Then he started grabbing hold of … some of — first of all he started threatening all the animals and kill myself. Then he hit me in the face. And then he grabbed some of my belongings and took them out and lit a fire and started burning them. And while that was happening, I quickly grabbed my mobile phone, my dog and a bag with a few clothes in and took off down the road.

Naomi was later able to find accommodation for her horses. However, initially she had been forced to leave them behind on the night she took flight. The serious nature of the threat to both Naomi and her pets cannot be underestimated. Mulroney (2003) reports that in Australia, '20.8% of all homicides involve intimate partners' (p. 5).

In recognition of the difficulties faced by victims of domestic abuse who own and love their pets, in 2005 the RSPCA took steps to establish 'Pets in Crisis', a program through which the safety of pets can be ensured through the provision of immediate, but temporary, accommodation with caring volunteers. Such action allows victims of abuse to seek refuge and remain safe while being secure in the knowledge that their pets are also housed in a safe environment (RSPCA, 2008).

Child Abuse

The difficulties surrounding the issue of children who actually witness domestic violence are enormous (Cooper & Vetere, 2005). Rosenbaum and Leisring (2003, p. 7) and Burke (1999, p. 257) all describe the impact of domestic abuse on children as 'devastating', while Geldard and Geldard (2009) maintain that it is inevitable that children caught in this situation will be 'traumatized' (p. 235). Approximately 90% of children living in homes where domestic violence is an issue are painfully aware of the situation (Adams, 1994; Education Queensland, 2000; Horton, Cruise, Graybill & Cornett, 1999; James, 1994), moving daily through the minefield of life trying desperately not to trigger an incident or become caught up in one. At times, the need for clinical intervention can be crucial (Cummings, Pepler & Moore, 1999), as children are forced to deal with the complexities of domestic abuse at a variety of levels (Peled, 1998). Many children are able to provide specific accounts of the incidents they have witnessed (Cooper & Vetere; Ericksen & Henderson, 1998). Other children develop a means by which they are able to dissociate from the violence, and as a result remember only broken images of the events (Silvern & Kaersvang, 1989). It has also been found that children who are compelled to live in violent surroundings can also develop symptoms associated with posttraumatic stress (Hughes & Graham-Bermann, 1998; Kilpatrick, Litt & Williams, 1997; McCue, 2008; Osofsky, 1995; Somer & Braunstein, 1999). The pressures of such an existence take their toll physically, emotionally and psychologically, ultimately pervading every aspect of life as fear becomes their constant companion (Clark & Miller, 1998; Margolin & Gordis, 2000).

Ruth, a nurse whose children were witnesses to the abuse within the household, explains why she chose many years of night work:

I would be there for the children of a daytime and in the evenings. Especially when he didn't want to cope with them and put them to bed at 5 o'clock in the night … and there they would have to stay until the morning. That was the lifestyle.

Rachel's two sons were also witnesses to some of the abuse she suffered. However, unknown to Rachel until some years later, the older son also fell victim to the violent abuse of his father. Like a number of young people who find themselves in this type of situation (Bahr, 2007a; Gary & Campbell, 1998), he left home and lived on the street for some years until Rachel was finally able to leave her husband.

Children who observe violence within the home often begin to imitate the behaviour of the perpetrator (Bahr, 2007b; Ericksen & Henderson, 1998; Miller & Knudsen, 2007). Role models that exemplify violence as a means of resolving conflict or achieving one's own desires are unhealthy, and provide children with an understanding that violence is an acceptable means of expression (Mills, 2008; White, 1991). Thus, violence becomes a learned response to conflict and an accepted part of the problem-solving process (Baumeister, 1997; Browne & Herbert, 1997; Von Steen, 1997). Gradually, as an outworking of this response, the social development of the child may become inhibited (Graham-Bermann, 1998). The child may become entangled with issues of bullying, and thereby face further difficulty within the school environment (Fisher, 1999; Landes, Siegel, & Foster, 1993). In considering the results of numerous studies, there appears to be a significant connection between child aggression, child delinquency and child interpersonal difficulties, and the psychological abuse of that child (Black, Heyman, & Slep, 2001; Black, Slep, & Heyman, 2001).

Anna spoke of the manner in which her now adult son emulates his father in the verbal abuse he directs at her. She is unable to reason with him in some areas, and says, 'You're just shouted down with awful verbal abuse'. In effect, her son has learned that verbal abuse is an acceptable means by which to address his mother. McDonald and Brown (1996) maintain that 'children whose parents are violent towards each other are also more likely to behave violently than children reared in non-violent homes' (p. 13). Adolescents may turn to alcohol, drugs, gang membership or even suicide in an endeavour to escape the physical and emotional trauma of a violent home (Blanchard, 1999; Gary & Campbell, 1998).

As a direct result of the secrecy surrounding incidents of domestic violence, children forced to live in such circumstances feel themselves to be totally alone. There is no emotional support, no comfort and no guidance (Cooper & Vetere, 2005). Trapped in this form of desert wasteland, many children of abused women begin to blame themselves for the violence that occurs in their lives (Humphreys, 1998; James, 1994; Kearney, 1999). These children are isolated, often forced to conceal their emotions for fear of reprisal from the perpetrator. Many suffer from anxiety, withdrawal and/or stress-related illnesses such as headaches, stomach pain or asthma (Blanchard, 1999; Fortune, 1991; Miller, Veltkamp & Raines, 1998), while others view their surroundings as 'threatening and hostile' (Browne & Herbert, 1997, p. 82). Reynolds, Wallace, Hill, Weist and Nabors (2001) found symptoms of post-traumatic stress, depression and low self-esteem in the 21 primary school-aged boys included in their study of child witnesses of domestic abuse. Silvern et al. (1995) also report a strong tendency for internalisation to be present among college students who had witnessed domestic abuse as children. Such reactions can last for years, and have the potential to be quite debilitating for the individual (Cooper & Vetere; McCloskey, Southwick, Fernandez-Esquer & Locke, 1995; Yule, 1998).

In a study conducted by Levendosky, Lynch and Graham-Bermann (2000), a number of women who were victims of abuse expressed the belief that, although they were compassionate and caring towards their children, their parenting style would change dramatically in a nonhostile environment. Suggested differences included a decrease in anger, more consistent discipline, and an increase in the time available for positive interaction with the children.

Miriam explains how frightened she was for the wellbeing of her children. She tells of the pain she suffered as she watched her own two sons being emotionally, and at times physically, abused by their father. Any interference on her part could easily bring repercussions for the boys. Miriam says:

> My biggest fear was that I'd be the one that'd die and leave
> him with the two boys, and then what would happen to

the boys ... I knew, if I — if anything happened to me, I would dread to think what happened to those two boys.

Feng, Giarrusso, Bengston and Frye (1999) found that in families similar to Miriam's, where high levels of abuse were typical, separation and subsequent divorce could have a positive impact on the wellbeing of the children concerned.

Miriam also expresses concern that, by remaining too long in the abusive situation, she may have jeopardised the wellbeing of her children. This is confirmed, many years later, in a conversation with the younger of her two sons. Miriam, now clear in her convictions, says:

> Don't hang in too far, thinking you'll fix it this week. It must get fixed. Because it goes from year to year until you end up doing more harm than good. I hung around too far. And ... yes, I can see that in the boys. The boys tell me, you know. The youngest told me not so long back. He said, you know, he said, 'I blamed you for a long time, Mum'. So ... there's such a thing as cutting your losses.

This illustration supports the concept that children who are abused as a result of living in a violent home can sometimes hold the nonperpetrating parent responsible for the ongoing abuse (Sternberg et al., 1994). In the case of Miriam, it is possible that her lack of interference may have been perceived by her younger son not as a form of concern or protection, but rather as evidence of a lack of concern, thus making her, in his eyes, at least partially accountable for the abusive actions of her husband.

While domestic abuse did not begin as an educational issue, it was transported into the educational arena as a result of the overall effect it has on children. Often, children who are subjected to trauma, such as that of witnessing domestic abuse or being abused themselves, are unable to perform well academically (Mills, 2008; Wolfe, Zak, Wilson & Jaffe, 1986), experience a variety of adjustment problems (Cummings, Davies & Simpson, 1994), and, as previously mentioned, experience difficulty relating to others (Blanchard, 1999; Schwarz, McNally & Yeh, 1998; Wittwer, 1995). Huth-Bocks, Levendosky and Semel (2001) suggest that witnessing domestic abuse can significantly affect the intellectual development of preschool-aged children, resulting in far more limited language skills than their nontraumatised counterparts. Further, children of battered women are often unable to attend school for security reasons, and may be forced to adjust to living with numerous others in a protective shelter (Hoff, 1990).

Dealing with the varied forms of domestic abuse on a day-to-day basis has been described by the women affected as extremely difficult. However, the presence of the cycle of violence within abusive relationships serves only to complicate matters for the individuals involved as they endeavour to deal with the repetitive and often unpredictable cycles of abuse.

The Cycle of Violence

The cycle of violence may well be the most confusing yet binding force for the victim as violent episodes are intermingled with acts of love. The cycle itself may be broken down into three basic stages: tension, explosion and 'loving contrition' (Miles, 2000, p. 71; Walker, 1979), although other authors (Gott, 1995; JCDVPP, 2002) include additional elements or stages, such as remorse and helplessness. In an effort to remain succinct, and to provide a clear overall view, I have chosen to deal only with the three key phases of the cycle.

Of the 20 women interviewed, 14 in some way identified the presence of the cycle of violence in their relationships. Often, without being directly questioned, a woman would share information that would indicate a specific stage in the cycle (Hannah, Susanna). Others, such as Naomi and Eve, clearly stated that they were very aware of the cycle of violence being prevalent in their marriage. In the case of Sarah, discovering the presence of the cycle of violence within her marriage, and developing an understanding of the nature of the cycle, assisted her in rethinking the options available to her.

Lois tells how she came to quite an enlightening realisation regarding the presence of the cycle of violence in her marriage:

> I wouldn't have totally been aware of how often it was happening until I read the domestic violence booklet that I was given, and I totally identified with this cyclic idea that we would go in ... I just went, 'Oh wow! Is this what it is? They actually write information about this and' ... and it happens this way.

Tension

During the first phase of the cycle of violence, the victim is very aware of the tension building within the relationship and may endeavour to offset the pressure and the potential explosion by attempting to control the external environment (Berry, 1998). Family members and activities are juggled in an often futile attempt to avoid an incident. Children learn restrictive and limiting behaviour patterns as they become conditioned to placate the perpetrator (Beattie, 1989; Humphreys, 1998), while the victim is forced into a role that is not only stressful but ultimately damaging to her emotional, mental and physical health (Barnett & LaViolette, 1993). The actual length of the tension phase, including the fear accompanying it, may vary significantly from days to even years (Berry). Walker (1979) indicates that even individuals who have lived in a violent relationship for a substantial length of time, and have experienced many such cycles, are often still unable to determine when the explosion will occur.

Explosion

The explosion, as the second phase of the cycle, may occur at any time and for any, or no apparent or seemingly legitimate, reason. It is unpredictable and therefore unavoidable for the victim, regardless of any lengths to which she might go to circumvent the situation. The explosion may be triggered by something as trivial as the nature of the evening meal, the spilt drink of a child, or the table setting (Berry, 1998: Browne, 1987). The degree of violence released against the victim is determined entirely by the perpetrator. A violent incident may be over in minutes, or alternatively become a lengthy session of battering and torture intermingled with extreme verbal abuse during which the perpetrator frequently places the blame for his despicable conduct upon the victim of his dishonourable, unscrupulous and criminal deeds (Dutton, 1995; Walker, 1979). The only consolation for the victim is the fact that the long-awaited explosion is finally over — until next time.

Hannah expresses not only the tension of the build-up of anger, but also the relief she used to feel once an explosive episode had taken place:

> It would build up. He would get angry about stuff. And he would get really annoyed and then it would be like you'd

be relieved when he finally did the lolly, 'cause you could
... you knew that he was annoyed and things were happening, and you're thinking — you're just waiting for it. So it
used to be a relief when he would do the lolly.

Even during the course of this conversation, Hannah's body language
indicated the relief she would feel after the explosion occurred.

Loving Contrition
The final phase is often referred to as the honeymoon period (Walker,
1979), during which the perpetrator may acknowledge feelings of
guilt and remorse in relation to his previous actions, and endeavour to
make it right through ongoing demonstrations of love and positive
attention towards the victim. Supposedly positive behavioural mani-
festations may include gifts or peace offerings such as flowers or
chocolates, attempts at gentleness, and increased levels of intimacy
(Gott, 1995).

Susanna explains her experience of the honeymoon phase of the
cycle of violence:

See he would abuse me and yell at me, but then he'd come
and he'd buy me a watch, or he'd buy me a piece of jew-
ellery or something. And I ... but see, that wasn't what I
wanted. I didn't want anything like that. I just wanted
some help.

Abigail has a similar experience:

It happened in a cycle, which I have learnt, there is a cycle.
It would happen and then the next day would be like ... he
would try to make it up to me and be extra nice. And then
you'd just get to the stage where you felt comfortable and
then it would happen again. And it just continued like
that.

The care and loving concern displayed by the perpetrator at this time
may result in the victim actually believing that he is truly repentant
and will not offend again. The two conflicting images of loving
behaviour and abusive behaviour are presented to the victim
(Landenburger, 1998). Many times, out of a deep desire for it to be
so, the victim may choose to believe that the loving personality is the
true person, and the angry and violent outbursts are simply a result of

surrounding circumstances (Berry, 1998; Hoff, 1990). Thus, the perpetrator himself is not viewed by the victim as being violent, but rather as having a problem that can be solved, perhaps with the assistance of the victim (Towns & Adams, 2000). Frequently, victims of domestic abuse will accept responsibility for the physical and psychologically debilitating actions of their partners (Bagshaw & Chung, 2000; Browne & Herbert, 1997; Walker, 1994), as they feel a sense of obligation to make the relationship work (Beall & Sternberg, 1993). Thus, the cycle continues, leaving the victim isolated and confused, alone in her plight, living only to please the perpetrator and avoid the explosion of his uncontrolled wrath.

The honeymoon phase brings with it only a fleeting moment of respite, without the benefit of true safety (Barnett & LaViolette, 1993). As clouds without rainfall, there is no time of refreshing, only a time of anticipatory stillness against the backdrop of a dormant volcano. This phase serves only to reinforce the hope of an ultimately happy union, thereby binding the victim all the more tightly to her tormentor (Ott, Graham & Rawlings, 1990, cited in Barnett & LaViolette, 1993). It is the abuse, intermingled with phases of kind and loving behaviour, that can eventually lead to a condition of 'learned helplessness' (Gott, 1995, p. 7).

Learned Helplessness

Learned helplessness is rooted in the belief that a situation cannot be controlled, regardless of the action taken. It comes as a result of uncontrollable events being experienced by the individual. In effect, the victim of domestic abuse can see no link between her own actions and subsequent consequences, and so applies this perception (regardless of its accuracy) to her expectations regarding future events; this ultimately results in passive behaviour even when that passivity may be considered inappropriate (Garber & Seligman, 1980; Lemon, 1996; Peterson, Maier & Seligman, 1993).

> A pure case of learned helplessness must have all three components: noncontingency between the person's actions and outcomes, the expectation that the outcome will not be contingent in the future and passive behaviour. (Peterson et al., 1993, p. 9)

In applying this concept to domestic abuse, the victim often endeavours to alter her own behaviour in an effort to prevent the abuse and/or violence, as was the case with Elizabeth (mentioned earlier) as she tried to follow the advice of her pastors. But, because the outbursts are specifically the choice of the perpetrator and are not contingent upon the behaviour of the victim (Sprenkle, 1994), the victim then perceives that the situation is outside her control and thus feels completely helpless (Cooper-White, 1995; Lemon, 1996). Thus, the lack of success she experiences 'causes an expectation of uncontrollability' (Witkowski & Stiensmeier-Pelster, 1998, p. 59). As a result, the victim may eventually adopt a passive behaviour pattern as a 'line of least resistance'. As this attitude becomes more generalised, it limits the ability of the victim to believe that anything she does will result in a positive outcome. Her power is minimised and she becomes trapped in the situation, without the belief that freedom is possible or even the motivation to seek it (Walker, 1979).

Further, Garber and Seligman (1980) consider learned helplessness and the associated lack of controllability to be a contributing factor to depression. The findings of Yost (2003) also tend to support a link between learned helplessness and depression in relation to victims of domestic abuse. This study indicated a connection between the severity of depression experienced by the victim as a result of high rates of physical abuse, and a subsequent decline in the intention of the victim to reject the abusive behaviour of the perpetrator. Peterson et al. (1993) list changes in the immune system, a decrease in both self-esteem and levels of aggression, and possible physical illness as issues that can also result from the expectation of ongoing helplessness and thus a total loss of hope or any form of positive outlook for the future. Lemon (1996) explains it this way: 'Once the women are operating from a belief of helplessness, the perception becomes reality and they become passive, submissive, helpless' (p. 75).

Susanna endeavoured to deal with her situation by constantly working harder. While nothing changed with regard to the perpetrator, Susanna ultimately became ill as a result of the stress she was experiencing. It was not until after separating from her husband of 28 years, and attending university as a mature age student, that Susanna sensed a strong feeling of personal liberation. Susanna describes her newfound freedom:

> Since going to university, I found out that ... I found out that I — people like me, and they enjoy being with me, and they think I'm great and fun and that I can learn things and pick up things and I've never felt like that. This is a whole new experience for me. I've never felt that.

Susanna's experience highlights the manner in which individuals can be held emotionally and psychologically captive as they are continually cloistered in an environment of constant negativity. Experiences such as those of Susanna and Elizabeth set the stage for the ultimate entrapment of an individual through the condition of learned helplessness.

Learned Hopefulness

While none of the women interviewed could be specifically classified as suffering from the condition of learned helplessness, most of them could certainly be classified as experiencing what may be referred to as a form of 'learned hopefulness' (Barnett & LaViolette, 1993, p. 16). Even though conditions in a number of cases may be described as virtually unbearable, many of the women lived with the constant hope of change in relation to perpetrator behaviour, and thus chose to remain in the situation (Gelles, 1987; Jaffe et al., 1996; Keys Young, 1998). Hannah lived with the constant hope that somehow, in some way, her husband would change. Hannah pinned her hope on her faith in God to bring about change in her husband. She explains it this way:

> I expected God to show him that this is not the way that you treat your wife. I — that's what I was hoping for. Somehow or other I thought, 'You'll have to see one day'. I mean, you know, you don't see him carrying on like that, or him [referring to the more acceptable behaviour of other male members of the church]. I just somehow expected it to rub off.

It would appear that learned hopefulness can be fostered in a number of ways. At times it appears as a result of the aforementioned honeymoon phase of the cycle of violence. During this stage, life can appear more positive, and the perpetrator more loving and/or caring. It is a natural response for the victim of abuse to want the honeymoon phase to continue. There is also an understandable desire for the victim to want to believe that the caring and loving spouse is the real person, as opposed to the aggressive, dominant and controlling personality frequently displayed by the perpetrator (Berry, 1998; Browne, 1987). The violence is often viewed by the victim as being beyond the control of the perpetrator, leaving the woman free to believe that her partner is essentially a good person at heart (Eisikovits & Buchbinder, 1999). Ultimately, the more pleasing aspects of the honeymoon phase fuel the ongoing hope for change. The repetitious nature of the cycle constantly reinforces the hope that accompanies the honeymoon phase (Barnett & LaViolette, 1993).

In other cases, hope can arise and be sustained as a result of the Christian faith of the women and the manner in which they approached the situation. Such elements as reliance upon prayer, in relation to either personal strength to cope with the difficulties or significant change in perpetrator behaviour, formed a significant foundation for hope and a pivotal point for decision-making.

Deborah has chosen to remain with her husband of 23 years. Apart from the hope for change, Deborah's faith has played a specific role in her choice. She explains it this way:

> I have to do all that I can so that I can stand at the judgment bar of God and say, 'I did everything I could. I forgave. I loved. I learned to be charitable. But he still abused me', and then God can with all His wrath take out whatever He wants on him. Now in the meantime, one day he might wake up and go, 'Oh I have been ...' — you know — 'pretty unkind over all these years' ... and change. I guess that's one of the reasons I'm still here.

While hope for change was still present, many of the women represented were reluctant to terminate the marriage. Though perhaps less debilitating than learned helplessness, the hopefulness that is learned as a result of repetitive cycles, or perhaps from only slight changes in perpetrator behaviour (possibly attributed to prayer, personal faith, or simply the strength of the individual to 'hang in there'), still serves to maintain the status quo by causing the person to remain in a truly untenable situation.

Usually, only the slightest glimmer of hope was required to cause any of the women to remain in the marriage. It was only when they came to the realisation that there was absolutely no real hope for change in the relationship that many of them were willing to make a decision to terminate the marriage (Short et al., 2000). Such behaviour supports the position that most women do not want the marriage to end; they simply want the abuse to cease (Borkowski et al., 1983; Magen, 1999). The power of hope is highlighted by Browne (1987), who indicates that a final loss of hope was one of the more commonly reported facts among women who finally resorted to killing their abusive husbands.

Reported Effects of Abuse

The effects of domestic abuse are many and varied, including such problems as low self-esteem, depression, stress-related illness, and the desire to commit suicide (Anderson, 2002; Browne & Herbert, 1997; Thorne-Finch, 1992; Tifft, 1993; Walker, 1979, 1994). Kirkwood (1995, p. 71) lists such things as chronic illness, hair loss and 'a higher susceptibility to infections' as being part of a reaction to the unrelenting stress and tension of living in an abusive environment. Humphreys and Thiara (2003) argue the existence of a strong causal link between symptoms of 'severe emotional distress' (p. 223) experienced by women and the fact that those women are living in a violent and abusive environment. While a report by VicHealth (2004) focused primarily on issues surrounding physical and sexual abuse, further insight was offered in the statement that 'an emerging body of evidence demonstrates that emotional abuse can have serious health impacts' (p. 15).

For the purpose of this volume, I have chosen to limit dealing with the effects of abuse to those key aspects that were reported by the women as they told their stories. Thus, the following areas will be included: change in the personality of the individual; depression; physical illness; and the desire to commit suicide. It is important to remember however, that in most cases interview questions were not specifically posed in these areas, and the information was volunteered as the stories unfolded. It is therefore quite possible that a greater number of the women than actually indicated may have experienced each of the effects mentioned.

Personality Change

Constantly living under extreme levels of stress and continually feeling out of control can contribute not only to physical but also to ongoing psychological difficulties (Walker, 1979, 1994), including changes in personality (Mertin & Mohr, 2000). Plath (2001) notes the substantial impact of abuse, specifically in reference to psychological abuse, on the mood and thought patterns of those who have been victims of abuse. Herman (1997), in her study of victims of captivity, in which she also includes the experiences of victims of domestic abuse, asserts that 'prolonged captivity also produces profound alterations in the victim's identity' (p. 91). Sixteen of the 20 women indicated that they experienced some form of change relating to their personality. Most reported some form of withdrawal into themselves; others used terms such as 'robotic', 'mechanical' (Ruth), 'squashed' (Esther) and 'died' (Elizabeth) to describe the manner in which they responded to the abuse in their lives.

Tifft (1993) describes the withdrawal into oneself as a way that provides the victim with a form of escape from the continual demands of the perpetrator. The 'self' of the victim is described as being 'almost completely annihilated through violence, degradation, and humiliation' (p. 60). Hence, Elizabeth's choice of the term 'died' can be considered quite apt.

Lynch and Graham-Bermann (2000) identify decreased self-esteem, and the lack of ability to trust either themselves or others, as part of the psychological difficulties faced by women who have become victims of abuse. Thorne-Finch (1992) views violated trust as a 'central issue for most adult victims of emotional, physical, and sexual violence' (p. 39).

Referring to the effects of abuse, Esther describes the change in herself as a person, but also acknowledges the substantial increase in freedom and independence that took place after separating from, and ultimately divorcing, her husband of six years:

> I am still today struggling with self-confidence, self-esteem
> ... even though I'm working full time. I know I have
> changed. I was probably — I was just squashed actually, I
> guess. I mean, I used to be a fairly happy-go-lucky, freer

type of person and then I think that just stifled me. And I know that it'll never be the same because you've gone through many circumstances. I definitely don't have trust.

A very open and cheerful Mary explained to me how a number of years earlier she had withdrawn from the difficulties facing her. Her words, 'I'd turned in on myself', were a stark contrast to the now happy and seemingly well-adjusted woman in her 60s who sat opposite me. Part of the reason for the change became apparent as Mary spoke of changes that had occurred since her four-year separation and subsequent divorce from her husband of 37 years:

> He was totally negative. And so since he's left me, if I want to sit in a chair and read a book all day, I can. And like, if I want to get on the phone and talk to my friends for hours, I can, you know. And nobody is checking up on me or telling me what to think. I'm free to think what I want to think. He was distorting my thinking and I didn't realise that. I was so unhappy. When he left I sort of could open up to my friends ... and be accepted by them, you know, for what I was.

Rachel identified a very strong change in her own personality as a result of her marriage:

> I wasn't happy. I was terrified. I'd always had quite a bubbly personality and ... outgoing and loved company and loved people and I was getting more reclusive and more reclusive.

Depression
Anxiety and depression are identified by a number of authors (Abrahams, 2007; Anderson, 2002; Barnett, 2001; Carlson, McNutt, Choi & Rose, 2002; Dutton & Painter, 1993; Golding, 1999; Kernic et al., 2003; Mertin & Mohr, 2000; 2001; Van Hook, 2000; VicHealth, 2004) as feelings associated with the trauma of abuse. Dienemann et al. (2000) describe depression as 'the most prevalent negative health consequence of domestic violence' (p. 499), and further highlight a cause-and-effect link between domestic abuse and 'diagnosed clinical depression in women' (p. 508). Such observations are noted to include both major and bipolar depression.

Symptoms of depression can result from a deep sense of powerlessness and feelings of loss of control in relation to abusive relationships (Barnett & LaViolette, 1993; Walker, 1979, 1994). Feelings of hopelessness can become overwhelming, paving the way for the onset of depression (Vernon, 2004). Such feelings have the potential to permeate the entire life of the individual, thereby affecting the ability to concentrate or function fully in either the home or the workplace environment (CEO Challenge, 2004d). The confidence of the victim is undermined, and any attempt at escape appears futile (Tifft, 1993). Keys Young (1998) lists depression as one of the reasons women remain in abusive relationships, while Cooper-White (1995) refers to depression as 'demobilising' (p. 115). Depression for women trapped in abusive relationships must, of necessity, be viewed differently from any 'normal depression' that can result from life events such as the death of a family member or close friend, a divorce or the loss of work. Depression resulting from these events is a natural outworking of grief and loss. Although this can be a difficult and painful experience, it does eventually pass, and most individuals tend to improve over time. However, depression resulting from abuse can be recurrent. Individuals may respond very slowly to treatment as they are constantly living amid the trauma of ongoing abuse (Hubbard, 1996). Eight of the women made clear reports relating to depression as a result of their abusive marriages.

Lois experienced a sense of overwhelming powerlessness as a result of intimidation on the part of her husband. The feelings of powerlessness and hopelessness progressively moved to depression, withdrawal and isolation:

> I just totally felt like there was nothing I could do. So I just moved within side myself. I just became very isolated within myself. And because I had no release for my anger, that turned into depression. You know, that build-up of anger, and I just became depressed ... I was very tired, very depressed, very isolated. I withdrew from the people at church — very much that withdrawing, isolating ...

Anna suffered with severe depression and was subsequently prescribed antidepressant medication. She describes the cause of her depression as 'totally because of my sadness in my marriage'. Deborah also experienced a lengthy bout of depression. Her doctor suggested medication, but she was hesitant to accept the offer:

> I was very unhappy. It seemed to be 18 months or two years, and I used to be such a bubbly personality. I was a very happy person. And so I couldn't shake this cloud of unhappiness, this sadness that I was under. And I fought that for — it would have been maybe two years.

Physical Illness

Physical illness can result from the stress of living in an abusive environment (Campbell, 1998; McCue, 2008). Bagshaw and Chung (2000) report that many women live in constant fear on a daily basis. Barnett and LaViolette (1993) maintain that severe stress that is prolonged becomes debilitating to both 'the body and the soul' (p. 92). Diamond and Precin (2003) list, as a physical response to trauma, such things as physical tiredness or even exhaustion, digestive difficulties, headaches and a variety of other health complications. A number of the women (Anna, Hannah, Elizabeth, Leah) commonly turned to the phrase 'walking on eggshells' to describe their own daily behaviour as they continually endeavoured to survive while living under the perpetually looming shadow of perpetrator control and domination. This phrase, 'walking on eggshells', has also been used by other victims of domestic abuse (Walker 1993, p. 136), and graphically depicts the tentative and uneasy lifestyle of any victim of domestic abuse.

For 23 years, Susanna tried to deal with the pressures of the situation herself. She speaks of the stressful tightening of her stomach, in addition to suffering from diarrhoea for years, and openly acknowledges that it is only since the departure of her husband that her stomach has finally started to settle. Susanna also states decisively, 'I got cancer, and I think that that was directly as a result of the amount of pressure and stress I was living with'. McCue (2008) lists cancer as a possible outcome for individuals who are forced to live in extremely stressful situations, such as in the case of domestic abuse, because stress has the capacity to reduce the effectiveness of the immune system.

Rachel explained that her asthma condition escalated considerably as a result of the severe anxiety she experienced in her marriage. After eight years away from her husband, she reported that she has been asthma free except for times of significant stress, such as the near death of her mother.

Suicide

"Suicide is one of the coping mechanisms chosen by many abuse victims' (Abrahams, 2007; Thorne-Finch, 1992, p. 37). Golding (1999) reports the contemplation of suicide to be common among victims of domestic abuse. VicHealth (2004) lists suicide and attempted suicide as a 'known health outcome of intimate partner violence' (p. 21). Suicide brings with it a final close to the suffering of the victim of abuse, but how desperate does an individual have to be to truly contemplate suicide? Six of the women indicated that they had considered using suicide as a means of total escape from the situation in which they believed themselves trapped. Again, it is important at this point to note that not one question relating to suicide was posed during the interviews. The information gleaned was purely the result of testimony offered voluntarily by the women involved as they told their stories. Thus the question is raised as to how many of the remaining 14 women had in fact also contemplated suicide but failed to mention it because the subject was not openly addressed during the course of the interview.

Five years into an 11-year marriage, Abigail speaks of her desire to commit suicide:

> Well, I just thought, 'What's life all about?' I mean there ... there was a couple of times where I just wanted to end it. And I sat on the end of my bed with a belt thinking, 'How can I rig this up to ... put it?' ... 'cause you don't think, 'Well, what's there to look forward to?'

Hannah spent time planning aspects of a suicide attempt:

> I was suicidal at the time. And it was like for a few months there I was planning how, whether there was enough tablets and stuff and whether ... when I should take them because I didn't want the kids finding me and stuff like that. That went on for a few months.

As a result of the abuse she was experiencing, in addition to ongoing health issues, Susanna states calmly:

> I felt at times ... I felt great despair and I have felt ... and I must admit, I have felt suicidal, because I felt that I couldn't cope with it any more, and didn't want to cope with it any more ... I would think, 'I don't want to be here any more'.

Many of the symptoms described by the women appear also to be characteristic of individuals suffering from posttraumatic stress disorder. While the disorder itself was not directly discussed, a number of the symptoms were apparent.

Posttraumatic Stress Disorder

Posttraumatic stress disorder (PTSD) is a condition that can occur at any age as a result of experiencing or witnessing an extremely traumatic event, including injury or threat of injury (DSM-IV; Millard, 1993; Wade & Tavris, 1996). Miller (1998) describes the likelihood of an individual developing PTSD being directly associated with the degree of threat or injury experienced by that individual. For example, victims of more violent crime, such as physical or sexual abuse, were more likely to develop PTSD. Thus, women who have become victims of violent domestic abuse may develop symptoms associated with PTSD (Abrahams, 2007; Barnett, 2001; Humphreys & Thiara, 2003; Nelson, 1997; O'Leary, 1999; VicHealth, 2004; Yoshihama & Horrocks, 2002). An Australian study (Mertin & Mohr, 2000) found that 45% of female domestic violence victims studied met the complete criteria for PTSD according to the DSM-IV definition. These same women reported that their experiences were not restricted to physical abuse, but also included emotional and psychological abuse.

Douglas (1987) suggests that PTSD provides a foundational framework for understanding the effects of battered woman syndrome (BWS), which may be classified as a subcategory of PTSD (Walker, 1995); while Walker (1993) describes a number of symptoms, such as hypervigilance and exaggerated startle response, as being characteristic of both PTSD and BWS. Walker (1993) further explains the connection between the hypervigilance and high anxiety state in which an abused woman finds herself is often linked to a variety of chronic illnesses that are often reported by victims of abuse. Included in the list of symptoms are invasive thoughts, sleep disturbances, difficulty concentrating (Mertin & Mohr, 2000, 2001), gastrointestinal disorders (as mentioned by Susanna above) and 'chronic pelvic pain' (Walker, 1993, p. 143).

Anna describes the intense pain she experienced during the time of her marriage, and continues to experience even now when confronted with verbal abuse or so much as a somewhat tense encounter. She directly attributes the physical pain to issues of fear and stress:

> And the amazing thing is, I still get that — the physical feeling if someone did something angry with me. It goes straight through from the bottom of my body right up into my chest — my private area — it just sits. This pain goes right up through me and I feel nauseous.

Summary

This chapter has considered some of the experiences of Christian women who have been faced with a variety of forms of domestic abuse. Based on their reports of physical, verbal, emotional, sexual, social, financial, spiritual, property and child abuse, the impact of domestic abuse on Christian women and their families can be viewed as significant.

Further, the cycle of violence has been shown as a factor contributing to why women choose to remain in a domestic abuse situation. Moreover, the role of the cycle of violence in contributing to conditions such as learned helplessness and learned hopefulness has also been indicated.

Finally, while the effects of living in a domestic abuse situation may be many and varied, issues specifically relevant to the women interviewed were presented. Changes in personality, depression, stress-related conditions and physical illness, and in some cases the desire to commit suicide were all clearly identified by the women as being closely related to their experiences of domestic abuse.

Reflections for the Counsellor

1. How would the fact that the women have 'no frame of reference' for domestic abuse affect their perception of abuse and/or the experience of domestic abuse?
   - Why is this significant?
2. Consider the impact of additional issues faced by committed Christian women who are confronted with the ongoing nature of abuse.

Client Discussion

1. What sort of indications did you have of domestic abuse?
   - When do you believe it started?
   - At what point did you realise it was domestic abuse?
2. How do you define domestic abuse?
   - Has your view of domestic violence changed over a period of time? If so, what contributed to the change?
3. What examples of domestic abuse are/were relevant to your experience?
   - What behaviours would you identify as contributing to a 'cluster'? (These may differ from client to client.)
   - What covert forms of abuse are you now able to identify?
4. What are your strengths (past and present)?
   - Did you find these were targeted by your partner? If so, how?
5. How did the abuse escalate over time in your situation?
   - How did it start?
   - What early actions either pointed towards or signified abuse?
   - Were there things (e.g. events, actions, behaviours) that you did not then identify as abuse but would now?
6. With what forms of abuse (e.g. physical, financial) do you most identify? Reflect upon examples of these in your own experience.
   - What situations had the most impact? Why?
7. Consider a normal day in your relationship. Do you feel abuse was present? If so, in what form (e.g. a look, a frown, a word, withholding affection)?
8. Consider your social/support network. Draw it (e.g. using an atom diagram).
   - Consider any changes or differences before marriage, during marriage and after marriage.

- Was your support network minimised at any time? If so, when and how?

9. Have you noticed anything in particular regarding your children, either in the domestic abuse situation or, if relevant, after leaving the relationship (e.g. behavioural changes at home or school, changes in academic results or friendships)?
   - How would you describe or identify any changes in your approach to parenting?

10. Discuss the three key stages in the cycle of violence.
    - Can you identify these stages in your relationship? Share your experiences.
    - How do you feel as the tension rises? Where is your focus? What are you thinking at that time?

11. Think of the honeymoon phase of the cycle. What is your experience? How do you feel at that time (e.g. relief, the need to stay, hopeful, confused)?

12. Did you experience feelings of helplessness or hopefulness in your situation? If so, what sustained those feelings? If relevant, what fed the hope?
    - At what point, if any, did you lose hope? Share your thoughts.

13. Do you believe you experienced any stress reactions as a result of your situation? If so, what? Were you taking medication and for how long?

CHAPTER 4

Perpetrators and the Pursuit of Power

This chapter presents images of perpetrators of domestic abuse, as reported by the women whose experiences are included in this book. It is to be noted that the treatment of perpetrator characteristics in this chapter is limited to a brief overview of the literature, as this particular book has been designed to focus primarily on the victims of domestic abuse rather than the perpetrators. However, to provide a suitable background and a clear overall picture of the experiences of the women involved, it is necessary to include not only examples relating to the behaviour of the perpetrators but also the manner in which the women perceived their perpetrator husbands. In an effort to create a clear voice for the women, excerpts from the interview transcripts have been used to illustrate the significance of the various issues raised throughout the chapter.

This chapter considers the nature of perpetrator violence first as a learned response in the family of origin, and then as a matter of choice on the part of the individual. It further considers the manner in which perpetrators of domestic abuse often blame their victims for the abuse, and highlights the significance of domestic abuse as a means of control. Power maintenance within the cycle of violence is addressed, focusing primarily on the seemingly more positive but very deceptive phase of loving contrition, otherwise identified as the honeymoon or buyback phase of the cycle.

The conflicting image of perpetrators of domestic abuse as professing Christians is presented as a very current and also very confusing issue for the women represented in this book. This chapter further considers the way in which the image of perpetrators of abuse as professing Christians can prove extremely challenging for any members of the clergy who are called upon to assist in cases of domestic abuse within their congregations. Finally, this chapter questions the role played by the lack of any significant level of consequence in relation to the continuing abusive behaviour of the perpetrator. It also suggests that the absence of such consequence could be viewed as a contributing factor to the ongoing nature of abuse. While acknowledging some of the substantial difficulties involved, this chapter further advocates the need for perpetrator change based upon confrontation, willingness and a commitment to long-term lifestyle transformation.

Perpetrator Violence

'To produce violence, it is not necessary to promote it actively. All that is necessary is to stop restraining or preventing it' (Baumeister, 1997). Baumeister further refers to violence as 'evil' (p. 263) and suggests that while evil forces may be extremely powerful, equally powerful positive forces are available within the individual to bring a balance and act as a means of restraint. Aggression takes place when individuals 'fail to exert control over their feelings and responses' (Baumeister & Boden, 1998, p. 128). Thus, perpetrator violence could be viewed as a choice by the perpetrator not to take control over his emotions and the manner in which he reacts to given situations. In the following case, the choice made by the perpetrator in relation to both when and how to abuse is made particularly clear.

Miriam explains the cold and calculated actions of her husband in relation to physical abuse. As a perpetrator of abuse, Miriam's husband chose to rely upon the effects of her laminectomy (spinal surgery involving the removal of intervertebral disc/s and subsequent spinal fusion: O'Toole, 1992) as he calculated the degree to which Miriam was able to defend herself:

> I've still got scar tissue in a breast where the iron — he threw the iron at me and it was the point of it ... and there's still, you know, injuries there. And he used to count a bit on the fact that I have a ... I had a laminectomy back in 1970. So, of course, I've never been physically quick or that and I was a bit slow so and ... yes, that used to come into it too. He knew how fast I could go and what I could do and what I couldn't do.

Of the 20 women interviewed, 14 described their husbands as being either violent or threatening, or both. However, 17 of them reported having suffered in some way as a result of physical abuse. This difference in reporting could be due to a discrepancy regarding the manner in which each individual chose to define the term violence. Hannah tells of the frequent threats made by her husband and the reason she took them seriously:

> He did punch me in the side of, in the ear once. I couldn't hear properly for a week. And he would threaten a lot. He would threaten to hit me. And because he had done it before, then I would ... he wouldn't even have to hit and I'd be frightened.

Domestic Abuse as a Learned Response

Domestic abuse can be viewed as a learned response (Adams, 1994; Bahr, 2007b; Caesar, 1988; Fortune, 1991; Walker, 1984), commencing first of all in the family of origin. As children watch abuse take place as their parents fight, either physically or verbally, they learn that physical violence is an accepted method by which to solve problems or to gain control (Jouriles et al., 1998; Sullivan, Basta, Tan & Davidson, 1992). Through role-modelling, it becomes possible for children to behave in a similar manner to their parents, losing control at sometimes only the slightest provocation (Baumeister, 1997; Browne & Herbert, 1997; Brownridge & Halli, 2000; Miller & Knudsen, 2007; White, 1991). Violence and abuse may well be seen by children who witness it as an acceptable means by which to vent their emotions. This can be particularly so when the boys of the household begin to identify with the male abuser (Browne, 1987; Landes et al., 1993), and further increases the risk of the child becoming a perpetrator of domestic abuse (Borkowski et al., 1983; Dutton, 1995; Fortune, 1991; Gelles, 1987; Hofeller, 1987; Mills, 2008; O'Leary, 1993; Walker, 1979; Werner-Wilson, Schindler-Zimmerman & Whalen, 2000).

Anna speaks of her horror at her grown son's response to her during a visit to her home. As Anna had chosen to remain married for 38 years, her three children had been raised in the marital home and so became constant witnesses to the ongoing abuse:

Two years ago when my son came home, who was very close to me and everything, he saw his father. He stayed with his father for a couple of days and then came back around here and was ... a tiny little thing annoyed him, and my son just abused me in the same way and ... oh I just ... I was just ill, and I can't speak. I am just, am speechless. And it's no good speaking anyway — you're just shouted down with awful verbal abuse.

Domestic Abuse as a Choice

Domestic abuse is often depicted as a choice on the part of the perpetrator (Adams, 1994; Blanchard, 1999). Fortune (1991) states quite plainly that 'men choose to batter their partners because the choice is there to make' (p. 122). The issue of domestic abuse being a choice arises when one considers the fact that the perpetrator is usually well able to control his behaviour outside the home. In some cases, perpetrators of abuse have been categorised according to the type of abuse, or the manner in which the abuse is manifested (Huss & Langhinrichsen-Rohling, 2000). Unlike the more generalised abuser, the 'family only' abuser does not abuse his work colleagues, friends, or others within the community. The actions of the perpetrator remain controlled while the threat of consequence is present (Nolan, 1994; Randall, 1991; Tifft, 1993; Walker, 1979). A 'Jeckyll and Hyde' (Susanna) concept is one that would appear appropriate, as often the partners of perpetrators of abuse describe them as 'two different people' (Dutton, 1995, p. 103; Hegstrom, 2004).

Miriam supports this position as she speaks of her experiences of abuse with her husband of 15 years, including the speed with which his demeanour could change:

> ... verbal abuse towards myself and mainly the older of the two boys, but sometimes the youngest as well ... was just constant. At anything and everything. It was more or less — it was like a split personality. And you could go along thinking everything was rosy and just in a matter of 30 seconds ...

Rachel describes how the behaviour of her husband differed, depending on whether the setting was his workplace, a social venue or the marital home:

> But at work they're the perfect gentleman and they don't — you know, they control their temper, their anger. They don't hit out at work. They don't hit out, you know, when they're out socially.

Anna, too, is able to illustrate the changing behaviour of her husband when he would bring the children to visit her while she was in the hospital:

> You know, my daughter said, when I was in hospital all those weeks, she said how he was just like sugar and honey at the hospital, and as he leaves all the nasty anger was there and everything. And so, people were saying how wonderful he was, and how supportive and caring.

Anna later goes on to say that she was actually too afraid to go home, so she made the request to return to the sanctuary of the hospital. She explains the manner in which her husband, a lay preacher who constantly presented an excellent public image, treated her on the occasion of her own mother's funeral, during which time she was suffering from severe stress and shock. Anna had been lying down recovering, when her specialist, who was some distance away, had been contacted by phone:

> And that's when my husband, when everyone went out to say goodbye to everybody, he dug his fingers into my shoulders and dragged me up on the bed and shook and shook me and said, 'You're coming back to [home town]'. And I just cried and cried, and I was meant to have the weekend at home.

Perpetrators and the Projection of Blame

Perpetrators rarely choose to accept responsibility for their abusive actions, but rather choose to blame others, usually their spouses (Fleming, 1996; JCDVPP, 2002; McCue, 2008; Miles, 2000; NiCarthy, 1986; Ptacek, 1988; Rinck, 1990, 1998; Stewart, 2004). Gregory and Erez (2002) found that perpetrators who were part of a court-ordered treatment program frequently blamed their victims for the inconvenience of having to attend the mandatory sessions. Dutton (1995) suggests that abusers may go through the process of mentally reconstructing the act of abuse 'in order to blame the victim for having provoked the aggression' (p. 49). Blaming the victim can also be a means by which the perpetrator is able to offset feelings of guilt or shame that have arisen as a result of the angry and abusive outbursts (Dutton). Frequently, the abusive incident is triggered by an extremely small and possibly insignificant event. At times there can appear to be no link whatsoever between the abusive incident and any other action (Browne, 1987). Unfortunately, an individual who chooses to behave in an abusive manner is able to move from one relationship to another, constantly blaming each new partner for the problems he faces. Gradually, as a pattern is established, it becomes far easier to move the blame from individual women and apply a broader generalisation, thereby blaming all women and placing the responsibility for the abusive conduct on women as a gender group (Dutton).

Linked with blaming the victim is the fact that perpetrators have been found to significantly minimise, or even deny, their own use of violence while substantially exaggerating the behaviour of the victim (Browning & Dutton, 1986; Claes & Rosenthal, 1990; Dutton, 1995; Eisikovits, Goldblatt & Winstok, 1999; Fleming, 1996; Heckert & Gondolf, 2000; McCue, 2008). Further, many perpetrators of abuse see nothing wrong with the actions they have taken (Hopkins & McGregor, 1991). Perpetrators who profess to be Christian will often use the Scriptures and theology in general in an effort to justify and support not only their own viewpoint, but also their behaviour (Fleming; Rinck, 1998).

Due to the incredible stress under which she was forced to live, Susanna dreaded walking into the family home if her husband was at home:

> My whole life was incredibly stressful. I just didn't like dealing with him because he was always down on me, or he's negative. And if he was unhappy, it was my fault that he was unhappy. And so it was very difficult to deal with.

Later, Susanna explains more of the manner in which her husband constantly blamed others for his own choices and decisions. Blaming others had become a rather constant theme in his life:

> See, even at this stage he doesn't recognise that he has made mistakes. It's other people that have made ... done things to him that's got him into this situation. He hasn't taken responsibility for it. That's why we're getting divorced, because I cannot see any way of him improving because he doesn't realise it and he's not humble enough to try to do better.

Domestic Abuse as a Means of Control

One of the primary aims of domestic abuse — be it physical, verbal or any other form — is the exertion of power and control over the victim and other members of the household (Adams, 1988; Barnett & LaViolette, 1993; Bowker, Arbitell & McFerron, 1988; Dutton, 1995; DVPC, 2008a; Miles, 2000, 2002; Nelson, 1997; Walker, 1994). Anderson et al. (2003) describe domestic abuse as a 'specific strategy used to subjugate the victim for the gain of the abuser' (p. 151), while Adams (1994) writes succinctly, 'when a man hits a woman, he has not lost control; he achieves and maintains control' (p. 11). Nabi and Horner (2001) found that women who had personal experience of abuse considered the need for the perpetrator to maintain control over the victim as being a central issue of domestic abuse. The desire for the perpetrator to control the victim often extends beyond the relationship, as perpetrators continue to abuse their partners even after separation or divorce (DVPC; Fleury, Sullivan & Bybee, 2000).

Perpetrators are often described as dominating, intimidating and controlling — even to the point of demanding total control over each and every aspect of the relationship — and can become extremely angry if their wives are not agreeable and compliant (Bagshaw & Chung, 2000; Hofeller, 1987; JCDVPP, 2002; Meloy, 1998; Nelson, 1997; Stewart, 2004; Tifft, 1993). Such an outlook can present serious difficulty if the wife is more educated or better qualified, or in some way seemingly more capable than the perpetrator (Claes & Rosenthal, 1990). Her ability can become a constant

(even daily) challenge to the perpetrator, whose self-concept is continually under threat as he is confronted with the reality of the
situation (Baumeister, 1986). According to Baumeister (1997), 'the
violent husband is the man who thinks his daily life is not confirming
his exalted opinion of himself' (p. 146). However, other writers
(Martin, 1976; Thorne-Finch, 1992; Walker, 1979) suggest that the
perpetrator may suffer from low self-esteem. Thus, the low self-
esteem of the perpetrator may be constantly reinforced by the
superior capabilities of his wife. In a study of male perpetrators who
violently abused their partners, Rosenbaum and Leisring (2003)
found that many of the men had grown up in abusive and unstable
homes with little if any affection or security. As adults, the perpetrators exhibited a wide range of psychological problems in addition to
low self-esteem and limited self-confidence.

Eve shares a time in her marriage when she experienced success
in her chosen sport, only to have her achievements minimised and
criticised because her success had highlighted the lack of achievement
on the part of her husband:

> I've always mostly played netball, and when I came home,
> I had two trophies and I was so excited about it and then
> when he saw them he just said, 'Oh well. That's fine for
> you, but I don't have any so …'. It was just like it cut me
> down and so I just put it in the cupboard sort of thing,
> instead of thinking, 'Oh that's really great and …'

The abuse of power over another is a means by which a perpetrator
can increase his control and therefore his power base within the relationship. However, when a husband chooses to violate his wife, the
damage to the relationship is often irreparable (Baumeister, 1997). At
this point, it is interesting to note that 17 of the 20 women are either
already divorced or separated with divorce pending. Only three
remained married to their husbands at the time of the interviews.
Thus, it may be considered that as a direct result of the abuse experienced by these women, the damage to their marital relationships was
indeed irreparable.

Ruth, a nurse, describes a number of situations where her husband
simply had to be in control throughout their 20-year marriage:

> We were both working, but he was in control and he was
> the power ... that turned the wheel, and made everything
> work ... and whether it was physical, mental, emotional
> or everything. He required the woman to be in the home.

Ruth explains how her husband dictated which church the family
would attend and also the manner in which he would make all the
decisions for the household. Ruth was given no choice or control over
the distribution of financial resources, regardless of the fact that she
earned a substantial portion of the family income. Further, Ruth was
permitted no input in the naming of her five children. Her husband
chose all the names based on his own Pacific Island cultural heritage,
exhibiting a flagrant disregard for Ruth's wishes in the matter.

Control was taken to the extreme when Ruth's husband constantly expected her to produce children even against the advice of her
doctor, and then ultimately sought female companionship elsewhere:

> I would have never had all the children I had if I could
> have produced a boy at the beginning. I would have never
> had any more children. But, because I had three girls, I had
> to keep going. And even my GP had told him to stop
> having children. My health was suffering. And ... the age
> of 37 and 40, I still had children. And fortunately my last
> child was a male. And the day I had the male, that was the
> day he looked elsewhere for his green pastures, or looked
> for what he wanted.

All the women interviewed either specifically described their husbands as being controlling, intimidating, threatening or violent, or
alternatively described situations in which their husbands did in fact
exhibit these behaviours. The most prevalent description provided,
which appeared in 17 of the 20 cases, was that of being controlling.

As seen in the abovementioned example of Ruth, the desire for
the perpetrator to control, exert authority or simply prove who is
'boss' can manifest itself in a variety of ways other than physical violence or the threat of it. Lois describes her feelings of powerlessness in
relation to her marriage. While her husband could certainly be
violent, threatening and intimidating, he also employed other means
by which to increase her feelings of helplessness and powerlessness:

> He bought a motorbike that set us back about $3000 when we were on a very low income. And he let that bike sit out in the yard and just rust and be destroyed and sold it for $300. And every time I would say to him, 'You really need to do something about that motorbike. You need to sell it. You just need to put it in our shed'. He would refuse to do that. So those sort of things make you feel powerless ...

Anna speaks of her experience regarding a similar situation, where simply because she wanted something, her husband refused to comply:

> If you wanted anything, especially in the latter years there was always that power game. An example being, I know it sounds simple, but it's all part of the whole picture now I realise. You know, we needed, really needed a new side fence. I mean we kept it nice, and he knew I really would like that side fence. And it was like I just knew if I made the slightest comments that it'd be totally ignored ... so that was held over me. Like, you know, we could easily afford it. So it was held over you. You know, you wouldn't even talk about it.

Lois and Anna were both painfully aware that any desire they had was subject to the will of their husbands. Even in seemingly small things, the perpetrators were clearly able to exert their authority and maintain their own exalted position while, in no small way, reinforcing the position of subjugation and powerlessness already felt by their wives.

Power Maintenance Within the Cycle of Violence

While the cycle of violence contains three basic phases — tension, explosion and loving contrition (Miles, 2000) — here I would like to consider specifically the power of the loving contrition or honeymoon phase. Usually, the honeymoon phase is free of violence, and is denoted by kind and more considerate behaviour by the perpetrator. It often contains demonstrations of love and future good intentions (Gott, 1995). However, the absence of violence does not necessarily constitute a time when the victim feels truly safe. It has been acknowledged that living in the cycle of violence can be similar to living on the edge of a volcano, in so much as an eruption is eventually inevitable (Barnett & LaViolette, 1993).

The period of loving contrition is part of the power and control issue. Miles (2000) views it as a further attempt at the manipulation of both the victim and the relationship. Any remorse on the part of the perpetrator is often accompanied by blaming the victim for his angry and destructive outburst, and minimising his own role in the assault. Although the victim may be confused, the desire for her relationship to work can override the need to escape. Thus, the seemingly caring gestures of the perpetrator serve only to further hold the victim captive (JCDVPP, 2002).

Abigail found that during the honeymoon phase she was often lulled into a false sense of security, feeling more relaxed in the relationship, until the tension started again. She states, 'you'd just get to the stage where you felt comfortable and then it would happen again'. Rachel explains how it could be easier for her to weaken and be drawn back into the situation during the honeymoon or buyback phase, as her husband exhibited seemingly acceptable behaviour and was even congenial at times:

> There were some nice times when he was half human kind of thing ... and I guess in that buyback period too — you know, they're particularly nice then, and you know they can do it when they want to.

Perpetrators as Professing Christians

It has been fairly well established that men who are professing Christians are not only capable of domestic abuse (Buxton, 2000; King, 1999; Miles, 1997; Nason-Clark, 1997; Ramsay, 1999; Smith, 1995) but also, like their non-Christian counterparts, are capable of employing extreme measures such as lies, deception and the manipulation of others (including members of the clergy) to hide their actions and ultimately avoid any undesirable consequences (Miles, 2000). Stewart (2004), a former detective sergeant in the police force of Wisconsin, refers to these individuals as 'cowards in the Kingdom' and describes their behaviour as 'inexcusable' (p. 97). Miles (2002) further suggests that, regardless of what many Christians would like to think, the likelihood of both victims and perpetrators of domestic abuse being present in every congregation is extremely high. In relation to churches in the Unites States, Miles (2002) paints this vivid picture:

> Hidden securely behind the ornate stained glass windows, and buried deep within the hearts of many people seated in the pews of churches across the United States, incidents of domestic violence flourish like a raging fire out of control. (p. 24)

The characteristics attributed to perpetrators in general are equally attributable to perpetrators within the religious community. All the women represented referred to their perpetrator husbands as professing Christians, although two (Rachel and Naomi) did specify that they classified their husbands as being backslidden (turned aside from their Christian faith) in so much as they were no longer involved in the religious beliefs or practices of their denomination. It is therefore important to consider that all the examples of abuse provided by the women in this book were perpetrated by men professing to be Christian, some of whom were significantly involved in the life of their local church. In some cases (Anna, Elizabeth), the involvement of the perpetrators extended to leadership roles.

Anna speaks of the lengths to which her husband went to display a confident and positive public image as an active member of their local church:

> Of course we went to church every week and he was so involved. He always made sure he was one of the elders or he was the minister's mentor and that ... totally, deeply involved. My husband, you know, prides himself on his preaching ability. He'd practise for hours so he didn't have to read notes. He'd practise his prayers ... he was always the one the minister would ask to help serve the communion and he'd take it around, and he'd know all the right things to say, and he'd use the people's names. And then when he'd sit down, he'd make a big show of either putting his arm around my shoulder, or holding my hand.

This lack of congruence between her husband's public life as a lay preacher and his private life as a perpetrator of abuse proved extremely painful for Anna. She not only found the behaviour of her husband confusing, but also experienced substantial pressure as a result of the constant pretence at happiness. Anna expresses her inner turmoil as she describes her feelings in relation to the ongoing charade:

> Sundays I would feel very upset inside and I was putting on a mask. A total mask of happiness. I absolutely fooled everybody.

Deborah faced a similar problem as her husband's profession of faith was in constant conflict with his lifestyle within the family. Deborah's husband was extremely well educated, holding a masters degree and being employed as a school principal. Despite being economically secure, he controlled and withheld finance from the family. Deborah explains how she was totally unprepared for the manner in which her husband was able to manipulate the local minister:

> He arranged for us to go and see our local minister. We went. He went with his diary of the things that he had been doing. And I had gone with nothing. Now I could have taken years of diaries to say that you've done this, this and this, and I went with nothing. Then it boiled down to the bishop saying, 'You should be really grateful you're married to such a man'. I knew that I couldn't go back there again for any support.

The conflict between the profession of faith of the perpetrators and the lifestyles led by them proved confusing for many of the women. Domestic abuse in general — in addition to such activities as the husband's involvement in pornography (Joanna, Leah, Lydia), adultery (Susanna, Lois, Rebekah), masturbation (Eve), homosexuality (Mary, Sarah), nudism (Elizabeth) and alcohol and/or drug abuse (Hannah, Naomi, Rebekah, Eunice) — was not in any way part of the frame of reference of any of the women, much less so in relation to men who were considered to be Christian and also actively involved in their local churches.

Based on the premise of identifying an individual by the fruit each one produces, a concept found in both the Gospel of Matthew (12:33) and also the Gospel of Luke (6:44) (Carson, 1984; Earle, 1964; Liefield, 1984), Rinck (1998) suggests that it is the behaviour of the perpetrators that must be considered far more than the words they speak. She carefully explains that if behaviour indicates hostility or abuse, spoken declarations become empty and meaningless.

Perpetrators: Benefit Versus Consequence

In October 2000, during a training seminar focusing on domestic violence and the assistance of women who had become victims of abuse, a question was posed relating to why some men become perpetrators of domestic abuse. The presenter responded in a very frank and open manner with the words, 'Because they can'. While such a response may be considered a gross simplification of an extremely complex issue, it does appear to reflect the thought that abuse is indeed a choice on the part of the perpetrator not to control his own responses to given situations (Adams, 1994; Baumeister, 1997; Baumeister & Boden, 1998; Blanchard, 1999; Stewart, 2004). It also tends to highlight the limited likelihood of a wife, whether as a result of fear or feelings of moral commitment (Bagshaw & Chung, 2000), reporting the actions of her husband to the police or anyone else in a significant position of authority who is both willing and able to confront the perpetrator and attach consequences to the abusive actions. Thus, any negative consequences for unacceptable behaviour become minimal or at least somewhat delayed, leaving the perpetrator unchallenged in his pursuit of power and control (Monson & Langhinrichsen-Rohling, 1998). In essence, abusive behaviour provides the perpetrator with that which he desires (Adams, 1994; Koss et al., 1994). He benefits from increased attention, control over others, and possibly a boost in self-esteem through his own experience of power in addition to the helplessness of others (Browne & Herbert, 1997). Often the victim will endeavour to cater to every possible whim of the perpetrator in an effort to keep a reasonable level of harmony within the relationship (Dutton, 1995). In effect, the benefits for the perpetrator appear to far outweigh the cost.

The case of Elizabeth clearly illustrates the total lack of consequence for the perpetrator. Of the 20 women represented, all of whom experienced some form of physical abuse, Elizabeth was the only one to mention actually contacting the police after being brutally attacked by her husband. Even then, the results for Elizabeth were devastating:

I rang the police, and two police constables came, and one of them decided to take me in the police car down to the hospital to see … I did have a broken bone in my nose, but they can't do much with noses. And my face was very damaged … and the other one stayed with him. And while I was there at the hospital, I was counselled by a Salvation Army person who encouraged me that I could lay charges, but if I did I would ruin him for life. And then the policeman basically said the same. He said, 'Look, you could lay charges, but you would ruin him for life'. You know, he would have a bad mark against his name and … and I thought, 'Well, I don't want to do that to him'. I didn't want to sort of have long-lasting effects on his life or his career so I decided not to lay any charges, and I was taken home. And when we got home the other policeman came to the door and he just looked at me and he said, 'Everything will be all right now because your husband's got some tablets to settle you down'. And I didn't realise at the time what that meant to me. But at that point, something in me died, because, you see, I had done … I had stood up for what I thought I needed. Then I had gone to where I thought I could get help — two people, the church and the police were involved — and everyone concerned was indicating to me, in one way or another, that there was something wrong with what I had done.

Regardless of the police presence, Elizabeth's husband faced no consequences whatsoever for his vicious and brutal attack upon his young wife, and continued to reoffend over a period of 20 years until the marriage finally dissolved. This incident left Elizabeth feeling totally disillusioned with both the church and the legal system. She speaks of the pain and isolation of the weeks following the attack:

I couldn't go to playgroup. I couldn't go anywhere. I was trapped for quite a long time [sigh], weeks and weeks, waiting for, you know, my eyes were slits — you know, it was just so painful, and of course there was no sympathy.

As a result of this incident, Elizabeth learned that she was expected to obey her husband and comply with his demands. Unfortunately, but understandably, Elizabeth also learned that she could not rely on either the church or the legal system to provide her with any meaningful assistance. Ultimately, the assistance, understanding and actual enlightenment Elizabeth needed came from a secular organisation. It was a very shocked Elizabeth who realised that 'there were answers out there, but they weren't in the church'.

More recently, in an effort to establish an appropriate consequence for perpetrators of abuse and to ensure some level of safety for the victim, there is an increasing move in the United States for law-enforcement officers to build an evidence-based prosecution. As a result, cases of abuse can be prosecuted on a purely evidentiary basis without the need to rely on any testimony from the victim. One very significant outcome of this strategy is the freeing of victims of abuse from the pressure and danger of having to give evidence against their abusive spouse (Gwinn, 2003; Stewart, 2004).

Perpetrators and Change

Miles (2000) clearly states that change in perpetrator behaviour is solely the responsibility of the perpetrator himself. The victim is neither capable of, nor responsible for, initiating or sustaining any change in perpetrator behaviour (Dutton, 1994, 1995; Dutton, Saunders, Starzomski & Bartholomew, 1994). Unfortunately, perpetrators of abuse often deny that they have a problem, or endeavour to justify their actions (Gondolf, 1988; Rinck, 1990; Walker, 1979). To this end, a perpetrator will frequently tell others (such as friends, wives or clergy) whatever he thinks is appropriate in an effort to either avoid taking responsibility for his behaviour or convince them of personal change, again resulting in an avoidance of responsibility (Miles). It is therefore necessary for the counsellor or clergy person to be aware of the strong tendency of the perpetrator towards manipulation, charm and persuasion, lest they too become caught in the web of deception (Miles; Nason-Clark, 1998; Rinck). Protecting the perpetrator from the consequences of his actions is neither a caring nor charitable act (Kroeger & Nason-Clark, 2001). Without confrontation, the perpetrator is able to continue to pursue his lifestyle of abuse without challenge and therefore without the opportunity to receive the assistance he so desperately needs (Fleming, 1996).

Elizabeth constantly kept her minister informed of the abuse she was suffering. She frequently asked for prayer, in the hope of change in her husband, their relationship and their marriage. However, her husband was never confronted regarding his abuse. Even when he forced Elizabeth to accompany him one evening to the home of their minister in an effort to prove her to be a disobedient wife, he was not told that his behaviour was unreasonable or unacceptable. Instead, the minister and his wife became a part of the charade as they endeavoured to decide, at the request of the perpetrator, whether or not Elizabeth should be permitted to wear a secondhand, one-piece black bathing suit she had been given.

As a backdrop to this event, Elizabeth explains the manner in which her husband exerted control in every area, including her behaviour and her dress:

> Everything I wore, I was either a slut or provocative, men were watching me, I was so stupid I didn't even realise. I had to be watched all the time. I couldn't be trusted. I bent over the wrong way. I just, you know, everything I did was ... was wrong.

Later, Elizabeth says:

> He was quite cranky because I was wearing ... He'd been away and he found out I was wearing ... It's a one-piece, like, black bathing suit. And ... he believed in holding it up to the light, it was see-through. So, he decided to march me down there and tell them about it. The four of us sat round one night, in their lounge room ... The pastor's wife held it up to the light. Everyone looked at it to see whether it was acceptable that I should wear it. Pastor actually himself said very little ... but I was literally hauled over the coals for ... doing something that he said I shouldn't do.

Elizabeth's husband later left the marriage to be with another woman, whom he also left before becoming involved with and finally marrying yet another woman. Despite committing constantly violent acts of domestic abuse, becoming a nudist and leaving Elizabeth for another woman, Elizabeth's husband retained his leadership role in the church and was ultimately provided with his pastor's credentials. Due to lack of confrontation and appropriate assistance on the part of the minister, Elizabeth was left unaided in a tormenting and torturous situation for the duration of her 20-year marriage. Moreover, her husband was never challenged, and as a result was never provided with the opportunity to face both the truth and the consequences of his behaviour. Instead, he was permitted to continue his lifestyle without ever taking responsibility for his actions or endeavouring to address the root issues of his problems. Schissel (2000) states emphatically that the society that holds perpetrators accountable for their actions establishes the foundation for 'the most effective violence prevention strategy: high demand for nonviolent behavior' (p. 971). Such a statement suggests that the reverse is also true, in that a society that refuses to hold perpetrators accountable is providing a foundation for the acceptance of violence and aggression.

Rinck (1990, 1998) maintains that often the only reason a perpetrator will seek any form of assistance is as a result of his wife either threatening to leave him or actually doing so, thereby creating a crisis situation for the perpetrator. The threat of unpleasant consequences can motivate the perpetrator to action; however, many of those Rinck classifies as misogynist may be willing to lose everything, through separation and subsequent divorce, rather than choose to admit they have a problem and deal with the issues involved. She further notes that success in dealing with such individuals is 'rare' (1990, p. 140). Individuals in this category will often become involved in a new relationship, thereby jeopardising their chances of truly addressing and dealing with the root issues of their problem (as in the case of Elizabeth). Kroeger and Nason-Clark (2001) state plainly that 'most abusers do not change' (p. 125), while Walker (1979) maintains that relationships that have their foundation in a strong power imbalance, which favours the perpetrator, are very unlikely to be resolved to a point of ongoing equality.

In relation to perpetrator change, Gondolf (1988) highlights a willingness to change on the part of the perpetrator as being paramount. He acknowledges that a personal transformation is necessary to sustain any changes that have taken place, and further emphasises the importance of support groups to help encourage and maintain perpetrator commitment to change. The utilisation of group therapy for perpetrators of abuse is supported by a number of authors (Dutton, 1995; Fleming, 1996; Geldard & Geldard, 2009; Kroeger & Nason-Clark, 2001; Rinck, 1990, 1998; Sullivan, 2003). However, the challenge to maintain a lifestyle change can prove exceedingly difficult for the perpetrator whose daily environment is one that conflicts with the more positive concepts fostered within the support group (Shaw, Bouris & Pye, 1999).

While many Christian authors (JCDVPP, 2002; Kroeger & Nason-Clark, 2001; Miles, 2000; Rinck, 1990, 1998) believe that, in God, there is hope for perpetrator change, they also acknowledge that the road to healing is fraught with difficulties and there are no absolute guarantees. Regarding the restoration of the marital relationship that has suffered substantially as a result of abuse, Rinck (1998) writes, 'it takes a lot of time, therapy and prayer to renew the marriage relationship' (p. 88). In many cases, the relationship is lost completely. Of the women in this book, only three (Hannah, Deborah, Abigail) remained married after enduring many years of abuse. Of those, only one (Abigail) reported any marked level of change sustained over a period of time, in her case three-and-a-half years. At the close of the interview, Abigail had this to say:

> Miracles are possible. I never thought that my husband would change in the way ... that he did. So it is possible for something to happen. My husband's actually ... gone so far the other way, that he helps me with my faith. He's brought me closer to God. He's made um ... God seem more real for me.

Abigail also highlights the fact that she confronted her husband's behaviour by leaving the marriage for a short period of time, and as a result of that confrontation her husband chose to seek help in the form of a 10-week course with Centacare. Abigail's husband also exhibited an ongoing desire to change and maintain a long-term commitment to the marriage. Abigail too accepted the opportunity of attending a short course, lasting approximately five weeks. The aim of the course she attended was to help women gain an understanding of the various forms of abuse, power and control, gender issues, and the manner in which the cycle of violence operates.

In the case of Abigail, the following points are clearly defined: first, the initial confrontation in the form of Abigail's departure; second, a sincere desire and willingness by her husband to accept responsibility for his actions and make the necessary changes; and third, a strong commitment on the part of the perpetrator to both the program and the marriage. Finally, as an outworking of these things, a positive result emerged.

Summary

This chapter has provided an overview of the images of perpetrators of domestic abuse as reported by the women who shared their experiences. Illustrations provided by a number of the women have been used to describe the manner in which perpetrator abuse can be viewed as a choice and a definite violation of the person of the victim. As each of the women experienced projection of blame; domestic abuse as a perpetual and powerful means of domination, intimidation and control; and ongoing power maintenance through the cycle of violence, the image of their perpetrator husbands as professing Christians and God-fearing men became both confusing and seemingly inappropriate.

Finally, confrontation and ultimate consequence have been suggested as necessary strategies when dealing with the individual who chooses to abuse. Such strategies can be further enhanced by the role of helping professionals and associated support groups. While total lifestyle change for the perpetrator of abuse has been presented as a difficult challenge for all concerned, it is openly acknowledged that such change is indeed possible. However, this only applies when and if the individual concerned is willing to take responsibility for his actions, and commit to dealing with the root issues of his problems.

Reflections for the Counsellor

1. How would you explain to a client the actions of a perpetrator, particularly one professing to be a Christian?
   - What possible types of conflict do you see in this situation?

2. How might you go about helping a client to understand the dynamics of this type of relationship?

Client Discussion

1. How do you see violence as being the choice of the perpetrator?
   - Discuss some examples of violence from the chapter and also from your own relationship. Are there any parallels?
   - Compare and contrast your partner's behaviour inside and outside the home.
   - What does he say?
   - How does he act?
   - What does he tell people?
   - How does he treat others?

3. What words would you use to describe his behaviour (i) inside the home and (ii) outside the home? You may use drawings, words or other representations as you wish.
   - How do you account for these differences?

4. What types of events or incidents would trigger abuse? Share some examples from your relationship.
   - How would you rate these trigger events (e.g. minor, insignificant)?

5. How did your partner try to control you (e.g. by actions, threats, looks)? Discuss.
   - How did you feel at these times?
   - Did your partner endeavour to minimise your achievements, maximise your failures, destroy your interests or rob you of satisfaction or success? If so, how? Discuss.

7. Perpetrators do not need to actually speak the words 'I am the boss' but can demonstrate that same concept in a number of ways. Discuss the ways in which this may have happened in your relationship.

CHAPTER 5

Discovering Forgiveness

This chapter provides an overview of the way in which the Christian teachings relating to forgiveness have the capacity to affect the lives of Christian women who have become victims of domestic abuse. The teaching of forgiveness is defined according to biblical principles which include the need to forgive an offender, and the relevance of sincere repentance in relation to the desire to receive forgiveness.

Key issues surrounding forgiveness with specific reference to domestic abuse are discussed. These include the manner in which forgiveness is linked to repentance, the definition of repentance, and the subsequent call for genuine repentance on the part of the perpetrator. Inaccurate interpretations of the biblical principles of forgiveness are presented, focusing on the potential harm of applying such interpretations to situations of domestic abuse. Inaccurate interpretations of forgiveness encompass: the requirement to not only forgive but also forget the offence; excusing perpetrator behaviour; the restoration of trust in an abusive relationship; and the demand on the victim for either mediation or reconciliation on the basis of forgiveness. The need for positive action on the part of both the victim and members of the clergy is indicated, emphasising the necessity of ongoing victim support.

Finally, forgiveness in its most practical form is viewed as a process that can ultimately produce positive effects that contribute to the healing and restoration of the victim. In contrast, the act of pressuring the victim to forgive or take any other action that is not in her best interest is presented as yet another form of abuse.

Overview

Forgiveness is an issue that remains very significant but also deeply confusing for the Christian woman who is a victim of domestic abuse.

The concept can challenge her faith to the point where she is torn between her 'Christian duty' to forgive the perpetrator and her own inability to do so. Such pressure can bring with it feelings of guilt, condemnation and great personal frustration, which ultimately adds to the emotional distress of the individual as she feels she is not only failing in her marriage but also in her spirituality.

The subject of forgiveness is a complex issue which requires a significant degree of understanding of the issues of domestic abuse (Tracy, 1999). In some settings, the victim may be instructed by members of the clergy to provide ongoing forgiveness in a perpetual, unlimited and unconditional manner, regardless of the deed or activity of the perpetrator. Such an expectation can be extremely damaging to the individual who sincerely wishes to practise her faith, but is torn between her own survival and confusion regarding the needless pressure to extend forgiveness to a possibly unrepentant perpetrator.

Defining Forgiveness

The concept of forgiveness is a basic tenet of the Christian faith (Casey, 1998; Rye et al., 2000). It is described by Barabas (1981a) as the 'giving up of resentment or claim to requital on account of an offense' (p. 289). He further explains that forgiveness carries with it the ideal of total restoration of the relationship. Usually this is achieved partly as a result of the offending party repenting of their role in the offence, and endeavouring to make some form of reparation to the victim. Repentance requires a change in attitude (Turner, 1975; Rye et al.). The New Testament uses two Greek words to define the act of repentance more precisely because each word focuses on a different aspect of the act of repentance. Bass (1981) points out the connection between the Greek word *metanoeo*, which focuses primarily on a change of mind in relation to the situation, and the Greek word *metameleia*, which he refers to as a 'change of soul' (p. 711) that ultimately leads to a turning away from the particular sin or deed in question. The first presents itself more as an intellectual realisation or acknowledgment, while the second is the behavioural commitment which follows through as a direct result of the initial realisation.

A variety of examples from the Scriptures are used to illustrate the need for forgiveness to be an active part of the belief system for those choosing to identify with the Christian faith. Among them is the parable found in the Gospel of Matthew (18:23–35), which depicts the plight of a servant who is in debt to his master for an incomprehensible amount of money. The figure stated is 10,000 talents. It has been suggested that this sum could have been roughly equivalent to perhaps $10 million (Earle, 1964), but other calculations suggest that it could have been substantially more (Wilkins, 2002). For example, a talent is listed by Huey (1975) as being the equivalent of 3000 shekels, while a shekel is described by Petersen (1981a) as being the equivalent of one day's wage at the time the parable is presented. Using these calculations, one talent alone has a value placed upon it of approximately 8.2 years of wages. The debt of 10,000 talents described in the parable is now depicted as a startlingly inconceivable 82,000 years of wages. The key point of the parable, and also the overwhelming aspect of the monetary amounts presented, is the fact that the inescapable and overburdening nature of the debt of sin owed by mankind to an all-powerful God is forgiven (Carson, 1984; Earle). Those who identify with the Christian faith are required to emulate such forgiveness in their dealings with others (Monsma, 1975; Patton, 1985). This parable not only illustrates the expectation of forgiveness between individuals, but also illustrates the conditional nature of forgiveness, by highlighting the fact that because the servant himself chose not to forgive a colleague of a debt that could be considered miniscule by comparison to the debt from which he had already been released, his forgiveness was revoked and he was ultimately imprisoned.

The concept of conditional forgiveness is also found in the well-known prayer, usually referred to as the Lord's Prayer, also taken from the Gospel of Matthew (6:9–13). This prayer is provided as a model for Christians to follow. Again, the focus in this passage is on the individual person being forgiven their debts by an omnipotent God in the same manner in which the person chooses to forgive the debts (or wrongdoing) of others (Barabas, 1981a).

A further extension of the mandate to forgive is indicated in the seemingly unlimited nature of that forgiveness. This point is illustrated when Christians are instructed to forgive 'seventy times seven'

(Matthew 18:21) or 'seven times in a day' (Luke 17:4). Authors agree that this instruction is not meant as a mathematical equation; but rather as an indication of the generous and caring spirit behind the act of forgiveness, and that forgiveness should be ongoing (Barabas, 1981a; Carson, 1984; Childers, 1964; Earle, 1964; Liefield, 1984; Murphy, 2003; Strauss, 2002).

These teachings of ongoing and constant forgiveness presented a substantial amount of difficulty for some of the women interviewed (Anna, Lydia, Sarah) as they placed themselves under enormous pressure to conform to the requirement of Scriptures and forgive their husbands. While Lydia expressed the difficulty she had wrestling with her Christian values in the light of the abuse she experienced, both Anna and Sarah spoke openly of the scriptural mandate to forgive. Anna explains her position:

> That's what makes it, I've said over and over, a thousand times worse, trying to do something about an unhappy, abusive marriage when you are totally involved in the church. Because if you do have your Christian principles, you're thinking of Jesus' words of 'forgive seven times seventy'. 'Do not judge.' All those things kept coming into this. They influence you.

Sarah became quite upset when speaking of the battle she experienced in endeavouring to apply the Christian principles of forgiveness to the violence that confronted her very early in the marriage. Her confusion and distress became even more apparent when she recalled the manner in which she prayerfully sought the will of God regarding the relationship before making a marital commitment:

> You know, I prayed about this and this is what I thought was the path that I was to take, and here it is … and it's falling apart and I'm terrified … It was like — am I meant to stay with this? I've made vows … and in the prayer it's forgive us our trespasses as we forgive those who trespass against us. And that's the part I thought well, I can't forgive this person. I can't forgive the injustice that's been done and continues.

Sarah was eventually able to find peace in this aspect of her faith after receiving assistance from her minister in the form of an article about another victim of abuse. Sarah believes the provision of the article to be one of the most helpful things her minister was able to do for her. Reflecting on the content of the article, Sarah recalls:

> That the forgiveness part, it was written in such a way that it was like, maybe, you as a person don't have to forgive, that you hand that over to God. And that made a lot of sense to me ... 'cause I was really grappling with ... well you know, this is how I see it. How can I not forgive this? And it just really ... it was a balm for me.

The situations described by both Anna and Sarah highlight the necessity of viewing the Scriptural teachings regarding forgiveness in the light of domestic abuse. A woman whose life and faith are firmly grounded in Christian teaching is presented with a major dilemma when confronted with domestic abuse.

Forgiveness in Cases of Domestic Abuse

The practice of forgiveness in the case of domestic abuse raises a number of searching questions: is forgiveness, or should it be, conditional upon repentance; how does one define and identify true repentance within the context of domestic abuse; does remorse constitute repentance; and what action should one take when faced with the challenge of forgiving a perpetrator of abuse? Such questions can prove confusing for victims of abuse who desire to know exactly what forgiveness is, and what they are expected to do about it from a biblical standpoint. The following section will consider the connection between forgiveness and repentance, some common but inaccurate interpretations of the concept of forgiveness, and positive action that can be taken to assist the victim of abuse.

Linking Forgiveness to Repentance

'Forgiveness which does not call for repentance is barren' (Kerr, 1991, p. 45). Monsma (1975) maintains that, while in some cases there is no specific criteria mentioned in the Scriptures, there is strong evidence to suggest that the act of forgiveness on the part of the wronged person can be linked to the act of repentance and the subsequent request for forgiveness on the part of the offender. Cooper-White (1995) views repentance as a necessary prerequisite to forgiveness. She states plainly that victims of abuse require justice, which includes the calling to account of the perpetrator. Horsfield (1994) argues that even the forgiveness of God is conditional upon repentance, and notes further that both honest confession and repentance on the part of the perpetrator are essential if forgiveness is to be sought. Keene (1995) develops the concept of forgiveness further, explaining that the structure of forgiveness in the New Testament is one in which the individual holding the greater position or power is the one who is expected to forgive. Alternatively, forgiveness by those of equal status is also acceptable. According to Keene, if this concept is applied to a domestic abuse setting, the victim is under no obligation to forgive her abuser as she is clearly the weaker individual in a completely unequal power relationship.

Esther provides a particularly clear illustration of herself as the weaker individual in the power dynamic as she expresses her feelings of being constantly abused by her husband's ongoing demands for her forgiveness. In response to a question regarding the need to forgive her husband, Esther says:

> Yes, but then he would tell me to. He would say that, you know, the Bible says to forgive, to forgive seventy times seven, or whatever that one [Scripture] is. But I felt that I was being abused, because I felt that you couldn't ... do the same thing over and over again, and then ask forgiveness for the same thing over and over again, knowing that it hurt the person over and over again.

Genuine Repentance

Repentance has already been described as a change of attitude followed by an appropriate change in behaviour (Woodbridge, 1995), a focus emphasised by the prophet Ezekiel (18:30–32) when he declares that one must turn aside from harmful and ungodly practices if one is to live (Alexander, 1986; Grider, 1966). Miles (2000) explains that in many cases perpetrators will claim to be changed by the power of God, without making any personal effort to initiate or maintain the behavioural change. He cites one case where a short time after the victim had separated from her perpetrator husband, who was then confronted with the loss of his family, the husband claimed God had brought about a miraculous change in his life and behaviour. While the husband did express remorse for his actions, he refused to accept any assistance from either a therapist or a support group, and became angry when such action was suggested. It must be clearly understood that remorse does not constitute repentance (Cooper-White, 1995; Fortune, 1995a).

Smedes (1984) presents a view of repentance that encompasses four levels, each motivated by a choice on the part of the offender. Initially the perpetrator must perceive the offence through the eyes of the victim and develop an empathic understanding of the pain that has been experienced. This is followed by honest confession made directly to the person who has been wronged, and then a genuine promise to sincerely undertake not to reoffend. Smedes describes this final step as a 'passionate desire not to hurt again' (p. 67), explaining that it is only this level of repentance that opens the way to forgiveness. Thus, a simple apology does not constitute either confession or repentance (Cooper-White, 1995).

Eve's church expressed an interesting understanding of repentance and the subsequent need for her forgiveness toward her husband to be forthcoming. Apparently, an apology coupled with joining the prayer line conducted during the weekly church service was assumed to constitute an acceptable level of repentance. In speaking about her duty of forgiveness, Eve says:

> That was a big issue too. Yeah. Saying I had to forgive him for how he — you know the lies he lived and what he'd done to me — that's a big thing. Well, he's doing the wrong thing and he's come and said he's sorry and you know, he's been out ... the church and the prayer line. Well, I've got to forgive him because he's trying to do the right thing and you know it puts you in a bad position if you don't. You feel pretty bad.

Added to this was the fact that Eve was constantly reminded that her husband had been expected to forgive her for a substantial indiscretion that had taken place during the very early stages of their marriage. The contrast between these two situations is that Eve had indeed repented with sincerity and did not repeat that behaviour, whereas the behaviour of her husband — which included verbal, emotional and sexual abuse — continued unchanged.

In the absence of genuine repentance, it is reasonable to assume that the injustice will continue to be perpetrated (Education Psychology Study Group, 1990). Therefore, regardless of demonstrations of remorse or expressions of apology, the ongoing nature of domestic abuse must call into question the authenticity of claims of repentance on the part of a perpetrator who continually rejects any attempt to actively engage in counselling or behavioural change.

Regardless of any action taken by Anna, the abuse continued. Her husband, a lay preacher in the church, did not seem to regard his actions as unacceptable and therefore saw no reason to repent of them. Anna illustrates the futility of ongoing forgiveness in the absence of genuine repentance when she states:

> I know what forgiveness is about. I must have forgiven him a million times in 38 years ... And always coupled with that was trying to see the best in him, only expressing the best about him and hoping he would change.

Anna reports that there was never any change in her husband's behaviour. Ultimately, she ended the marriage after 38 years.

Inaccurate Interpretations of Forgiveness

Unfortunately, at times, forgiveness has been inaccurately interpreted in a variety of ways. It is therefore necessary to consider a number of actions that should not be classified as forgiveness. First and foremost is the erroneous concept of forgiveness being paralleled to forgetting. Other areas of concern include excusing perpetrator behaviour, restoration of trust, mediation, and the expectation of reconciliation. The following section will address these issues and endeavour to highlight the pitfalls of such expectations being placed upon victims of domestic abuse.

Forgive and Forget

Forgiveness does not require the victim to forget those things that have been perpetrated against her (Bishop & Grunte, 1993; Cooper-White, 1995; Enright & Zell, 1989; Hallowell, 2004; Henderson, 2002; Pearson, 1998; Smedes, 1984). Such a requirement has the potential to inhibit the healing process for the victim by causing her to remain enmeshed in the events of the past, thereby creating a powerlessness to initiate positive change (Walker, Bratton & Acquaviva,

1998). Further, the concept of forgiving and forgetting presents an unrealistic expectation for victims, trivialises the pain of the experience (Stoop & Masteller, 1991), does not have its roots in the Scriptures but rather in the writings of Shakespeare (Fortune, 1998; Miles, 2002), and contributes significantly to the already diminished levels of accountability for the perpetrator (Nason-Clark, 1997). Therefore, by encouraging the victim to adopt an attitude of forgive and forget, misguided individuals are not fostering the application of scriptural principles but instead are inadvertently cultivating the perpetuation of abuse (Casey, 1998).

Although Leah's minister did not actually say 'forgive and forget', it would appear that the message was the same. Leah was not only expected to forgive the constant physical, emotional and sexual abuse perpetrated by her husband, she was pressured to do so. Forgiveness was portrayed as possessing an almost magical quality, in that the problem would disappear if only she did the 'right thing'. Leah was further expected to continue her daily life as if all the offences had been dealt with as a result of forgiveness. Leah describes the counsel she was given:

> I was always told I had to forgive him for anything that happened …I guess that would make everything right. That'd give me the right attitude to do the right thing as a woman should do.

The ineffective nature of this form of counsel is evident when Leah reports that while some attention was paid to her husband, she found no benefit in the counselling that continued on and off for the entire 12-year period of church attendance. She comments:

> Nothing seemed to change. Everything seemed to be the same, so I kind of thought, well I mustn't be doing it right [sigh] … Nothing changed. Well that's the reason why I didn't go back … Also I was made to think, well, you know, there must be something wrong with me.

In an effort to make her marriage work, Leah attended numerous marriage seminars and endeavoured to follow the advice she was given by her minister. Some years after her divorce, when she was still being pressured by her minister to reconcile with her former husband, she decided, 'This is all a load of crap' and left the church. As a victim of domestic abuse, Leah was not supported but rather bullied further, as she was held accountable for the failure of her marriage.

In contrast to Leah's situation, Abigail's minister made time to listen to her and did not pressure her to forgive or ignore the behaviour of her husband, as he was well aware of the issues that were present in the marriage. Abigail explains that her minister chose to confront her husband and state clearly 'that if he was going to keep going in the way that he was going, that he would lose me'. She further reports that she felt supported and encouraged as a result of the meeting with the minister. Over time, Abigail's husband did receive counselling and also managed to sustain long-term behavioural change.

Excusing Behaviour

Forgiveness does not extend to excusing the abusive behaviour of the perpetrator or putting on a brave face and continuing life as if nothing has occurred (Cooper-White, 1995; Dowrick, 1997; Hallowell, 2004; Henderson, 2002; Kroeger & Nason-Clark, 2001; Patton, 2000; Safer, 1999; Smedes, 1984). While this action may prove effective in maintaining a form of peace, and may also assist in hiding the guilt and shame associated with domestic abuse (Bagshaw & Chung, 2000; King, 1998; Lynch & Graham-Bermann, 2000), it also enables the perpetrator to deny the situation and avoid seeking an honest solution. A number of the women interviewed found themselves constantly making excuses for the unacceptable behaviour of their perpetrator husbands (Mary, Ruth, Susanna). A popular excuse was often the background or early family life of the individual (Anna, Elizabeth, Rachel, Joanna, Lois).

In her attempt to be charitable, caring and forgiving, Susanna developed a long list of excuses for the inappropriate, and at times, criminal behaviour of her husband. Having experienced the benefits of a positive family environment herself, Susanna was very sensitive to the difficulties her husband had encountered during his early life:

> I just thought, 'Oh well, he's had a pretty difficult child-
> hood, and ... he's got, you know, his mother isn't a very
> pleasant person at all'. So I sort of made excuses.

In relation to her husband's fraudulent acquisition of finance, Susanna said:

> He explained that to me very well ... and I thought, 'Oh, right. OK'. And I believed him. Oh he was put into a corner. He didn't have any option, so that's why he did this. See, I've always made excuses for him.

At other times, in an effort to make sense of what was happening with her husband, Susanna told herself, 'Well he's under stress or this is the stage he's going through'.

Leah found herself excusing the apparent inability of her husband to change his behaviour:

> I just thought that he could change if he would ... like he was weak and ... he was trying, but there was ... like ... he couldn't do it because ... maybe oh ... things in his past, like maybe he needed more counselling. He needed more help to help him to change and all that sort of thing. I guess that's what I thought.

Like many women in similar situations, Leah felt that if only her husband could receive those things he needed, such as enough time, enough love or enough counselling, then he would naturally improve and their lives together could be reasonably free of incident. Unfortunately, this was not the case.

While Hannah did admit to making partial excuses for her husband at times, and certainly questioned the possible relevance of attention deficit disorder in relation to the abuse she endured, she discovered that her minister was more than prepared to make excuses for her husband:

> The response from the church we were going to was very much his way. And it was like he was frustrated. There were reasons for him to behave like that ... He just said, 'He's doing that because he's frustrated' ... and he ... I was left feeling that I had to be more understanding and I had to pray for him and he [the minister] would pray that I knew the things to say and how to behave. It was more that I was the one who had to ...

This minister not only made excuses for the perpetrator, he also made Hannah accountable for the behaviour of her husband by suggesting that she needed to pray more and to understand how to behave in order to prevent the violent outbursts.

Restoration of Trust

Trust within a relationship must be earned (Tracy, 1999). However, forgiveness does not require that trust be restored between the victim and the perpetrator (Bishop & Grunte, 1993; Fortune, 1995a). When an individual has been victimised and abused — not once but repeatedly over a long period of time — trust has been violated to the deepest and most intimate of levels, and as a result is not easily reestablished (Wilson, 1988). For trust to be rebuilt, evidence of behavioural change must be consistently apparent over a substantial period of time (Pearson, 1998). Hegstrom (2004) writes of his own experience as a recovering perpetrator of abuse, and explains the significance of time in rebuilding a trust that had been shattered during 16 years of emotional and physical abuse. After seven years of separation and divorce, during which he received assistance from a support program and also endeavoured to demonstrate his commitment to change by interacting and communicating appropriately with his former wife, he was finally reunited with her. Nason-Clark (1997) emphasises the need for this form of change, explaining that the perpetrator must not only renounce his violent behaviour but also 'move toward a new way of relating to the wife he once abused' (p. 53).

Lydia learned very quickly not to trust her husband's claims of repentance. After leaving the marriage once and returning only to find nothing had changed, she was advised by her father, a former minister, to leave a second time and endeavour to work out her own values, beliefs and faith while in a safe environment. This advice proved extremely helpful to Lydia. She did not return to the marriage after her second move. Lydia speaks of the repentance strategy employed by her husband, and her own lack of trust in his promises and claims of repentance:

> He just writes some sob story saying 'I'm really sorry. I'm
> ... please forgive me. I'll never do it again da-da-da-da-da.
> Come back and we'll, you know, have a look at those
> things ... and you're right, I did this that and the other
> and ... ' He can do all the repenting he likes, but if it's
> not ... I've been through that. I've had the letters. I've
> thought, you know, nothing you write to me is going to
> make me believe you now [laugh].

Mediation

The act of forgiveness does not pave the way for members of the clergy to expect the victim of abuse to attend mediation in an effort to resolve issues that have been inaccurately classified as marital difficulties. Domestic abuse is not a result of superficial or general forms of conflict, but has its roots in far deeper issues that have been discussed in earlier chapters (Adams, 1994; Anderson et al., 2003; Bagshaw & Chung, 2000; Dutton, 1995; JCDVPP, 2002; Miles, 2002; Walker, 1994). Neither the willingness of the victim to attend mediation or be reconciled with the perpetrator should be viewed as proof of forgiveness having taken place. The reverse is also true, in that an unwillingness by the victim to attend mediation or be reconciled with the perpetrator does not indicate an unwillingness to forgive. Mediation is not a practical alternative, as this form of intervention assumes equality within the relationship, aims at conflict resolution, and can prove to be a covert means by which to avoid criminal charges being brought against the perpetrator (Fortune, 1995a).

Reconciliation

Forgiveness does not necessarily lead to reconciliation, and reconciliation should not be demanded of the victim (Dowrick, 1997; Enright & Zell, 1989; Jantz, 2003; Miles, 2000, 2002; Murphy, 2003; Safer, 1999). In cases of domestic abuse, reconciliation is often impossible (Alsdurf & Alsdurf, 1989; Walker, 1979), and can potentially threaten or even harm the victim by restricting the consequences for the perpetrator and contributing to an increase in abuse for the victim (Kroeger & Nason-Clark, 2001; Smedes, 1996). While reconciliation, and thus an apparent restoration of the family unit, is often a primary focus of members of the clergy (Nason-Clark, 2000b), reconciliation is similar to trust in that it must be earned (Miles, 2000; Worthington, Sandage & Berry, 2000). The perpetrator does not have the right to expect a swift reconciliation based solely on the grounds of remorse, apology or the expectation that the victim should forgive him. Reconciliation is not a one-off event that culminates in the external reunion of two individuals, thereby creating the illusion of the problem being solved. Instead, it is often an arduous and painful process (Alsdurf & Alsdurf). Cooper-White (1995) states emphatically that 'forgiveness is not a right' (p. 256); ultimately, the choice to attempt to reconcile must always remain with the victim (Miles, 2002).

While Joanna stated that she was not placed under any direct pressure to forgive her husband, she also said that her minister was pressing her for a reconciliation, which she agreed was tantamount to expecting forgiveness to be forthcoming. Joanna explains the situation in which she found herself:

> I should believe that God can do anything and that He could change him and then I should have him back ... I suppose at the end of the day, yeah. It ... it would have to [link up with forgiveness]. I mean you can't be healed unless it ... there's forgiveness anyway.

Further to this, Joanna speaks of how she was forbidden to play any part at all in the music ministry of the church if she was not willing to reconsider reconciliation with her husband at some future date:

> I think no matter what I say, or no matter what I do, or no matter how I try and change my attitude about things that ... that they're not going to accept me. 'Cause they, like, totally took me off everything and I'm not allowed to be part of any music at all now. Like, I'm not even allowed to sing, play keyboard. I'm not allowed to have anything to do with it. That's what they told me, because I won't say that I want to look at things in a couple of years. I've given no hope for the marriage.

Joanna loved being part of the music ministry team, and loved to worship with her voice and also with her instrument. However, as a victim of abuse, instead of being supported and encouraged, she was further victimised by her minister, who chose to deprive her of one of the things that was most helpful in keeping her going. As a result, Joanna says she felt 'terrible ... Like I was worthless'.

Positive Action
The potential ramifications of premature forgiveness in the case of domestic abuse are substantial. Such action leaves the victim open to further abuse, and also hinders the possibility of the perpetrator choosing a path of genuine repentance by providing him with an immediate excuse not to pursue it (Smedes, 1984). Both Alsdurf and Alsdurf (1989, p. 102) and Fortune (1995a, p. 202) refer to this as

offering the perpetrator a form of 'cheap grace' whereby he is seemingly forgiven and free to continue his abusive lifestyle unchecked. Holding the perpetrator accountable is essential (Fortune, 1995b; Fortune & Poling, 1995). Horsfield (1994) advocates the need for the presence of justice for the victim, and views the extending of forgiveness without a justice that addresses the associated ethical, legal and moral issues as yet another form of 'condoning evil' (p. 1).

Miriam was prepared to forgive her husband for the abuse he had perpetrated against her and their two sons, and to remain in the marriage, but she did stipulate the need for her husband to seek professional assistance:

> I told him a few times, 'You know what you've done in the past, fair enough, you know … we can work that out. You know … I sort of wouldn't hold that totally against you. But you've got to try and do something about it. You've got to get help. You've got to … and, I, that includes both of us then … I'm more than willing'.

Miriam also recalls feeling very supported by her minister, who visited the marital home in an effort to convince her husband of the urgent need to modify his behaviour:

> He actually came to the house … He was trying to get my husband to see this just can't go on, because the longer it goes on, you know, the harder it is to do something about it —— to control it.

Miriam reports that she did not feel pressure from any source to forgive her husband, as both she and her minister were able to acknowledge that she had done everything possible to remain in the marriage. Miriam explains, 'It was a case of having to [leave]. There was just no option left because I'd spent 15 years of … exploring all the options'. Miriam felt supported and released to follow whatever course of action she deemed necessary, and left the marriage.

Positive action demands that the offence itself should be taken seriously, as should the need for genuine repentance. Neither should ever be minimised. Nor should the concept or function of forgiveness be trivialised. In order to accomplish this, one needs to understand the truth regarding the nature of domestic abuse and the manner in which perpetrators tend to behave, in addition to the aim and purpose of forgiveness. In some cases the victim may need assistance in seeking restitution from her abuser, perhaps in the area of medical, counselling or other expenses. Alternatively, she may require support if she wishes to leave or lay charges against him (Fortune, 1995a). These two issues are not indicative of a lack of forgiveness, but lie within the realm of the personal and moral right of the victim to receive justice (Horsfield, 1994; Smedes, 1996), the absence of which can severely inhibit the ability of the victim to forgive and ultimately to experience healing (Horsfield). Forgiveness is not designed to prevent the perpetrator from reaping the consequences of his actions (Tracy, 1999). While forgiveness can sometimes foster the renegotiation and possible restoration of a relationship, it also has the capacity to release the victim to terminate the relationship in favour of moving forward with her own life (Cunningham, 1985).

Rebekah offered an insightful analogy, drawing a parallel between the principles of forgiveness and the simple event of borrowing a motor vehicle from a neighbour or friend. She describes her present understanding of forgiveness thus:

> Someone tried to use the example with me, if someone keeps borrowing your car and they bring it back a few days later [instead of on time] and just say 'I'm sorry, I'm sorry', and then come back again and borrow the car, that doesn't mean the next time that you lend the car, because they're showing that they're not really sorry. You forgive them, but you don't allow it to continue ... So I realise that yes, I have forgiven him, but it doesn't mean that I stay in that situation.

Encapsulated within a number of the inaccurate interpretations of forgiveness seems to be the concept that forgiveness is, can be or should be an instantaneous event. As Smedes (1984) points out, such expectations 'only trivialize a wrong that should not be trifled with' (p. 66).

Forgiveness as a Process

A recurrent theme in the literature is that forgiveness must be viewed as a process that occurs over time as opposed to an event that takes place at a given moment (Alsdurf & Alsdurf, 1989; Bishop & Grunte,

1993; Gordon, 1999; Gordon, Baucom & Snyder, 2000; Horsfield, 1994; Kroeger & Nason-Clark, 2001; Malcolm & Greenberg, 2000; McCord-Adams, 1991; Miles, 2000; Safer, 1999; Smedes, 1984, 1996; Stoop & Masteller, 1991; Tracy, 1999). This concept is supported by information provided by a number of the women (Anna, Mary, Ruth). To finally reach the point at which a victim is able to forgive her abuser is described by Kerr (1991, p. 45) as a 'long pilgrimage', through which the victim should be permitted to move at her own pace (Miles). Cooper-White (1995) describes the process leading to forgiveness as one that includes the expression of the anger, pain and grief that has surrounded the experience of abuse. It involves a transition from victim to survivor as her personal story is acknowledged in its fullness. A hasty move towards forgiveness does not allow for the necessary release of emotion (Enright & Zell, 1989). Acquaviva (Walker et al., 1998) states that forgiveness is a choice made by the individual, and suggests that a victim should not place unreasonable demands upon herself but rather start at a point that is comfortable for her. Forgiveness is not the point at which recovery commences (Horsfield), but should be regarded more appropriately as the final step in a lengthy healing process (Fortune, 1995a).

Anna does describe her understanding of forgiveness as a process. Unfortunately, there does not appear to be a similar understanding on the part of the clergy. Anna finally left her marriage and her church. She felt rejected because the perpetrator (her lay preacher husband) was constantly supported by the church while she was eventually left isolated. She speaks of the final visit she received from the minister's wife, and the pressure she was placed under to forgive her husband:

> She came over here and she started on about forgiveness — you know, 'Anna, you're going to have to forgive him'. And I remember sitting at this table and saying, 'I know what forgiveness is all about, and you can't just do it straight away'.

In contrast to Anna, Mary describes a very positive experience with her minister, who made himself available as required and helped her to work through the emotions associated with her experience, finally assisting her to come to a more complete understanding of forgiveness. During our time together, Mary reflected on that experience:

I felt, 'No! I don't want to forgive him'. And I thought, like, why has he done this to me? He can't love me. Does he feel he has any reason to do these sorts of things, and what did … made him justify his actions? And then I realised, it's in your person — like, that's his person. If I can step aside from the personal experience, into the whole of life experience, I can let him go and I can do it, but it's taken … not until he left me did I feel that I could actually do that, 'cause while ever he was with me I kept feeling that I had rights and he wasn't giving me those rights … and I was justified in not forgiving him. So I suppose in one way it was the way — it wasn't until the separation, the physical separation actually took place that I felt that I could let go of the anger, the hurt and the anger I felt towards him … and let it go.

In finding her way through the maze of forgiveness, Mary frequently sought the counsel of her minister:

I had discussions with Father about it. Whether it was forgiveness or being able to forget, because if I count — like would I ever be able to forget … like, it's happened — like, I'm a human being with a mind. Can I forget? And what part is forgiveness or forgetting? And I kept saying to Father, like, 'What is forgiveness?' and he said, 'It's actually wishing that no harm would come to him'. I said, 'Well on that basis, I can forgive him … that way. Like, I'm angry that it happened, but I don't wish him any harm from here on, like, I don't — I've got no desire to kill him or to have anything happen to him now that he's out of my life, like … I can let him go'.

Throughout this lengthy excerpt, it is possible to visualise Mary working through the process of forgiveness. Initially, she admits she does not want to forgive her husband, and feels totally justified in her position. Gradually, she is able to let go of her anger and pain. However, this does not occur until he has left the marital home and is effectively out of her life, as the constant contact with her husband and thus the continuation of the offence inhibited Mary's ability to let go. In accordance with the advice of Cooper-White (1995) regarding the release of emotion, Mary's minister assisted the healing process by exhibiting a willingness to actively listen, show compassion and encourage the release of pent-up anger, rather than condemn Mary for having such feelings. It would appear that Mary's minister walked her through the process, step by step, allowing her the time and freedom to sort through the issues and arrive at her own conclusions. Mary actually reports that her minister encouraged her to express her anger. 'He said to me, "You were given the right to be angry." He said, "Christ got angry, so get angry … get angry."' Mary's minister further offered her a definition of forgiveness that she could understand, accept and ultimately adopt for herself, thereby providing yet another stepping stone in the 'long pilgrimage' (Kerr, 1991, p. 45).

In this situation, it is possible to gain further insight into some of the benefits that can flow from unification between a genuinely caring minister and a member of his parish who is suffering deeply and requires assistance. In the absence of pressure to forgive, Mary was able to eventually come to the point where she could release her former husband from any obligation to her, an action that reflects the original definition of forgiveness provided at the beginning of this chapter.

Effects of Forgiveness

The act of forgiveness cannot change the events of the past. However, it does have the capacity to affect present and future aspects of the life of the victim as it contributes substantially to the physical and mental health (Exline & Baumeister, 2000), as well as the spiritual and emotional wellbeing, of the individual (Stoop & Masteller, 1991). Based on a neuropsychological model of forgiveness, Newberg, d'Aquili, Newberg and deMarici (2000) maintain that it is possible that forgiveness and healing could work 'hand in hand' (p. 108). Speculation also exists that as a result of a decrease in anger, blaming and a tendency toward negative thoughts and feelings, brought about by the act of forgiveness, levels of stress may be reduced thus creating a positive effect on the health of the individual concerned (Thoresen, Harris & Luskin, 2000). Cunningham (1985) draws a parallel between forgiveness and the counselling concept of reframing an event, which enables the victim to reconceptualise the event and view it from a different perspective, thereby experiencing an increased sense of empowerment. This in turn, allows the victim to disengage from the ongoing struggle, be free from the 'gripping control of past events' (Enright & Zell,

1989, p. 58) and gradually move on with her life (Jantz, 2003). Smedes (1984) refers to this process as a 'spiritual surgery' (p. 27) of the soul, which fosters change within the victim (McCullough, Pargament & Thoresen, 2000) and promotes an wholistic restoration of the individual (Fortune, 1995a).

As reported in the previous section, the constant barrage of abuse has the tendency to inhibit the ability of the individual to move through the process of forgiveness, and thus the ability to finally arrive at a place of rest and healing. Without this, the victim is unable to effectively move forward with her life. A number of women (Susanna, Mary, Anna, Rachel, Esther) reported how much better they felt within themselves once they had been able to separate themselves from their husbands and thus from the abuse. This action formed a foundation from which they could begin to disengage from the harmful effects of domestic abuse. Many of the women interviewed, particularly those who had been separated for lengthy periods (Eunice, Miriam, Ruth, Rachel), appeared to have released their former husbands to their own choice of existence. Those who were separated were pleased to finally have the freedom available to move on with their own lives.

Forgiveness as a Form of Abuse

Initially, it may appear unusual for a seemingly virtuous biblical principle to be classified as a form of abuse. However, this is precisely the result when the principles of forgiveness are interpreted and applied inaccurately. Victims of abuse can be further abused if inappropriate demands are made of them to extend forgiveness to their abusers (Patton, 2000).

In the case of Elizabeth, her ministers contributed significantly to the constant nature of the abuse she suffered. In addition, they were guilty of perpetuating their own form of abuse by actually blaming her for her husband's ongoing violence, and demanding that she search her own soul and repent of whatever she might be doing to cause him to behave in such a way. Elizabeth explains:

> As far as my forgiving him — whenever I would have gone [to the ministers] I always had to put everything right, which always involved repenting and whatever was necessary. I mean, you know, where did this come from in me?

> Why am I like this? What in me caused him to have to do that? What was I doing? What was my part?

In response to my question, 'You always had to forgive him, though, for anything that he did?' Elizabeth answered strongly, '*Well of course … of course*'.

The incorrect application of the concept of forgiveness, as indicated above, can lead to an increased vulnerability for victims of abuse as they begin to feel they have no means of protection from the perpetrator if they choose to forgive him. If embracing the act of forgiveness is understood to mean forgetting, trusting or reconciling with their abuser, victims of abuse could be excused for fearing the possible consequences of a decision to extend forgiveness to an unrepentant and unchanged perpetrator. It is therefore necessary for victims of domestic abuse as well as members of the clergy to have a clear understanding of both the biblical teachings of forgiveness and their relevance, and the manner in which these teachings need to operate to be most effective in cases where domestic abuse is prevalent.

Summary

This chapter has considered a biblical definition of the concept of forgiveness, and the impact of teachings surrounding this concept on the lives and wellbeing of Christian women who have become victims of domestic abuse. The potential ramifications of inaccurate interpretations of forgiveness (such as forgive and forget, premature mediation or reconciliation), and the hasty restoration of trust in a relationship that has proven untrustworthy, have been presented as harmful to victims and should thus be avoided.

In contrast, the need for positive action is considered a necessity. Positive action includes the implementation of strategies helpful to the physical and emotional safety and security of the victim, and must therefore be tailored to the needs of the individual. Ideally, the role of the clergy is one of support and encouragement.

Throughout this chapter, forgiveness has been presented as a biblical concept that functions as a process rather than being a one-off event. Any attempt to move away from this view by endeavouring to enforce conformity on the part of the victim is potentially harmful. Indeed, it may be considered a further act of abuse.

Reflections for the Counsellor

1. What is your concept of forgiveness?
   - Has this view changed? How?
2. How would you explain forgiveness to a victim of domestic abuse?
   - What expectations might you have of her?

Client Discussion

1. What is your experience of the expectation for forgiveness in your relationship? Consider the attitudes/expectations of your partner, members of the clergy and yourself.
2. What excuses were made for your partner's behaviour by (i) yourself and (ii) others? Share some examples.
3. What concerns do you have regarding the topic of forgiveness? For example, the Lord's Prayer states that we should be forgiven as we forgive others.
4. What roadblocks to forgiveness (e.g. ongoing nature of abuse, possible reconciliation) were apparent in your relationship?
   - What steps did/could you take to help overcome these roadblocks (e.g. possible separation from your partner)?
   - Do you feel differently about forgiveness knowing that it does not mean you must reconcile with your partner? If so, how?
5. What does forgiveness mean for you? How would you explain it to a friend?
6. Imagine a continuum or forgiveness, ranging from *Completely unwilling or unable to forgive* at one end to *Completely willing or able to forgive at the other.*
   - At what point on the continuum do you see yourself?
7. When considering the concept of forgiveness, is there anything that you feel you would still like help to accomplish? If so, what?

CHAPTER 6

Breaking the Covenant

Initially, this chapter presents a brief overview of marriage as a sacred union, and the relevance of this concept to Christian women who have become victims of domestic abuse. It then defines the concept of the covenant relationship and provides an explanation of the historical perspective of the covenant, ultimately drawing the conclusion that the marital union does qualify as a binding covenant.

This chapter identifies key biblical issues surrounding the concepts of divorce and remarriage, with a specific focus on the words of Jesus in the New Testament but also including the diversity of opinion among authors and the biblical provision for a bill of divorce to be granted, thus opening the way for remarriage should it be so desired. Throughout the chapter, and with specific reference to both Old and New Testament Scriptures, the original design and ultimate purpose of marriage is presented as an enduring and intimate union, paralleling the relationship existing between Christ and the church.

Finally, the legal termination of the marriage is addressed as an acceptable option for women who find themselves in an unacceptable marriage as a result of domestic abuse, as it is considered that the covenant relationship has not been broken by the choice of the victim to separate and/or divorce but rather by the unacceptable and, in some cases, violent and criminal conduct of the perpetrator. Once again, excerpts from the transcripts, indicating the specific experiences of Christian women, are used to highlight the issues presented.

Overview

The sanctity of the marital union presents another issue of interest when considering the difficulties faced by Christian women who are victims of domestic abuse. The Christian marriage may be viewed as a binding covenant, sacred to death and not to be broken except as the result of marital unfaithfulness (Matthew 19:9). Marriage vows made in good faith, with a positive expectation regarding the future, are severely challenged as the victim of domestic abuse is confronted with the shocking reality of violence and aggression in her own home, and in a relationship that was designed to mirror the self-sacrificing love of Jesus Christ for His people, the church (Taylor, 1965; Wood, 1978). Often there is tremendous pressure for the woman to remain in the marriage because of the sanctity with which the union is regarded. Such pressure can come from a variety of sources — the perpetrator, members of the clergy or congregation, society in general and the victim herself — as any breakdown of the marriage may be viewed by the woman as her own failure as a wife (Anderson et al., 2003). Further, the concept that God hates divorce (Malachi 2:16) presents a strong argument against the breaking of the marriage covenant (Alden, 1985).

The conflict that can arise within congregations regarding issues surrounding domestic abuse and the sanctity of marriage is illustrated in a story shared by Reverend Al Miles in his book, *Domestic Violence: What Every Pastor Needs to Know*. Miles (2000) shares the story of a woman who was almost killed by her husband. The woman was highly respected and extremely active within the church, but the congregation became divided over whether or not the sanctity of the marriage itself was more important than the potential risk to the life of the victim. So intense was the disagreement that it resulted in a church split. It is interesting to note that throughout the duration of Miles' study, ministers constantly insisted that 'a marriage must be saved at all costs' (p. 149).

Defining the Covenant Relationship

The earliest biblical reference to marriage as a covenant relationship can be found in the book of Genesis (2:23–24) (Hugenberger, 1994), where it is stated, 'Therefore shall a man leave his father and his mother, and shall cleave unto his wife: and they shall become one flesh'. The first loyalty of the man initially lies with his parents but, upon entering into a marriage, it is then transferred to his wife

(Cornes, 2002; Henry & Scott, 1979a). The intended permanency, intimacy and exclusivity of the relationship are seen in the concept of the 'one flesh' union, which involves a complete meshing together of one individual with the other (Atkinson, 1979; Kroeger, 1996; Livingston, 1969; Martz, 2002; Sandage & Worthington, 1997; Trutza, 1975).

The expectation of the permanency of the marital relationship was voiced by most of the women interviewed. Although such an expectation may exist outside the Christian church, the belief of the women was reinforced by the fact that many of them had been raised in a strong Christian environment and as a result had accepted the prevailing values (Mary, Ruth, Anna, Deborah, Susanna, Lydia). Each one had made vows, which she took seriously, and thus committed herself to the union in the fullest possible way. This attitude can be quite typical for Christian women (Nason-Clark, 2000a). Eunice describes herself as a 'very good Catholic girl who was a 21-year-old virgin' when she was married. She chose not to divorce her husband but, after 17 years of abuse, lived separately from him until his death 19 years later. Eunice explains her belief and her experience regarding the sanctity of marriage:

> I felt married to my husband till the day he died. I never, ever … have been with another man. I can remember thinking the day I knew he was dead — I thought, 'My goodness. I'm a free woman'. That was an amazing thing for me. I always felt totally married, and knew that I would never find another, never look for another man.

Elizabeth also presents a very strong position in relation to the binding commitment of her vows, and the seriousness with which she viewed the marital union:

> I would never have thought of terminating the marriage then, because I believed the vows that I took and they said, 'Till death unto us, till death do us part'. So, that for me was … that was it. Anywhere along the line in the 20 years … when I really did believe that it was right and it … was *never to divorce* or end the marriage.

Historically, covenants were viewed as legally and morally binding agreements that were in force for the duration of the period agreed upon prior to the establishing of the specific covenant (Conner & Malmin, 1983; Payne, 1962, 1975a). Many covenants were binding unto death, and were therefore carefully and thoughtfully undertaken. A blood covenant was considered indissoluble, the partakers of which were expected to lay down their life for the other should it be deemed necessary (Trumbull, 1975). While not all Christian denominations view marriage as a covenant, or even as a blood covenant (Martz, 2002), there are those who teach that marriage is not only a sacred union but also a blood covenant. The concept of marriage being considered a blood covenant is drawn from the shedding of blood that occurs on the occasion of the first conjugal act (Martin, 2001; Trumbull, 1896; Twelve Tribes, n.d.). A differing representation of marriage as a blood covenant is indicated in the concept of the threshold covenant, whereby an animal was slaughtered in the doorway of the home and the blood allowed to pour onto the threshold as a welcome extended to the new bride, who stepped over the blood upon entering the home (Trumbull, 1896).

A covenant relationship involves mutuality, obligation and responsibility. Hugenberger (1994) lists the requirements of a covenant as follows: initially, entering into a covenant involves forming a deep and binding relationship with an individual who is not already a relative. Such a commitment involves obligations that are included in the terms of the covenant. In the case of a covenant between two individuals of equal standing, the terms are mutually agreed upon (Payne, 1981). The covenantal relationship is established by means of a solemn oath or set of promises that are declared before witnesses (Dumbrell, 1993). While it was not mandatory for the covenant-ratifying oath to be self-maledictory, in some cases the oath contains conditions that will apply if the covenant is broken. In relation to primitive tribal covenants, Trumbull (1975) explains that the individuals who covenant together openly invite trouble to come upon them should they be guilty of breaking the promises, proving themselves to be unfaithful and thus dishonouring the covenant. A similar concept is reflected in the book of Ruth, when Ruth covenants to remain with Naomi, her mother-in-law (Ruth 1:16). Ruth not only took a solemn oath to remain with Naomi (Linafelt, 1989), she also invited a curse upon herself should she break that oath. As a witness to her oath, she calls upon the name of God (Huey, 1992). A further biblical example of covenant responsibilities and consequences is described in the Old Testament book of Deuteronomy (chapter 28). In this case, God is the one who initiates the covenant. If the nation of Israel is obedient and faithful to the covenant between her and God, then Israel will benefit from the blessings that are linked to the terms of the covenant. If Israel proves unfaithful, then she will suffer as a result of the curses that are also linked to the covenant agreement (Ford & Deasley, 1969; Kalland, E.S., 1992; Sherwood, 2002). Thus, the terms of the covenant served to act as both an encouragement and a warning to those involved.

Trumbull (1975) further reports that it was customary to exchange gifts as part of the covenant ceremony. Such gifts acted as a visible sign of the oath taken. In the case of a bracelet or ring, the symbolism was that of a 'boundless bond between giver and receiver; the tokens of a mutual, unending covenant' (p. 65).

Marriage as a Covenant

Hugenberger (1994) views the marital relationship as a covenant, a position supported by a number of authors (Atkinson, 1979; Eilts, 1995; Mason, 1977; Miles, 2002; Payne, 1962; Robinson, 1990; Sohn, 1999; Sprinkle, 1997; Trumbull, 1999; Wilson, 1995, 1999a). He maintains the use of the terminology 'leave and cleave' (Genesis 2:24) to be indicative of a covenantal union. He further highlights the emphasis placed by the prophet Malachi on the fact that marriage is more than a relationship, but is indeed a covenant. Malachi uses the term 'wife of thy covenant' (Malachi 2:14) to emphasise the seriousness of the offence committed by unfaithful husbands who have chosen to break the covenant relationship with their wives. In the same verse, God is also declared as being a witness to the marriage covenant, thus indicating the sacred nature of the union (Greathouse, 1966; Jones, 1962). Hill (1998) suggests that the concept of God acting as witness brings with it a strong judicial tone that emphatically condemns the violation of the marriage covenant.

Hugenberger (1994) maintains that the marital union does meet the necessary criteria for a covenant, in that it is the cementing of a relationship between individuals who are not blood relatives, and its obligations are established through a covenant-ratifying oath. In addition to these requirements, it was customary for what Hugenberger refers to as an 'oath sign' (p. 247) to accompany the oath or solemn vow. Such signs include sharing a meal, shaking hands or perhaps displaying an uplifted hand. In the case of the marriage covenant, Hugenberger suggests that the actual consummation of the marriage could be recognised as the oath sign.

Having established the concept that the marital union does qualify as a covenant, it is necessary to consider the conditions and potential ramifications if the covenant relationship is broken for any reason. Divorce serves as a means by which a covenant can be legally terminated. For the Christian woman experiencing domestic abuse, it is important to understand the biblical issues surrounding the choice to divorce.

Biblical Issues Surrounding Divorce

The question of divorce is a complex issue for most scholars (Olender, 1998). However, it becomes even more complex for members of the clergy, and also for victims of domestic abuse who are told emphatically that divorce is not an acceptable option. To consider the argument from a Christian perspective, it is necessary to focus on the teachings of Jesus with regard to divorce. These can be found in the Gospels of Matthew (19:3–12), Mark (10:2–12), and Luke (16:18).

In the passages of Scripture located in Matthew and Mark, it is recorded that Jesus was approached by the Pharisees, a strict sect of influential religious separatists (Hagner, 1975; Petersen, 1981b), and questioned regarding his opinion on divorce. Carson (1984) points out that it is important to focus on the correct setting of the discussion. He maintains that the ensuing discussion is based entirely on a theological dispute regarding the definition of divorce and the reasons for which a divorce might be obtained, as opposed to a more generalised question regarding the act of divorce. The question put to Jesus in the Gospel of Matthew is whether or not it is permissible according to the law for a man to divorce his wife for any reason.

Again, it is important to note the phrase 'for any reason', which is present in the account in Matthew but not in Mark. It has been suggested that the inclusion of this phrase in Matthew is because this gospel was specifically written for a Jewish audience who would be familiar with the existing debate (Earle, 1964). The debate between the Shammaite and Hillelite schools of thought was not in relation to whether or not divorce was permissible, but instead centred around the reasons a divorce might be granted and considered legal according to Jewish law. Adherents of the Shammaite school of thought believed divorce was permissible only on the grounds of uncleanness or adultery, whereas devotees of Hillel supported divorce for any reason whatsoever, including something as simple as preparing an unsatisfactory meal (Carson; Cornes, 2002; Earle; Hoekstra, 1990; Instone-Brewer, 2002; Robinson, 1984; Sanner, 1964; Wessel, 1984; Zodhiates, 1984a).

It is in this context that Jesus responds with his views on divorce. Initially, the focus is brought back to Genesis (2:24) and the original design for marriage (Forster, 2000). Jesus reiterates the 'leave and cleave' concept and emphasises the nature of the 'one flesh' union of marriage. The union is, in effect, witnessed and sealed by God (Small, 1981). The 'one flesh' union is not something the couple achieves for themselves but rather something that happens to them as a result of their covenant union (Cornes, 2002). This concept leads into the direct statement by Jesus, 'What therefore God hath joined together, let not man put asunder' (Matthew 19:6b). Most authors agree that the divine plan and purpose of God was for marriage to be a permanent and indissoluble union (Earle, 1964; Farley, 1975; Keener, 1996; Livingston, 1969; Matthews, 1990; Meilaender, 1995; O'Donoghue, 1990; Olthuis, 1995; Owen, 1997; Sandage & Worthington, 1997; Small, 1981; Trutza, 1975; Wilkins 2002; Zodhiates, 1984a).

Upon hearing this, the Pharisees challenge Jesus still further by pointing out that the law of Moses (Deuteronomy 24:1) did allow for divorce (Matthew 19:7). While Jesus agrees that Moses did permit divorce, he makes two very definite points. First, he clarifies the reason divorce was permitted, this being the hardness of the human heart. Jesus then reiterates his initial response that divorce was not part of God's original design for mankind (Matthew 19:8) (Garland, 2002; Wenham, 1995). Jesus continues his response with yet another very challenging statement, declaring that a man who divorced his wife for any reason other than that of adultery, and who chose to remarry, would be guilty of committing adultery with his new wife (Matthew 19:9) (Strauss, 2002). Further to this, he would also be guilty of forcing his former wife into an adulterous situation.

From this discussion the question may arise as to whether or not Jesus was explaining the existing law, or creating a new law that prohibited divorce and subsequent remarriage regardless of circumstance (Sanner, 1964). In light of the fact that during 'the first century a valid divorce always included the right to remarry' (Heth, 1995 p. 72), Farley (1975) suggests the possibility that in this instance Jesus could be employing the use of hyperbole in an effort to emphasise the serious nature of the situation.

Remarriage

If one chooses to adopt the teaching of Jesus as a new law, and therefore a position that prohibits divorce and remarriage, a number of questions arise. For example, is divorce ever an acceptable alternative for a Christian? If divorced, should a Christian be permitted to remarry and, if so, under what circumstances? What circumstances apply if the divorce and/or remarriage occurred prior to the individual becoming a Christian? Once again, scholars present varying opinions on these issues.

Diversity of Opinion

Even within the Christian church, across denominations and between members of the clergy, there is great diversity of opinion on the subject of divorce and possible remarriage (Alsdurf, 1985; Atkinson, 1995; Meilaender, 1995; Olthuis, 1995). However, some authors identify a number of categories that can provide a general overview of existing beliefs. These range from the total permanency of the marital union without any allowance for either divorce or remarriage, thereby classifying any relationship other than the original marriage as adulterous; to a more liberal approach whereby a marriage may be annulled, leaving the parties free to remarry. Situated between these two extremes is, firstly, the opinion that divorce and subsequent remarriage is permissible within the limits of biblical specifications; and secondly, the view that in some cases, for the ultimate welfare of either the spouse or the children, divorce is a necessity (Collins, 1988; Sandage & Worthington, 1997).

No Option for Divorce

Toon (1996) adopts the first position, describing divorce as a 'severe disease of the soul' (p. 20). He not only identifies the act of divorcing one's spouse as sin because divorce is viewed as contrary to the divine will of God, but also advocates church discipline for those who are guilty of such sin and cites as an example 'exclusion from the Lord's Table' (p. 20). Similarly, Warden (1997) classifies both divorce and remarriage as sin, based on the fact that it is contrary to the divine will and purpose of God.

For a church to adopt an attitude similar to that of Toon (1996) places it open to the criticism of revictimising the already traumatised victim. Such an act could be construed as forcing the victim to choose between remaining trapped in an abusive relationship or facing the condemnation and rejection of the church. Often this form of teaching leaves the woman feeling as if she does not have a choice in the matter (Cassiday-Shaw, 2002), leaving her alone, spiritually and emotionally isolated, to decide which is the lesser of the two evils. This form of unwarranted pressure parallels the violence already perpetrated against the victim and, far from championing a righteous cause, proves nothing more than a 'subtle form of collusion with evil' (Alsdurf & Alsdurf, 1989 p. 123). Hynson (1998) maintains that even God does not expect individuals to remain in a marriage that consists of nothing beyond the legalisation of 'misery, abuse, torture, and tragedy' (p. 82).

Esther's experience was one of 'no go' regarding divorce. The sanctity of the marriage was regarded as a 'big thing', and her church ruled out the option of divorce except as a result of adultery. Even then, it was expected that one should overlook the situation and attempt to reconcile. As a result, Esther was given no reasonable option to escape from the ongoing verbal, emotional and sexual abuse she was experiencing. Ester explains her position:

> By the biblical thing, like, you know, if they commit adultery et cetera then yes it's OK sort of thing. But even some of the other churches I've been to in my little search around … really even … didn't see that as a major thing. Sort of, that you can still overcome that.

Joanna also suffered as a result of the 'no go' position adopted by her minister, telling of an experience very similar to that of Esther. However, the pressure of her situation was compounded even further when it appeared that her minister was using his position to make her the specific target of his weekly sermons. Joanna shares her experience:

> In the time that I had separated, [the minister] decided to do a series, a six-week series on marriage … which I thought was a little bit suss. And it was hard to sit through, but I sat there through it … basically that it's [marriage] more than a covenant and God takes it very, very seriously. At the end of the day and … you know, God just does not break covenants like that.

Joanna responds a little later to a question regarding divorce,

> Ohhh!! No. The only … God hates divorce and the only grounds the minister would see for divorce would be adultery. There's no, like — none of this … none of what I've been through is any grounds for divorce. He just told me yesterday that, you know, you just need to stay single.

This position not only restricted any means of escape for the 31-year-old Joanna (short of displeasing God entirely), but also treated her as the guilty party in the marriage by prohibiting any form of remarriage and perhaps the hope of future happiness for her and her four children. Further to this is the fact that a member of the clergy chose to use his position of authority to take undue advantage and seemingly browbeat an already victimised woman. Shackelford and Sanders (1997) clearly classify such conduct as an 'abuse of power' (p. 93). While this choice of action could certainly be construed as manipulative (Wiest & Smith, 1990), Beed (1998) suggests that because members of the clergy are often viewed as 'ambassadors of God' (p. 44), any form of betrayal or abuse can result in undermining the faith of the victim. At the very least, a church community should be able to liaise with refuges and aid organisations in an effort to provide much needed assistance for families who have fallen victim to abuse (Bolden, 1997; Fortune & Poling, 1995). Tidball (1995) asserts that the church should be 'the best therapeutic community in the world' (p. 46), providing a healing and nurturing environment of love, grace and compassion. Unfortunately for Joanna, this was not the case.

Divorce as a Necessity

Keener (1991) takes a more compassionate stand. While still maintaining that divorce is wrong, he acknowledges that there can be legitimate reasons for divorce and that innocent parties can be devastated as a result of the tragedy. He also suggests that the church who judges those who are divorced is guilty of revictimising individuals who have already suffered, 'wounded first by the very persons in the world they had most trusted, and second by the impersonal ecclesiastical policies that kicked them when they were down' (p. 6). Keener further maintains that in the case of a valid divorce, which is one that meets the biblical criteria, the innocent party is at liberty to remarry.

Instone-Brewer (2002) supports the concept of a valid divorce opening the way for remarriage, but also extends the definition of the criteria suitable to qualify for such a divorce. The additional qualifications apply to emotional and/or material neglect, conditions that were supported by rabbis, or Jewish religious teachers (Holdridge, 1981; Wood, 1975), of the first century. This position is based initially on the instruction given in the book of Exodus (21:10–11), which explains that a man is expected to provide for his wife in both a material and an emotional sense (Cox, 1969). It is later reinforced by Paul (1 Corinthians 7:3–5) when he writes to the Corinthian church about the mutuality of marital obligations in relation to love, intimacy and sexuality (Gill, 2002; Mare, 1976; Metz, 1968). If suffering as a result of neglect, a woman was permitted to appeal to the court to negotiate with her husband with the aim of securing a legal divorce (Instone-Brewer).

'Physical and emotional abuse are extreme failures of material and emotional support' (Instone-Brewer, 2002 p. 308), and represent yet another form of marital infidelity (Alsdurf & Alsdurf, 1989; Miles, 2002). Zodhiates (1984b) maintains that 'it is not possible to love and mistreat a person at the same time' (p. 109). As members of the clergy come to terms with this reality, they will be far better equipped to provide assistance for victims of domestic abuse, as is demonstrated by the following reports.

Eve found assistance for her predicament as a result of a change in church leadership. Her new minister expressed a more liberal attitude towards divorce and the reasons such action might be considered. Eve speaks of her situation before the arrival of the new minister:

> There was no sanctity in our marriage at all. But it was ...
> it was ... preached. Yes. Definitely. So I felt locked into the
> marriage even though I just felt it was a sham.

In response to the question, 'What about divorce?' Eve exclaimed emphatically:

> Ohhh! No! No! That was just an absolute ... yeah, dirty
> word. And ... no. That's just not acceptable.

Eve reports that her situation changed dramatically with the arrival of the new minister, who not only supported her in her desire for a divorce, but also assisted her with safe and practical strategies through which she could have her husband removed from the marital residence. Eve expresses her absolute relief at receiving the long overdue, and much needed support:

> Ohh ... I was just over the moon. I thought, 'I can't
> believe this'. I don't know how it's all going to come about,
> but finally I'm going to ... you know, all these years of
> people not really seeing how devastating this was for me.
> Someone who I really, you know, respected in the church
> was going to say, 'I see you have a real problem here, and
> he hasn't, you know, pulled his weight enough' ... So that
> ... that was really great.

Pellauer (1986) maintains that there are times when some form of intervention by a member of the clergy can be so significant that it can make the difference between life and death to the victim of abuse. Sarah received a great deal of practical assistance from her priest, who chose to put the safety of the victim and her baby first and foremost. Although separated by three states, the priest was willing to assist via telephone and, upon receiving a panicked and fearful call from Sarah, helped her to arrive at some quick decisions that would ensure her ongoing safety. Speaking of her conversation with her priest, Sarah relates her story:

> In no way did he force me [to decide]. It was, like, well, how safe do you feel? Do you think — you know, do you want to move to another place? I said, 'Look. I don't feel safe. I don't know anyone here. Even if we go somewhere else, there's no guarantee that he won't follow us or find us or ...' I said, 'I just want to leave'. He said, 'Oh. How fast can you pack a bag?' And that was it. It was like a very — to me it felt impulsive to just go. But then I thought, 'Look. At the end of the day ... I'll be safer in Brisbane. I'm going back'.

Marriage Annulment

A decree of nullity can be granted when a marriage is deemed to be invalid. This can occur for a number of reasons: the inability to assume the obligations of marriage; defects of consent; or defects of the will (Harman, 1990; Stuart, 1994). Marriage annulment requires a lengthy process of tribunal investigation to fully determine the original state of the marriage, and to establish if an annulment would be in accordance with the appropriate laws of the Catholic church (Price, 1990). Each case is considered to be unique and must therefore be evaluated on its own merits (Robinson, 1990). To arrive at an accurate conclusion regarding the state of the marriage, a substantial amount of detailed information pertaining to the entire marital relationship must be obtained (McGuckin, 1992; Power, 1990; Sheehy, 1990). The respondent (partner who did not initiate the application for annulment) has the right to know about the proceedings, and may be required for interview by the tribunal in an effort to provide further insight into the marital relationship and the reasons for the ultimate breakdown of the marriage (McGuckin, 1990; Robinson, 1984). The need may also arise for witnesses (nominated by the parties involved) to testify, not necessarily to the character of the individuals but to their own specific knowledge of the relationship (Reynolds, 1990). Witnesses may consist of family, friends or professionals (Vondenberger, 2004). In specific cases, access to psychological and medical reports may prove helpful in determining an outcome (Connors, 1990), and at times either the plaintiff or the respondent could be referred for psychological assessment. This can be a lengthy process involving both psychological testing and interviews by qualified professionals (Coram, 1990). Ultimately, if a marriage is found to be invalid, an annulment of that marriage does allow the individuals involved the opportunity for remarriage (Vondenberger).

The annulment procedure is a serious matter for those who wish to follow this course of action. Depending on the circumstances, a formal case may take as long as 18 months to be finalised (Vondenberger, 2004). While an annulment of marriage cannot erase the difficulties faced by the plaintiff, it does provide her with the opportunity to tell her story (Reynolds, 1990; Sheehy, 1990), and eventually (if granted) the acknowledgment that one or both parties were without the capacity to fully commit to a permanent union at the time of the marriage (Power, 1990). It is possible that such an acknowledgment may assist in alleviating the plaintiff of feelings relating to guilt or failure.

Miriam, although divorced by her husband some 14 years ago, explained that she was still considering seeking an annulment of her marriage through her church. While Miriam did not legally require an annulment, nor did she wish to remarry, she did feel that obtaining an annulment could assist her in finding some form of closure in relation to her marriage. Miriam shares her thoughts regarding a possible annulment of her marriage:

> I've since found out that I could get an annulment. There is
> — you know — only three or four reasons for an annulment and apparently, I cover the whole three. So it's there if I want it ... [The grounds include] mental instability. The other is ... and I forget the wording but it's not knowing of something that happened before the marriage. You went into the marriage not knowing that something had happened that affected it. I forget what the other one was, but there's only a couple. I have looked into it, for no particular reason than to put a closure on everything. Because after he got a divorce I thought, well ... yeah ... maybe that's what I should do too. 'Cause I was still picking up the pieces at the time. But I've never gone ahead with it ... and I'm still contemplating doing that.

Miriam's thoughts on obtaining an annulment perhaps highlight the extent to which she regards the spiritual authority of her church. For a woman of strong faith, it is possible that the seal of such authority could secure for her a more complete personal release, thereby fostering a finality to the marriage that could not be acquired through legal means.

While diversity of opinion is to be both expected and respected, it is nevertheless necessary to consider the circumstances under which some individuals are expected to live, in addition to the possible ramifications of such expectations. The bill of divorce was set in place in an effort to provide some release from extreme marital difficulties.

Bill of Divorce

Divorce and remarriage during Old Testament times is described by E.S. Kalland (1992) as 'a fact of social life' (p. 145), and therefore needed to be regulated (Mason, 1977). To accomplish this, Moses provided strict guidelines for the divorce procedure. One such requirement was a bill of divorce that Moses commanded a husband to give to his wife if he found it necessary to divorce her on the grounds of indecency or uncleanness (Ford & Deasley, 1969). The bill of divorce served as a source of protection for the woman, as it provided proof that if she remarried she would not be in an adulterous relationship (Borchert, 1999), which at that time was a capital offence (Leviticus 18:20; 20:20) (Harris, 1990; Kinlaw, 1969; Lambert, 1975; Russell, 1981a). Borchert also views the bill of divorce as a source of liberation for the woman, as prior to this regulation, men were in the habit of 'putting away', or evicting, their wives without affording them the formality of a divorce. This meant that the woman remained the property of her husband but was left without any means of support other than begging or prostitution (Lake, 1975). The bill of divorce brought a sense of legality to the situation as it clearly indicated the formal severing of the marriage bonds (Wilkins, 2002; Wilson, 1999b) and permitted the woman to remarry without penalty. This regulation recognised not only the humanity of individuals, but also the possibility that there could be mitigating circumstances within a marriage that could lead to the desire or need to dissolve the marital union. Hynson (1998) maintains that because such provision was made for divorce, it should not be considered unlawful.

To obtain a deeper and more accurate understanding of marriage, not only as a permanent union but also as a personal 'one flesh' union, it is necessary to consider the biblical view of the intimacy contained within the union when such a union is functioning in the manner originally intended. To accomplish this, it is helpful to consider some biblical examples of marriage as an intimate union. As Christian women, most of those sharing their experiences here had an expectation of what could be defined as a Christian marriage, consisting of such elements as trust, equality and oneness. The concept of a Christian marriage is illustrated in its purest sense in the Song of Solomon.

Marriage as an Intimate Union

The Song of Solomon provides images of love that depict the highest order of intimacy, highlighting the beauty and power of sexuality and personal interaction between the leading characters in the song, the bride and the bridegroom (Bergant, 2001; Kinlaw, 1991; Kroeger & Nason Clark, 2001). The Song of Solomon shows the purity and uninhibited nature of love within marriage as it was first intended and ordained by God (DeVries, 1981; Harrison, 1975; Knight, 1955). Some authors draw a parallel between the garden setting presented here and the garden setting of Eden, where the newly created man and woman were free to enjoy the intimate pleasures of each other's company (Carr, 1984; Kinlaw; Kroeger & Nason-Clark).

Clearly the marriage relationship, complete with intimate and passionate encounters, is designed to enhance the lives of the individuals concerned, bringing joy, harmony and a sense of wellbeing to the union (Harper, 1967a; Kinlaw, 1991; Knight, 1955). Each partner 'seeks and cherishes a communion of mind, soul and body' (Kroeger & Nason-Clark, 2001, p. 86). It is a relationship based on equality and mutuality. Although the imagery, which employs substantial use of simile and metaphor (Bergant, 2001), differs substantially from the terminology that might be employed in the more modern setting of the 21st century, the message of love and the beauty of love are unmistakably conveyed. The author uses poetic language to describe the bride. For example, 'Thy hair is as a flock of goats, that appear from mount Gilead. Thy teeth are like a flock of sheep that are shorn, which come up from the washing' (Song of Solomon 4:1f–2). The bride is beautiful. Her hair is black and shining, and her teeth are stunningly white and correctly positioned. The author then continues with an extremely detailed account of her magnificence — described by Kinlaw as an 'erotic physical inventory' (p. 1228) — which describes the thighs, naval, belly and breasts of the woman (Song of Solomon 7:1–4).

The level of unrestrained openness and intimacy portrayed throughout the Song of Solomon is one in which total trust between the lovers is paramount. In the absence of absolute trust, such levels of intimacy could be neither attained nor maintained (Conway, 1998; Keener, 1996). The intimacy described is far more than the physical union of two individuals. It is the meshing together of body, soul and spirit; of mind, will and emotions. It is allowing another into the deepest recesses of one's own being (Bergant, 2002). Knight (1955) describes the ultimate 'wedding night' experience by drawing a strong parallel between the physical expression of love and the spiritual expression of love, which through intimacy blend together in the 'ecstasy of union' (p. 63).

In stark contrast to the conjugal pleasures poetically enunciated by the bride and bridegroom of Scripture, Abigail speaks of her own wedding night as an inexperienced virgin:

> Well, I … I was a virgin when I got married, and he'd had a child in a previous relationship. I was quite … I wasn't … well I was timid I suppose, and I didn't know what to expect really. I'd read certain things about it … and I'd … it had been a very tiring day. And we got up to the honeymoon place at about 11 o'clock and … it's like he just wanted to do this thing. And … well, he didn't treat me very good that night. So I ended up crying myself to sleep. He was insensitive. I just remember him being … or getting angry, but then falling asleep. I just felt ripped off.

Abigail stated without hesitation that the abuse, which became ongoing, commenced on her wedding night. Abuse on any level violates trust and thus mars even the slightest attempt to achieve an intimate connection. Domestic abuse creates severe emotional distress and contributes greatly to depression, withdrawal, physical illness and even the desire to commit suicide (see chapter 3). In an atmosphere that exudes inequality and degradation, intimacy cannot survive. The author of the song speaks of taking away 'the little foxes; that spoil the vines' (Song of Solomon 2:15), possibly referring to the need to remove any offence that could create an obstacle to the the marital union reaching its full potential (Bergant, 2001; Harper, 1967a; Pope, 1977). If 'little foxes' or smaller occurrences that can be covert and perhaps unexpected have the ability to interfere with the harmony and intimacy of a relationship, just as the actual little foxes of old could spoil the flourishing vineyards (Cansdale, 1975a; Mack, 1981), how much more does domestic abuse wield the power to totally destroy that which was intended for good?

In a similar vein, and based on Scripture located in the book of Hebrews (13:4) that states, 'Marriage is honourable in all, and the bed undefiled', Kroeger and Nason-Clark (2001) stress the need for the continual impartation of honour and respect to permeate the marital union. These sentiments are echoed by Zodhiates (1991, 1992) when he explains that the Greek word *timios*, which has been translated *honourable*, is making an assertion regarding the subject of the sentence — in this case the marriage itself. Honour is emphasised (Hill, 1987); and the marriage, described by Guthrie (2002) as 'valuable' (p. 80), should not be defiled as a result of unfaithful or dishonourable conduct (Morris, 1981; Taylor, 1967).

Coercion, manipulation, sexual abuse, violent sexual encounters and rape within marriage all violate the sanctity of the marriage covenant, dishonouring and defiling a union that was designed to remain pure and untainted. Such practices cannot be justified in any way (Kroeger & Nason-Clark, 2001). In a home where domestic abuse is present, instead of experiencing a loving and caring interaction, the victim is debased and dehumanised as the sexual encounter is used to violently abuse and punish, resulting in a total 'violation of trust and intimacy' (Finkelhor & Yllo, 1985, p. 126).

This assertion is particularly apparent in the case of Eunice. Regardless of the extensive abuse she experienced, upon reflection Eunice conveyed that one of the most difficult things for her to cope with was the lack of loving intimacy within her marriage. She was left feeling cheated and ripped off, as the visions and dreams she had for her marriage were never realised. Eunice says:

> I often wish I had had a really loving relationship, or a very sexually fulfilling relationship with my husband. I can't say that I did ... I'd like to have looked back and thought that that had been there. We didn't have that ... And when he died, I grieved for those because that was ... that was a huge sadness that I had, that that part of my married life had never ... I'd never had it'.

Marriage as a Reflection of Christ and the Church

A common denominator of the covenants initiated by God is the element of liberation. Covenants were designed to bring individuals and nations out of oppression and into an improved quality of life that reflected the original plan and purpose of God (Eilts, 1995). Numerous covenants offer blessings as part of the covenant agreement, while others, such as the Abrahamic, Davidic and New Covenants, point forward to the ultimate redemption of the human race (Conner & Malmin, 1983). Thus, it is reasonable to assume that the original intention of the marriage covenant was that of blessing (Grady, 2000).

In addition to the concept of marriage being designed as a blessing is the parallel drawn by numerous authors between the quality of the marital union and the manner in which that union is meant to represent the loving and caring relationship between Christ and the church (Arnold, 2002a; Conway, 1998; Rinck, 1990; Stuart, 1994; Taylor, 1965; Wilson, 1999a; Wood, 1978; Zodhiates, 1984a). The apostle Paul admonishes Christian husbands to love their wives 'even as Christ also loved the church' (Ephesians 5:25), this being the highest order of love, indicated by the use of the Greek verb *agapao* — as opposed to the Greek words *eros* or *philia*, which relate to sexuality or familial affection respectively (Wood). The agape love required of husbands, and demonstrated by Christ himself, is not a love that allows for abuse in any form, but is a sacrificial love that is 'sincere, pure and ardent', showing 'constant affection' (Henry & Scott, 1979b, p. 217).

Rachel explains how, three years after she left her husband, this and other biblical insights brought with them not only a fresh understanding of the biblical concept of marriage but also a release from guilt, together with a sense of acceptance and personal healing:

> There is a place in the Christian church for women to separate and to be divorced without losing their faith. I'm still God's child even though I'm divorced when all of this other teaching had said that you shouldn't divorce. And there's some Scripture that talks about in the Old Testament [Malachi 2:16] ... where God talks about — you know, I hate that a marriage would break up, but I hate even more that a man should hurt his wife. And that verse is always left out in the patriarchal churches. And I think that was the biggest thing for me is when someone pointed me to that part. Moses could declare them divorced. But more than that, I hate it when a husband hurts his wife. And ... and the other stuff too about ... you know, that Christ loves us ... and that our husbands are to love their wives just as Christ loves the church. And that parallel needs to be seen in marriages. And when that's not happening in marriages, it is necessary and it is OK to divorce and to separate. Because God just doesn't ... He doesn't want women to be put in that position. That's not what He's about.

The Scripture Rachel refers to initially is located in the book of Malachi (2:16), and is often quoted, but only in part, in an effort to accentuate the fact that divorce is not an acceptable alternative in the eyes of God. A number of the women (Hannah, Leah, Joanna) seemed very familiar with the concept presented in the first part of the verse, and even quoted the words, 'God hates divorce'. However, the same women appeared to be totally unfamiliar with the concluding portion of the verse. The New International Version (NIV) of the Bible presents the complete verse as follows, 'I hate divorce says the Lord God of Israel, and I hate a man's covering himself with violence as well as with his garment, says the Lord Almighty'. While there is some difference of opinion between authors over the exact interpretation of this verse, there is a general consensus that God is a God of justice who does indeed hate violence; and that a man should not wear violence as a garment (Alden, 1985), nor should he endeavour to cloak his sin (Henry & Scott, 1979c). In relation to the use of the term 'garment', Deane (1995) maintains that the man who divorces his wife, 'shows himself openly to all beholders as an iniquitous man … Iniquity attaches itself to him plainly, encircling and enfolding him; the clothing of iniquity is the mark of the foul soul within' (p. 23). Jones (1962) and Hill (1998) make a similar observation, suggesting that the state of the external garment is indicative of the internal, or spiritual, state of the individual. Other interpretations suggest that the violence indicated is specifically in relation to a man's wife, a consideration that fits with the overall context of the narrative (Alden; Greathouse, 1966). Churton (1903) presents a very vivid image of the verse, interpreting it thus:

> But this hiding of the wrong done to his wife in secret, although cloaked and covered over as with a garment, is seen and noticed by God. The expression 'violence' seems to signify distinct acts of violence and cruelty, and not the act of divorce only. (p. 4A2)

The partial use of Scripture to justify a given position, in this case the unacceptable nature of seeking a divorce, presents a significant problem for Christian women who are victims of domestic abuse. Hannah exhibited a strong awareness of the fact that God hates divorce and, although she was unable to remember ever hearing a sermon or teaching to that effect, she was well aware of the attitude of her church regarding divorce. When questioned in relation to her beliefs on marriage, Hannah responds:

> It was just that you got married, and God hated divorce, so you just worked on your marriage, you didn't … it's not something that you just back out of.

Hannah later goes on to say that she would have disappointed herself, or found herself 'lacking' had she endeavoured to seek a divorce. Hannah highlights the depth of her commitment to the divine will and purpose of God when she explains:

> Well, I just didn't want to do anything that He would be not happy about.

She was willing to tolerate ongoing physical and verbal abuse, rather than consider following any course of action that might not meet with divine approval.

Breaking the Marriage Covenant

In direct contrast to the positive and nurturing image of Christ and the church, a marriage that is submerged in a sea of abuse can reflect neither the divine purposes of God nor the relationship between Christ and the church. Abuse is in no way consistent with the biblical intent for marriage (Conway, 1998; Miles 2002). It is therefore necessary to question whether or not a marriage covenant remains valid under such circumstances.

This point is addressed quite fully by Eilts (1995), who maintains that the covenant is in fact broken at the time of the abuse. When abuse is present within a marriage, the liberating intent of the covenant is lost and the marriage 'becomes a setting of bondage and affliction' (p. 448). The divorce is simply the legal acknowledgment of the breach. However, as a further complication, Eilts explains that Christian women who are trapped in a domestic abuse situation face some very serious issues arising from what they perceive as the breaking of their own marriage vows, which were initially expected to result in a lifelong commitment. It is this very belief in promises and permanency that contributes significantly to the victim choosing to remain with her abuser, often for a period of years.

Raised in a strict Catholic home, Mary expected her marriage to be a lifelong union. Instead, she remained in a loveless marriage for 25 years after her husband announced his homosexual preferences. Eventually, she was able to accept the decision of her husband to divorce her, this acceptance based on the insight that the divorce was simply the legal recognition of the violation of the marriage vows that had occurred many years earlier. Mary captures her thoughts quite succinctly when she states, 'if there's no love there, there's no marriage there'. Mary recognised, firstly, that the marriage covenant had been broken by the actions of her husband; and secondly, that she had determinedly undertaken everything within her power to 'keep the marriage going'.

A similar thought is reflected in Susanna's comments. Her faith views marriage as a covenant that is everlasting, continuing even after death. However, there is also a recognition that the covenant can be broken and become void, thereby permitting the innocent party to seek a divorce without facing the condemnation of the church. As a result of this outlook, Susanna received the support of her church when she decided that to file for divorce was the most appropriate option available to her. Susanna elucidates her position:

> We were supposed to be married for the eternities. OK. And that's a binding sort of thing. But because he's doing what he's doing, then it's … it's discarded anyway. Because you can only be married to somebody if you're trying to do the right thing.

Over the years of her marriage, Elizabeth eventually experienced a paradigm shift in her view of how a covenant can function. Initially she expected her marriage to be permanent, but life experience provided her with a different perspective. Elizabeth shares her current insight:

> Well, the marriage is not a contract. It's a covenant. So a covenant is the same as the kind of covenant that God has with us. So you know, it is forever. But I … I now have come to believe that that covenant, it's made by two, and it can be broken by one. And when one breaks it, it's broken. And he broke it a long time ago.

Alsdurf and Alsdurf (1989) support the concept of the marriage covenant being broken by the abuse perpetrated against the victim when they assert that domestic abuse is offensive to the covenant relationship, and constitutes an absolute 'betrayal of his oath to love, honor and commit himself to her' (p. 118). Such betrayal has both physical and spiritual repercussions. The prophet Malachi makes a strong connection between the absence of the blessing of God in the life of an individual, and the fact that those same men had dishonoured their marriage covenant (Malachi 2:13; Alden, 1985; Hill, 1998; Jones, 1962). The apostle Peter draws a similar parallel, indicating that if a husband is not honouring and respecting his wife, his prayers, and thus the blessing of God on his life, can be hindered

(1 Peter 3:7; Blum, 1981; Davids, 2002; Deutsch, 1987; Kroeger, 1996; Kroeger & Nason-Clark, 2001; Nicholson, 1967).

Finally, Eilts (1995) presents the argument that:

> ... while marriage is a covenant that is meant to be lasting, there is nothing in Scripture that can be construed to justify a lifetime of meaningless suffering, and there is substantial evidence calling for covenants with God to be ended when their purpose has been forgotten, ignored, or transgressed. (p. 449)

Summary

This chapter has presented the Christian concept of marriage as both a sacred union and a binding covenant relationship, which was initially designed as a loving and supportive intermeshing of the lives of two individuals. The intimate nature of the marital union has been presented as one that is clearly depicted in Scripture, which also highlights the intended permanency of the commitment.

The issues of divorce and the subsequent choice to remarry have been discussed in the light of Scripture, with specific reference to the statements of Jesus on the subject. An overview of the diversity of opinion existing between authors has been presented, in conjunction with the potential outworking of such opinions when applied to cases of domestic abuse.

It has been considered that the legal termination of a marriage may be regarded as an acceptable choice for a woman who finds herself in an abusive relationship, as such a relationship does not abide by the requirement of the original covenant. The covenant is therefore broken prior to any legal action being sought. It has also been considered that a valid divorce, according to biblical requirements, provides the woman with the right to remarry should she so desire.

Reflections for the Counsellor

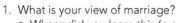

1. What is your view of marriage?
   • Where did you learn this (e.g. family, church)?

2. What is your view of divorce?

3. Have either of these views on marriage and divorce changed? How?

   Note: These questions may also be useful for client discussion.

Client Discussion

1. How would you describe your relationship?
   • List some words that describe your relationship.

2. What sort of love is required in marriage?
   • List some words that describe this form of love.

3. Compare your two lists from questions 1 and 2. Discuss.

4. What were your experiences regarding attitudes to divorce?
   • What were you told or advised, and by whom?
   • How did you feel about these suggestions?
   • How did they work for you?

5. If already divorced, how did you finally arrive at that decision?

6. What would help you to understand divorce better?

7. Do you think you would like to obtain a divorce?
   • If so, what would help you to come to this decision?

8. Do you believe that divorce is acceptable to God? If not, how would your situation be different if you believed it was acceptable?
   • Would you feel differently? How?

9. What challenges have you faced as a result of divorce, or what challenges might you face if you were to seek/obtain a divorce?

CHAPTER 7

Husband and Shepherd

> In the year 584, forty-three Catholic bishops and twenty
> men representing bishops voted, after a lengthy debate at
> the Council of Macon, whether women were human.
> Women were declared human by one vote in a count of 32
> to 31. (Cooper-White, 1995 p. 50)

This chapter provides an overview of the concept of female submission to male headship, and the manner in which the teaching and embracing of such philosophy can prove detrimental to the wellbeing of Christian women who are victims of domestic abuse. It then offers biblical examples upon which the teaching of female submission is based.

Accurate interpretation of Scripture is presented as a crucial element of scholarship. Three options for interpretation are presented: (1) the concept of mutual submission; (2) the relevance of both context and setting in relation to accurate interpretation of Scripture; and (3) the patriarchal position that embraces female submission to both the husband and members of the clergy. The potential connection between submission to one's husband and the husband's ultimate salvation, and the creation narrative are also considered.

Jesus' own treatment of women is examined in the light of breaking with patriarchal and cultural tradition and thus elevating the position of women. The image of Jesus as the good shepherd is also developed in an effort to highlight the parallel between the love Jesus has for His church, and the love a husband is expected to demonstrate to his wife. Finally, in relation to the church, an egalitarian focus is acknowledged as being the more productive and supportive choice when considering the wellbeing of women.

Overview

Female submission is a belief that openly supports male headship within the family and the need for the woman to submit to male authority. As with the concepts of forgiveness, and marriage as a sacred union, the issue of female submission to male headship is one that is fraught with difficulty for an individual trapped within an abusive relationship. Views on this subject vary significantly between denominations, and even then between individuals within a denomination. The concept of female submission to male headship is one that, according to the belief of some, promotes patriarchy and hierarchy (Seim, 1995), and contributes to violence against women (Ess, 1995). Others view female submission to male headship as a choice (Slaughter, 1996), or as part of the far more complimentary concept of a mutual submission (Mathis, 1992) that exists within a caring and loving relationship. However, in the case of domestic abuse, submission is rarely a choice, is certainly not mutual, and cannot be defined as existing within a caring and loving relationship.

Of the 20 women interviewed, 11 reported that female submission was considered an integral part of their Christian faith. Eight of those women identified themselves as attending a fundamentalist denomination. One other explained that, while not strictly fundamentalist in belief or practice, her church adopted a strong patriarchal position in relation to biblical teaching. In most cases, the manner in which the concept of female submission was either taught or practised acted as a hindrance to the wellbeing of the women, who sincerely wished to practise their faith but were also forced to deal with issues of domestic abuse. Such abuse appeared to gain strength from the restrictions placed upon women and the subsequent increase in liberty for the men.

Elizabeth constantly faced difficulties with the concept of female submission to male headship, particularly when it was used by her perpetrator husband either as a put-down or to dominate and control her behaviour. The following comments not only reflect Elizabeth's desire to make her marriage work by choosing to behave in a manner she understood to be correct, but also the desire of many Christian women who find themselves in a similar position. Elizabeth explains:

Submission was such a big thing. Like, he used to say to me 'You are a disobedient wife' if I wouldn't do what he wanted. And I thought, 'I don't want to be a disobedient wife. I'm really trying to be an obedient wife'. And that was my heart, because I wanted to do what was right in the marriage.

Biblical References to Submission

To consider the concept of female submission to male headship, it is first necessary to consider the key scriptural passages from which the teaching is drawn. In the New Testament, these include Ephesians 5:21–33, Colossians 3:18–19 and 1 Peter 3:1–12. Additionally, information from the creation narrative is sometimes drawn from the book of Genesis in an effort to support the argument in favour of female submission. The following section briefly outlines the content of these passages of Scripture.

Ephesians 5:22–24

This passage states that a wife should be in submission to her own husband just as she is to the Lord, and explains that the husband is the head of his wife just as Christ is the head of the church. Verse 24 accentuates the need for Christian wives to be subject to their husbands in 'every thing'.

Although the above passage is often used as a mandate for women, this exhortation is followed immediately by comments regarding the manner in which a Christian husband is expected to treat his wife. This instruction places the demand upon the husband to love his wife 'even as Christ also loved the church' (Vs. 25).

Colossians 3:18–19

This passage is quite short, but echoes the thought that wives are expected to be in submission to their own husbands. The author also takes time to reiterate the instruction to husbands to love their wives.

1 Peter 3:1–12

This passage of Scripture is a little longer. It includes not only the instruction that wives should be in submission to their husbands, but also a number of other directions regarding the general behaviour of Christian women and the manner in which they should attire themselves. Verse 1 indicates that appropriate behaviour by a wife may result in the conversion of her husband to Christianity. Finally, attention is turned to the husbands, who are instructed to honour their wives as the 'weaker vessel' (Vs. 7), accentuating the principle that both the man and the woman are considered to be heirs together in the Christian faith.

Genesis 2:20–3:15

Within the garden narrative contained in the book of Genesis, the woman (Eve) is created as a 'help meet' (2:20) for the man (Adam), who was created first. As the story unfolds, the woman is seen as being both deceived by the serpent and guilty of enticing her husband to sin (3:1–6). As a result of this action, the woman was told, among other things, that her husband would rule over her (Vs. 15).

Interpreting Scriptures on Submission

One may read the abovementioned Scriptures and subsequently determine that they appear very clear in their instruction that wives must be in submission to their husbands. However, one must not fail to consider the nature of the message being conveyed and the context in which it is presented. While all Scripture may be viewed as being inspired by God, through the Holy Spirit (Barabas, 1981b; Guthrie, 1975; Harris, 1981a; Lindsell, 1975), it remains possible that not all Scripture can be accepted literally and applied to all situations, but is relevant only for a specific situation at a specific point in time. For example, the prophet Isaiah speaks of a virgin who shall conceive and give birth to a son (7:14). While there are a number of possible interpretations of this verse (Grogan, 1986), the author of the Gospel of Matthew interprets it specifically in relation to the birth of Jesus Christ (Matthew 1:18–25) (Earle, 1964; Wilkins, 2002). Further, the terminology used later in the book of Isaiah depicts a more exact picture of the Messianic nature of the prophecy as it makes reference to the one who shall be called 'Wonderful, Counsellor, The mighty God, The everlasting Father, The Prince of Peace' (Isaiah 9:6) (Price, 1966). Thus, it remains exceedingly important to view Scripture as a whole, carefully considering the context and also the audience for whom it was initially provided (Drumwright, 1975; Grogan, 1975).

There are a number of positions regarding the interpretation of Scripture addressing the issue of female submission to male headship.

These include a positive view of mutual submission within a marital relationship, a consideration of the context and cultural setting pertaining to the relevant Scriptures, and a strong patriarchal stance that demands absolute submission of female to male.

Mutual Submission

Female submission to male headship can be viewed within the framework of mutual submission, which presents both individuals as equals before God and before each other (Browning, 2004a; Kroeger & Kroeger, 1992; Miller-McLemore, 2004; Osiek, 2004; Rinck, 1990). Of particular interest in this case is the passage in Ephesians 5. It should be noted that Bible scholars are not necessarily in agreement as to whether this section of the chapter should commence at Verse 21 (Arnold, 2002a; Miles, 2002; Scholer, 1996; Wood, 1978), which requires all Christians to submit lovingly to each other out of reverence for God; or at Verse 22 (Taylor, 1965), which focuses primarily on female submission. Wood explains that grammatically Verse 21 could connect quite adequately with the preceding verse, but it appears to flow more 'naturally' (p. 75) with the following section. Thus, a position of mutuality could be considered reasonable. Browning (2004b) presents submission and mutuality within marriage as being contained within the overall concept of Christian love and charity, as opposed to the hierarchical interpretation of the male being the sole head. Grenz and Kjesbo (1995) echo this thought in their emphatic declaration that mutual submission is the 'overarching principle for relationships among God's people' (p. 115).

The potential conflict that can arise regarding the positioning of Verses 21 and 22 of Ephesians 5 is powerfully illustrated in the story of Lydia. Raised in a liberal Christian home, she freely supported the concept of submission when contained within the parameters of mutual submission. However, her husband maintained a far more patriarchal viewpoint, which resulted in substantial levels of conflict, unreasonable demands and ongoing abuse. Lydia defines her understanding of Ephesians 5:

> That whole Ephesians 5:21–22 passage, I think it is — it's all good because of Verse 21. You know — it's all good. We can do it. If that's the context, then that's fine. You know,

and for me that was my exegesis of that whole situation was that it's in the context of equality, where both of you submit to each other, out of reverence for God.

Lydia also took the opportunity to explain her feelings, together with the questions that were raised for her when, prior to her wedding, her then fiancé became pedantic and demanding regarding the reading of Ephesians 5 during the wedding ceremony. Based on her understanding of the verses in the book of Ephesians (above), Lydia believed this would be acceptable, but she recalls:

> This is really … this is one of the first things that made me think, 'Ooo-ooo' [laugh]. The lights went on. Flags went out. I just thought, 'Hang on a minute'.

When viewing her relationship retrospectively, Lydia was easily able to identify one of the early warning signs of a potentially abusive situation. However, like many victims of domestic abuse, Lydia chose to overlook what appeared to be a reasonably small issue, choosing instead to believe that her relationship would unfold in a positive way.

Further to the debate regarding the grouping of verses within Ephesians 5 is the question surrounding the accurate interpretation of the Greek word *hupotasso*, which is translated as *submit*. Kroeger (1995) alerts the reader to the possible change in interpretation when a verb is used in the middle voice, as occurs in the Greek language. This is frequently the case when the verb *hupotasso* 'is applied to women or wives in the New Testament' (p. 138). This verb has a wide range of possible interpretations (Kroeger & Nason-Clark, 2001), and can also carry the meaning of being compliant or acting responsibly in relation to others (Kroeger, 1996; Miles, 2002). Thus, the interpretation should not be narrowed in an endeavour to support an expectancy of female submission to male headship. Miles refutes the legitimacy of a male-preferred hierarchical structure within a marriage, but instead argues that the primary focus of a Christian marriage is for both 'husbands and wives to behave responsibly toward one another in a meaningful and respectful way' (p. 73).

Another question arises in relation to the interpretation of the Greek word *kephale*, which is often translated as *head*. For example, 'the husband is the head of the wife' (Ephesians 5:23) or 'the head of the woman is the man' (1 Corinthians 11:3). While this issue has been long debated by scholars, Scholer (1996) offers the conclusion that there can be a variety of acceptable meanings for *kephale*, including 'authority over, preeminence and source' (p. 42). In favour of the use of *kephale* from a metaphorical perspective meaning *source*, Kroeger (1996) supports an interpretation of 1 Corinthians 11:3–12 in which the man is depicted as 'the source of woman, and woman as the source of man' (p. 209). This interpretation links closely to the same passage of Scripture where Paul expresses the obvious desire for 'mutual support and interdependence' (Kroeger, p. 209) between the man and the woman. Some scholars may choose to apply the 'authority over' interpretation in an effort to support a position of female submission to male headship; however, the context in which these Scriptures are set points clearly to a position of mutual submission (Scholer). Grenz and Kjesbo (1995) firmly reject any interpretation that embraces an 'authority over' perspective, highlighting moreover the egalitarian stand promoted by Paul regarding gender relationships within the Christian church. Perriman (1998) also offers an interpretation of *kephale* focused on 'pre-eminence', the outworking of which is based upon the cultural expectations of the era rather than on any degree of inequality between male and female.

Context and Setting

Keener (1992) and Borland (1991) argue in favour of the idea that an understanding of the context and setting of Scripture is relevant to the accurate interpretation of its meaning. Both authors set the concept of female submission squarely within the cultural traditions of the era. Keener stresses the fact that a radical turning away from the submissive role of the woman, considered to be standard practice in the ancient world (Richards & Richards, 1999; Wood, 1978), had the potential to create substantial opposition, and even conflict, for the newly forming Christian church of the time. Keener offers the argument that while Paul was the proponent of some radical concepts — including the equality of both men and women before God, and the idea that husbands should love their wives with an attitude of servanthood — he continued to maintain a strong sensitivity to the cultural issues at hand. By advising women to function within the prescribed cultural framework, Paul endeavoured to minimise any perceived threat to the Roman aristocracy and thus foster the ongoing development of the Christian church.

Van Leeuwen (2004) also supports the notion that adherence to cultural gender roles could have been considered a necessary compromise at the time. Paul's position on gender equality pointed more towards the liberation of women: challenging Christian husbands to step aside from the existing cultural mindsets that restricted women and placed them in a position of inferiority, and instead embrace a more loving and supporting attitude thereby modelling the example of Christ (Grady, 2000). Keener (1992) supports the need to consider Scripture in the light of the relevant culture, rather than attempt to forcefully impose concepts that were considered relevant to the authority structures of the first century onto situations existing within the very different authority structures of the twenty-first century. Keener (1992) further highlights the need to focus primarily on the principles of Kingdom living presented in the Bible, advocating the consideration of the book and teachings as a whole, as opposed to adopting the more restrictive position that has the potential to inhibit accurate interpretation and thereby limit the possible application of the principles involved. Cahill (2004) echoes these thoughts, suggesting that attention be turned to overarching themes and the relevant manner in which these themes may be utilised to provide insight into very present contemporary issues. Turning her attention to the often symbolic nature of Scripture, Osiek (2004) suggests that constantly embracing a strongly literal interpretation of Scripture, outside the consideration of context and setting, can easily minimise the influence and impact of the symbolism employed.

Patriarchal Position

The patriarchal position supports a very traditional societal framework that embraces the concept of male headship within the family, church and community. It places women in a position of inequality and subordination based solely on gender (Ezell, 1998; Luzzi, 1998). From a strict patriarchal viewpoint, the role of the husband may be described as 'the God-ordained role of full-time boss and provider' (Grady, 2000, p. 72; Knight, 1991), a position which Gallagher (2004) warns is likely to result in divorce as the wife is called upon to submit totally and lovingly to the God-ordained authority of her husband. Submission on the part of the woman is viewed as obedience to God. It is demonstrated through her obedience to all those He has set in authority over her, including her own husband and church ministers (Griffith, 1997).

Elizabeth not only experienced considerable difficulty with issues of submission regarding her husband, but also from her ministers. Regardless of the state of her marriage, she was not permitted to even contemplate a temporary separation. Elizabeth clarifies her situation:

> It wasn't OK for me to say I wanted a separation just to try and make something work. That wasn't an option for me. I was just — it was just an understanding there which, if it were me now, I would say, 'Could you tell me why?', but back then I just knew … I wasn't being submissive. See — so I was brainwashed into … Not an option for you. End of story. Don't even go there.

Hannah's story is particularly useful in illustrating the extreme degree to which the concept of female submission can be taken, negatively affecting not only the relationships of couples within the church but also the church itself. Like Elizabeth, Hannah reported a substantial amount of difficulty with the concept of female submission to both husband and ministers. However, the position adopted by Hannah's church appeared manipulative and provided the clergy with a power base that left Hannah feeling trapped. Hannah explains the problems she was experiencing:

> They used to say about how a wife should … how a husband should behave and how he should love his wife and treat her as his own body and all the rest … they say all that. But then they had the Jezebel spirit thing going, where women were supposed to not tell their husbands … they obeyed their husbands. They used to say that there was this independent spirit, and that to have an independent spirit was like witchcraft. And witchcraft — you know, God couldn't stand that. So somehow they screwed the whole thing around so that all the women in the church had to sit down and behave, and obey their husbands, regardless of what their husbands were doing. And that anybody who questioned things had an independent spirit … and that was rebellion. And God cannot stand rebellion. They would say … if you want to obey God, you obey your

> leaders. Listen to what your leaders say. So if we weren't listening and doing what they said, then we were rebellious and we were ... God hated us and all the rest of it.

For the purpose of clarification, the Jezebel spirit referred to by Hannah is viewed by some as one who usurps authority not rightfully belonging to them, and one who undermines the position of those in authority. This image is based on the biblical character of Queen Jezebel as depicted in 1 Kings 16–21 (Barabas, 1981c; Culver, 1975; Richards & Richards, 1999).

This situation created confusion for Hannah, who was able to identify a lack of congruence between the messages that were presented to her congregation. While there appeared to be an element of truth in the initial information presented, such as the requirement that a man should love his wife as his own body (Ephesians 5:28), in addition to the contorted interpretation of the Old Testament Scripture that states 'rebellion is as the sin of witchcraft' (1 Samuel 15:23), the principles of submission were extended to a degree that fostered exorbitant levels of control for the ministers involved. Eventually, the unrealistic nature of this particular perversion of the concept of submission resulted in a major church split.

Based on 1 Peter 3:1–12, which states that it is possible for a man to be won over by the appropriate conduct of his wife, there is a belief put forward by some that as a woman chooses to constantly defer to her husband, he in turn will perhaps convert to Christianity and begin to treat her with increased love and respect (Griffith & Harvey, 1998; Grudem, 1991). This belief can also be taken to the extreme by some organisations advocating that, regardless of the desire of the husband — even if those desires are not in accordance with the will of God — the wife should remain compliant and trust God to deal appropriately with her husband (Griffith, 1997). This position is resolutely opposed by a number of authors (Green, 1984; Grudem; Slaughter, 1996), particularly with regard to the submission of the woman to abusive behaviour perpetrated by her husband (Alsdurf & Alsdurf, 1989; Grady, 2000; Kroeger, 1996; Luzzi, 1998; Pearson, 1998).

The extreme nature of teaching on female submission was particularly evident in Leah's situation. Regardless of the continual presence of domestic abuse in her relationship, the leaders in Leah's church advised her as follows:

I was even told like I should maybe read *Cleo* magazines so I
could turn him on more. Yes. I should treat him — ah, he's
the head of the home and I should treat him accordingly. And
if I did that then everything else would follow on.

Leah further explains the philosophy of her church as:

The husband is the head of the home. Your attitude to
your husband is your attitude to God. So that if you …
[sigh] you have a bad attitude towards your husband, like
you don't like him or you speak badly against him, that's
like speaking badly against God … I was told, 'Well, you
have to support him. You have to keep showing him more
love. Maybe you should do something special for him'. It
was all that sort of thing, like the man is the head of the
home and you have to … it was up to me if there was a
problem. I was the one who had to do something about it.

For Leah, the final outworking of doctrines and advice founded in a
strong patriarchal position was disappointing and quite detrimental.
Left feeling confused, disillusioned and questioning, Leah chose not
to attend any denominational church. She expresses the confusion of
a woman whose faith has been severely undermined:

There's a whole pile of things that I've been taught that I
realise now are wrong. And so I feel like all my foundations
are all shaky and I don't know what to believe any more. I
don't know if they're wrong or they're right. This is the thing.
It's just heaps of all these little rules and I'm trying to say …
is this a rule … that is, a made-up man's rule, or is this a rule
… or is this an attitude that I should have because I'm a
Christian or something like that? You know, it's like I don't
know what's right and wrong any more. And you're kind of a
bit … [sigh] … feel a little mixed up.

In contrast to Leah's experience, Joanna was able to find some encouragement in the fact that her church supported the principle of
submission in a more balanced context that Joanna described as 'reasonable biblical teaching', thus freeing her from a seemingly impossible
expectation. After a brief pause, Joanna thoughtfully states:

They said submitting doesn't mean that you have to do
whatever your husband says — that, you know, if your

> husband's requesting you to do something really stupid that you don't do that just because he says it, and just because he's the husband. Yeah, he is the head of the house, but you know, submit does not mean control.

The patriarchal position is often connected to the creation narrative (Genesis 2–3; Miles, 2000), where the woman, Eve, is seen as the representation of all women and also as 'an agent of chaos' (Ess, 1995 p. 94) who, through her disobedience, paved the way for the fall of man. Some choose to view the subordination of women as a form of divine punishment for her act of disobedience. However Keener (1996) suggests that it was not the subordination that was the punishment, but rather ongoing conflict with her husband which would eventually result in her subordination. Woman is frequently depicted as being unreliable, careless, unthinking, not to be trusted and very much in need of male guidance or control. She is seen as holding a position inferior to that of the male, who was created first. Ess describes these beliefs as myths that minimise the position and power of women and ultimately provide a foundation for domestic abuse, a position clearly illustrated by Ruth in the following example.

The church that Ruth's husband required her to attend preached female submission, maintained a 'very old fashioned' interpretation of the Bible, and fostered a high level of gender inequality that Ruth reports contributed both to wife abuse and other forms of abuse within families. Ruth describes this church as being:

> Very much fundamentalist, very much male dominated, and very much the males sat on one side and the females on the other. It was also very well known because of their very strong ties, that extended families — incest and sexual abuse were very much common, everyday issues ... which I never realised until it happened to my child.

Kroeger (1996) highlights the danger of a strong patriarchal position that embraces a hierarchical philosophy and allows one individual to rule over another. Numerous authors believe that such a stand, steeped in gender-based hierarchy, has the potential to foster abuse in its many forms and even justify it for some perpetrators (Miles, 2002; Rinck, 1990; Roberts, 2002; Scholer, 1996), leaving the woman powerless to function effectively (Alsdurf & Alsdurf, 1989; Ess, 1995; Nason-Clark, 1997; Nesheim, 1998).

Raised in a fundamentalist household in which domestic abuse was not an issue, Eve was aware of the principles of female submission and male headship that were modelled by her parents. Eve describes it as 'an unspoken law':

> You just knew Dad was the head of the home. Mum was there, always there with meals and looking after us. And she never worked and, well, was very involved in the church, with Sunday school and things like that.

Eve's church presented female submission in a more definitive manner. Eve summarises the position:

> The man's the head of the home. And the wife is submissive, and what a great treasure it is for a man to have a submissive wife. It's the greatest thing and all this came through as a very strong thing that was preached.

However, the minister was totally unprepared for the issues surrounding domestic abuse. Eve tells of the attitude of the minister, and the manner in which her position was minimised and undermined when she endeavoured to confront the reality of her situation and expressed the desire to terminate her 20-year abusive marriage:

> When I get really strong they just go, 'Well you're just rebellious. You're just not prepared to work on this. I can see why he … he reacts to you'.

Based on a belief in female submission to male headship, the church plainly told Eve that she was rebellious and in possession of a wrong attitude, thus blaming Eve for her own victimisation. Further to this, Eve's husband received a great deal of sympathy, as Eve was judged to have rejected the appropriate role of the woman by not adopting the principle of female submission and actively applying it to her life and marriage.

In contrast to a strong patriarchal position, Ortlund (1991) and Piper and Grudem (1991) describe male headship as modelling the role of Christ while still retaining the authority, responsibility and leadership within the partnership. Although Ortlund emphasises the equality of male and female, he still appears to place the woman in a subservient role, claiming that she 'usurped Adam's headship and led the way into sin' (p. 107). Schreiner (1991) maintains that although both men and women are viewed as having equal worth before God, the male is in possession of the 'God-given responsibility to lead' (p. 136). It would appear that there is a very fine line between the theoretical concept of male headship and the behavioural outworking of the same concept in the form of male domination. Ortlund personally condemns male domination as a 'personal moral failure' (p. 102), but Miles (2002) describes male headship as 'a man-made concept designed to maintain a patriarchal social system' (p. 68). Lois, who received positive assistance from her minister, shares comments that seem to reflect the position held by Miles (2002):

> Our pastor, he would say ... he said that you can recognise a cult because it subjugates its women. So he was very pro-women. And the Salvation Army minister very much, they were very pro-women, very much family.

Jesus' Attitude Towards Women

To gain a more effective understanding of the appropriate treatment of women in relation to Christian teaching, it is necessary to consider, as a very positive and practical example, the manner in which Jesus' varying interactions reflected His respect and ongoing concern for the women of His day (Russell, 1981b). Jesus' treatment of women throughout the gospels set a standard that broke with the traditional patriarchal outlook of the period (Cahill, 2004; Richards & Richards, 1999). A number of passages of Scripture are useful for highlighting the considerate and even liberating attitude that Jesus demonstrated towards the women with whom He came in contact. Examples include Jesus' dealings with the woman experiencing an issue of blood (menstrual haemorrhage) (Matthew 9:20–22; Mark 5:25–34; Luke 8:41–49), Mary and Martha (Luke 10:38–42), and the woman of Samaria (John 4:7–9). A closer examination of these Scriptures testifies to the respect that Jesus offered to women, together with His willingness to step aside from traditions that both viewed and treated women as inferior members of society.

The Woman With the Issue of Blood

The situation for the woman experiencing the issue of blood is extremely difficult. The nature of the disorder is not specific, although it would appear she had been suffering an almost constant flow of menstrual blood for 12 years (Earle, 1964; Sanner, 1964; Wessel, 1984). Her condition was worsening, and the doctors were unable to help her (Childers, 1964; Strauss, 2002). To further complicate her situation, the woman was considered ceremonially unclean and therefore not permitted to attend social or religious gatherings (Lake, 1975; Wilkins, 2002). According to Jewish law (Leviticus 15:25–33), she was 'perpetually unclean' (Carson, 1984 p. 230; Harris, 1990) due to the constant haemorrhage, and should not have been in a public place lest others should become contaminated (Garland, 2002).

Instead of rebuking the woman for touching Him and thus causing Him to become ritually unclean, Jesus took time to encourage her (Liefield, 1984; Sanner, 1964), using the gentle and affectionate term 'daughter' (Luke 8:48) as he spoke openly with her (Strauss, 2002). In doing this, Jesus effectively caused Jairus, the ruler of the synagogue (Luke 8:41) — and a very important man whose daughter was near death — to wait for His attention while He ministered to the needs of a woman (Richards & Richards, 1999). The break with tradition is not only obvious (a Jewish leader would not normally be expected to wait for a mere woman) but also unexpected, as Jesus' disciples appear impatient to continue on to where they perceived more important work awaited them (Wessel, 1984).

Mary and Martha

It is reasonable to assume that both Mary and Martha were unmarried as they lived with their brother, possibly in the home of their late parents (Childers, 1964). As such, Mary and Martha were expected to serve in the household (Strauss, 2002). Instead, Mary chose to break with the social order and place herself at the feet of Jesus, as would a male disciple (Childers). In a society where girls were not provided with any formal education, and rabbis did not accept women as disciples (Liefield, 1984), Mary's actions are described by Strauss as 'particularly shocking' (p. 417). When Martha challenges Jesus regarding Mary's apparent shirking of household responsibilities, Jesus 'shatters cultural expectations' (Strauss, p. 417) by not only accepting, but encouraging Mary's choice to place herself in the position of a disciple, a position previously occupied solely by male members of society. While not minimising the existing cultural role expectation for women, Jesus offers an increased liberty for women as He utilises this opportunity to openly acknowledge their equal status in His eyes (Richards & Richards, 1999).

The Woman of Samaria

Jesus spoke freely with the woman at the well outside Samaria. The woman is described by Tenney (1988) as 'ignorant', 'sinful', 'poor', and a possible 'outcast' (p. 92), and by Mayfield (1965) as a woman of 'loose morals' (p. 96). She was a woman of low reputation, even in her own community. The woman herself was shocked at the fact that Jesus spoke with her because this was not considered appropriate behaviour for Jewish rabbis, who were firmly discouraged from speaking publicly with a woman (Richards & Richards, 1999; Tenney 1981a). To add to the complexity of the interaction, a great animosity existed between the Jews and the Samaritans (Blaiklock, 1981; Kelso, 1975), even to the point of 'bitter hostility' (Kostenberger, 2002 p. 45). A Samaritan woman had no privilege, was considered to be permanently ceremonially unclean, and should therefore be avoided (Kostenberger). Regardless of the social stigma attached to such an interaction, Jesus chose not only to speak with the woman but also to share with her deeper levels of spiritual truth, which ultimately led to the spreading of the gospel message in the area (Blaiklock).

Throughout the gospels, Jesus is seen to break with religious and social tradition, challenging the cultural expectations of the period, rejecting the denigration of women and elevating the status of women. Jesus' own attitude and actions, as reflected in His dealings with women, introduced a liberation for women that should not be ignored by those who wish to follow His example (Richards & Richards, 1999; Sly, 1992).

For the women interviewed in this book, a belief in the concept of female submission to male headship appeared to affect the manner in which members of the clergy dealt with the women who turned to them for assistance. Those members of the clergy who expressed a firm belief in female submission were reported to be far less helpful, often condemning the women for acting in a manner contrary to biblical teaching. These clergy members demonstrated their choice for what may be termed a legalistic position, basing their objections on the demand for submission rather than modelling the role of Jesus in choosing a compassionate, positive response designed to liberate those who were oppressed.

Love in the Form of Agape

Miles (2002) points out that while wives are frequently reminded of their Christian duties, very little time or energy is given to either sermons or teachings that clearly explain the behavioural expectations of men according to Scripture. Thus, the teaching on submission is seen to lack balance. In truth, there is a very high demand placed upon husbands with regard to the love they are expected to demonstrate in relation to their wives. Husbands are admonished to love their wives (Colossians 3:19) 'even as Christ also loved the church' (Ephesians 5:25), 'even as their own bodies' (Ephesians 5:28), and 'even as [he loves] himself' (Ephesians 5:33). In each of these cases, the Greek verb *agapao* (meaning *to love*) is used in either the present imperative active or the present infinitive active form (Zodhiates, 1991). The verb *agapao* is the highest form of love expressed (Nielson, 1965), contains a moral component, and indicates a choice of the will of the individual to delight in or seek the welfare of another (Thayer, 1996; Vaughan, 1978; Zodhiates, 1992). It is a self-giving, self-sacrificing form of love (Conway, 1998) that excludes 'bitterness, commands and selfishness' (Nielson, p. 419). The use of the present imperative active or the present infinitive active indicates a command involving 'continuous or repeated action' (Zodhiates, 1991 p. 869). Thus, the command for husbands to love their wives does not indicate a weak, inconsistent, on-again/off-again relationship based on sexual or romantic feelings or the prevailing emotion of the moment, but rather an ongoing moral commitment to fully and continuously love and seek the welfare of the wife with whom he has been joined through the covenant of marriage. The expectation to love unreservedly is illustrated more succinctly in the following section, where the role of the shepherd is used as a model for the Christlike love and devotion expected of the husband.

The Expectation to Love

A great deal of the argument in favour of female submission hinges on the analogy that is drawn from the relationship between Christ and the church. The wife is expected to respect and honour her husband as she would Christ. The husband, in turn, is expected to model the attitude and behaviour of Christ in his relationship with his wife (Arnold, 2002b). To develop a more accurate understanding of the New Testament relationship between Christ and His church — or in the case of the Old Testament, of God and His people Israel — it is helpful to consider the popular image of the shepherd caring for his sheep (Briggs & Briggs, 1906; Kirkpatrick, 1933; Kostenberger, 2002; Scott, 1975). Jesus referred to Himself as the 'good shepherd' (John 10:11) (Mayfield, 1965; Vos, 1999), the likeness of which is so aptly presented through the use of descriptive imagery in Psalm 23 (Cansdale, 1975b; Henry & Scott, 1979c). By thoughtfully reflecting upon the role of the shepherd, one may be better equipped to visualise and thereby understand the level of expectation placed upon the husband to care for his wife.

Traditionally, the role of the shepherd was to nurture, guard and protect the sheep in his care (Holdridge, 1981; Kirkpatrick, 1933). He usually spent his nights sleeping across the entrance to the fold as part of his duty of protection (Vos, 1999). The shepherd carried a rod, which could be used for support; or it could be used as a weapon, together with his sling, to defend the flock against would-be attackers; and a staff with which to guide or perhaps rescue a straying sheep (Funderburk, 1975a; Holdridge; White, 1975). The shepherd is depicted as one who is devoted to the wellbeing of his sheep (Eaton, 1967; VanGemeren, 1991). The shepherd will not run from danger as would a hired worker (Tenney, 1981a) but would instead risk his own life for the sake of his flock (Kostenberger, 2002), as demonstrated by David, a shepherd who eventually became King of Israel (1 Samuel 17:34–36) (Purkiser, 1965; Youngblood, 1992).

Psalm 23 paints a picture of peace and rest as the sheep feed, shelter and find refreshment in rich, lush pastures beside the quietness of the springs (Briggs & Briggs, 1906; Leslie, 1949; Spurgeon, n.d.). The sheep are provided for by the knowledge, wisdom and skill of the shepherd (Eaton 1967; Horne, n.d.). The psalmist more than adequately conveys an image of trust between the sheep and the shepherd. The sheep choose to follow in the path of the shepherd. They are led and guided in an attitude of love — not driven, pressured or bullied (Kostenberger, 2002; Spurgeon). They recognise his voice

(Holdridge, 1981; Tenney, 1988), and are reassured by his presence (Purkiser, 1967). Even in the most difficult terrain and most dangerous of circumstances, there remains a sense of confidence and safety (Horne; Schaefer, 2001; VanGemeren, 1991).

Husband and Shepherd

A number of parallels can be drawn between the image of the shepherd and his sheep, and the role of the husband in relation to his wife. These can be placed under the three key classifications of provision, protection and peace, all of which are the direct result of the steadfast nature of the commitment of the individual. This section will provide a brief overview of the possible connections between the role of a faithful and responsible shepherd and the role of a faithful and responsible husband.

Provision

The act of provision is one of the key roles of the shepherd. Without their basic needs of quality food and water being met, the sheep are likely to lose condition and become weak and potentially less able to fend off disease. The shepherd makes every effort possible to provide the very best for the sheep in his care (Psalm 23:2) (Briggs & Briggs, 1906). Modelling on the role of the shepherd as an image of Jesus Christ, the husband, in his Christlikeness, is expected to provide for the wellbeing of his wife in the best possible manner available to him. Such provision would clearly include suitable food, clothing and housing, but the principle may also be extended to perhaps include the nurturing of the woman as an individual, and the provision of an environment where she is able to cultivate her skills and talents, and develop effectively as one who possesses equal standing in the eyes of God as demonstrated by Jesus in his treatment of Mary (Luke 10:42) (Richards & Richards, 1999).

Protection

For the shepherd, the role of protection is secondary only to the role of provision. Even sheep of the highest quality are of no use if they are stolen by thieves or destroyed by wild animals. Thus, the duty to guard and defend is paramount. Unlike the times of the early shepherd (Holdridge, 1981), neither thieves nor wild animals present a common daily threat to the husband of the 21st century. However, protection and safety can assume a variety of forms. While a husband may be presented with the need to physically defend his wife from a would-be attacker, in the light of the prevalence of domestic abuse, a greater consideration might be the need for the woman to feel safe in her own home. Such safety can certainly be extended to include her emotional wellbeing, which in turn can be linked to the role of the shepherd whose responsibility it was to lead and guide the sheep in a loving manner, without pressure or bullying (Kostenberger, 2002; Spurgeon, n.d.). Even in the darkest, most traumatic moments of life, the relationship between husband and wife is expected to be such that the wife is confident that her husband will do all within his power to love (agape) and protect her in every way possible (Psalm 23:4).

Peace

The image of peace and contentment is clearly apparent throughout Psalm 23. Such peace appears to be the product of an environment of provision and protection, where the presence of unconditional love abounds. Briggs and Briggs (1906) note the present tense of the language, indicating not an experience of the future but a 'present habitual experience' (p. 208). It is in this environment that bonds of trust can be forged effectively. As a result of ongoing experience, the sheep are able to trust the shepherd, and are fully aware that they will be nurtured, cared for and protected as the shepherd continues to faithfully fulfil his professional duty. So too, as a result of experiencing the benefits of the Christlike behaviour of her husband, the wife should be able to trust that no harm will come to her while her husband is taking full responsibility for his role within the partnership.

Steadfast Commitment

As with the concept of love in the form of agape, the steadfast commitment required of the husband is again reflected in the Christlike role of the shepherd. The shepherd does not run from trouble, leaving the sheep helpless, but rather stands firmly and deals effectively with the problem at hand (1 Samuel 17:34–36; John 10:11–13) (Kostenberger, 2002; Tenney, 1981a). Such commitment and devotion was expected of a shepherd. In similar manner, neither should the husband flee from the difficulties of life, leaving his wife to assume the responsibility alone. Difficulties can range from simple daily issues with children, to the more pressing issues of finance or health. Still, the requirement remains the same: that of a steadfast commitment, in the form of agape love, to both the woman and the relationship.

An Egalitarian Focus

The women interviewed who reported having no difficulty with the concept of female submission to male headship came predominantly from churches that embraced a far more egalitarian philosophy, and did not emphasise this particular concept. While those women continued to face difficulties with their perpetrator husbands, they received considerably less condemnation from the church. For example, Mary's minister focused primarily on demonstrating an ongoing care and concern for Mary, as the victim of abuse. Mary describes him as 'unique'. Sarah's minister addressed her specific need, focusing on her physical safety and ultimate wellbeing in very practical ways, such as suggesting that Sarah seek a protection order and supporting her decision to geographically relocate.

Rebekah found that although her church did emphasise the need for female submission, at least some endeavour was made to present it within the more balanced context of a loving relationship. While female submission was not a frequent topic for sermons, Rebekah reports it was clearly expected, and also addressed during marriage seminars or private interviews with the minister. Rebekah expresses her understanding of the application of the concept:

> They do [teach submission]. But I guess they teach it in that the head is ... the husband is supposed to love the wife the way God loves us, and the way Jesus ... And so everything about Jesus is ... is, like, is love, whereas ... so it's not in a ... you'll do this or else kind of way.

The information provided by the women interviewed would appear to indicate that if churches do choose to adopt a policy that embraces the concept of female submission to male headship, then there exists an overwhelming need for the principle to be taught within the context of agape love on the part of the husband, providing a clearly and concisely illustrated definition and behavioural model for the role of the husband that does not hinge upon the behaviour of the wife, just as the accountability and behaviour of the shepherd is not contingent upon the behaviour of the sheep.

Within the framework of domestic abuse, the concept of female submission to male headship can be viewed as a weapon to be wielded at the will of the perpetrator. Therefore, perpetrators of abuse must not be provided with yet another weapon with which they are able to abuse, but must be confronted with the inexcusable shortcomings of their behaviour and challenged to make choices for which they alone are accountable.

Summary

This chapter has presented the concept of female submission to male headship as a teaching that, particularly when applied within a patriarchal framework, has the potential to create ongoing and significant difficulties for those women who are suffering as victims of domestic abuse. While the concept itself may initially appear to be set within Scripture, crucial elements of interpretation must be closely considered before arriving at any final conclusion.

Further, this chapter has emphasised the essential consideration that must be given to the position of Jesus and His own demonstrated treatment of women, together with the overarching principles of love, charity and mutual submission, and the manner in which these principles were constantly encouraged throughout the early stages of the growth of the Christian church.

Christian women have clearly reported the difficulties they have faced with both abusive husbands and those members of the clergy who have chosen to embrace the concept of female submission to male headship. Churches choosing to embrace this concept need to address it from a far more egalitarian perspective, teaching and preaching a balance of committed and demonstrated love on the part of the husband.

Reflections for the Counsellor

1. What are your thoughts regarding female submission to male headship?

2. How might a belief in this principle affect a client's actions or behaviour?

3. In the light of this chapter, how could you best help a client to understand this concept?

Client Discussion

1. How do you view female submission to male headship?
   - What actions define female submission?
   - Where did you learn this belief?
   - How was it taught?
   - What examples have you seen?

2. What new thoughts are of interest to you since reading this chapter? Jot down what you feel are the key points.

3. What are your experiences of female submission to male headship in your relationship? Consider the comments or advice of your partner, members of the clergy, yourself and others.
   - Who decided whether or not you were correct in your behaviour?
   - How was this determined (e.g. were you expected to 'do as you were told')?

4. Upon reflection, do you remember the presence of what could now be viewed as indications of male dominance or an expectation for you, as the female, to submit? If so, what were the signs?

5. What has been your understanding to date of the Scriptures relating to submission?
   - Do you feel the need to rethink your position? If so, what has prompted this?
   - What are your thoughts now?

6. What view of female submission was prevalent in your church or other areas?
   - How was this expressed?

7. How did Jesus perceive or treat women? Consider the three examples mentioned in the chapter.
   - What words would you use to describe the actions or attitudes of Jesus?

8. Reflect upon Psalm 23 and the obligations it raises regarding provision, protection and peace, and the caring role of the shepherd.
   - Were these obligations truly met in your relationship?
   - How do you view marriage in the light of the example in the psalm?

9. Is there a place for female submission today?
   - In what context do you consider female submission to be possible?

CHAPTER 8

A Faith for Coping

This chapter considers the specific coping strategies employed by Christian women who have experienced domestic abuse. Initially the potential benefits of a religious lifestyle are presented followed by an overview of the coping process with particular reference to the issue of stress in relation to coping. Methods of coping are addressed. These include appraisal and reappraisal; problem-focused and emotion-focused approaches; and the advantages of a blended approach to coping with difficult life events.

The concept of coping is presented within the context of religion and religious coping styles, including self-directing, deferring and collaborative approaches. This chapter briefly considers some of the potential difficulties associated with religious forms of coping when confronted with stressful life events, and also highlights the role of hope for individuals in crisis.

Finally, the chapter presents the coping strategies employed by the women interviewed, as they endeavoured to cope with the daily ordeal of living in an environment of domestic abuse. These women employed a blend of both religious and nonreligious coping strategies, depending on the specific nature of the presenting problem. Religious coping strategies include maintaining an active relationship with God, praying, seeking encouragement through the Scriptures and scriptural song. Nonreligious coping strategies include focusing primarily on the children of the marriage; seeking solace and distraction through a variety of activities; reading as a source of information, enlightenment and encouragement; and planning a course of action. Each of these strategies is presented according to its relevance to the women, and excerpts from the transcripts are utilised to illustrate the views and strategies of individual members of the group.

Benefits of a Religious Lifestyle

The Christian faith and the beliefs associated with it can offer a number of benefits to its adherents, such as an increased sense of security and hope for both the present and the future (Bjorck, 1997; Carson, Soeken, & Grimm, 1988; Van Uden & Pieper, 1994), a positive self-concept (Blaine & Trivedi, 1998), and an overall sense of wellbeing throughout life (Bergen & McConatha, 2000). Additionally, Christianity provides its followers with the opportunity to trust in a benevolent and loving God (Connors, Toscova, & Tonigan, 1999), develop an increased sense of purpose and meaning in their life (Koenig, McCullough, & Larson, 2001; Pargament, Koenig & Perez, 2000), and adopt a lifestyle that incorporates higher levels of positive social interaction (Strawbridge, Sherma, Cohen, & Kaplan, 2001), and fosters improved levels of both physical and mental health (George, Ellison, & Larson, 2002; Miller & Thoresen, 1999; Pargament, 1997). Strawbridge et al. also found a connection between active religious involvement and marital stability.

Religion also has the capacity to provide a substantial level of support by offering a sense of belonging and protecting individuals from feelings of isolation and loneliness (Weaver, 1998). Support networks can flow naturally from many church-based activities such as prayer groups, Bible studies, and other socially focused activities in which members of the congregation participate (Koenig et al., 2001). Many religious teachings offer a practical level of guidance for day-to-day living, interpersonal relationships, and business ethics (Blaine & Trivedi, 1998; Kubacka-Jasiecka, Dorczak & Opoczynska, 1994).

Mary chooses an amusing story to illustrate the manner in which church activity groups can effectively serve as support groups for those in need:

> When I joined the choir, the first week I went, they talked for about half an hour … and then they started to sing. And I thought, 'This is funny'. I've been to school choirs with the nuns. You go to choir, and you sing and you come home and that's it. So I never said anything. But the next week I went to choir and they started singing straight away and I thought, 'Ohh, that must be a once-off'. And halfway through, here they are all talking again … So anyway, I started to listen to

what they were saying and I realised that all of these wo— ... they were mostly ... yeah they were all women at that stage had had a problem and a serious crisis in their lives, and Father had helped each one of them through that crisis. And this was his way of building a support group. He brought them together in the choir ... and if they talked, well that was fine. And if we sang, that was fine ... And so I realised that, the choir wasn't the thing. If we sang, that was lovely. And if we sang in tune, that was a miracle. But he wasn't worried about that either [laugh]. It was ... he had this support group to help these people through their thing. So he was way ahead of his time.

Pargament (2002) maintains that the degree to which one chooses to embrace his or her faith, significantly influences the benefits that may be derived from any religious commitment. In effect, those who appropriate the more positive tenets of their faith, deeply integrating such aspects into their daily life, obtain the greatest benefit (Pargament & Brant, 1998; Pargament, Tarakeshaw, Ellison & Wulff, 2001). Brown (1994) also posits that religious involvement does appear to have the capacity to function effectively for those individuals who are able to accept it.

This is supported by the fact that 15 of the 20 women interviewed reported having a strong foundation in the Christian faith. Many were raised in homes where religion was practised, and the Christian faith formed the basis for the family lifestyle (Mary, Deborah, Susanna, Ruth, Lydia). Wilson (1998) maintains that biblical teaching and Sunday school attendance will avail very little for children who are unable to witness the application of such teaching on a daily basis or, alternatively, who witness behaviour that is contrary to those concepts being taught. The opposite, however, is also deemed to be true: those children who are raised in loving homes where religious beliefs are not only taught, but also practised, within the security of a warm and caring environment are more likely to experience a positive influence in relation to their faith.

Coping

Ganzevoort (1998) describes coping as a 'process' (p. 260) through which individuals endeavour to make sense of difficult life events and determine the most appropriate means by which to maintain a physical and emotional equilibrium in their lives, while mitigating any loss or potential loss (Pargament, 1994). The process of coping could be presented as being fluid, ever-changing and constantly reevaluated in the light of new information or a change in circumstance. For some, it could be described as a juggling act, the degree of difficulty of which is wholly dependent upon the nature of the life event and the degree of threat, challenge or loss it poses to the individual (Pargament, 1997). Gordon et al. (2002), in a study of chronically ill women, highlight the process of coping as one requiring ongoing adjustment throughout the course of the illness, as often the situation must be reassessed and the physical and emotional wellbeing of the individual readdressed if necessary. The concept of ongoing reassessment and subsequent adjustment could be paralleled to that of women who are residing permanently in an environment of domestic abuse, in which they describe their own lifestyle as one of 'walking on eggshells' (Anna, Hannah, Elizabeth, Leah). In this case, however, the situation is not being reassessed periodically, but rather constantly, as each woman endeavours to remain alert to any changes in the mood or attitude of the perpetrator and thereby make the necessary adjustments to deal with the presenting problem. Elizabeth emphasises the continual uncertainty of her daily life when she says:

> Even the unpredictability, I — I never knew when I was going to do something wrong. And you lived, like, on those eggshells.

When questioned regarding the frequency of the abuse she was experiencing, Leah also stresses the extreme levels of insecurity, and the need for constant vigilance when living in an abusive relationship:

> Well I would say it was all the time. It was just a way of life … it felt like you were walking on eggshells. I suppose I probably … yeah. You just couldn't really be yourself 'cause you were always thinking what the other person was going to do and then fitting in, acting accordingly so that you didn't get yourself upset or hurt and everything was smooth.

Stress and Coping

Life events vary for individuals, and sometimes those events that cause significant stress for one individual may not affect another individual in the same manner (Gore & Colten, 1991; Paton & Smith, 1996; Rutter, 1981). Stress frequently becomes part of the equation when a situation is perceived to reside outside the control of the individual affected. Feelings of uncontrollability may emerge as a result of a perceived lack of resources to deal with the stressor, or perhaps from the unpredictable nature of the stressor (Bickel et al., 1998). Resources may be classified as those positive elements that one is able to bring to a situation. Resources may be personal, such as personality, self-confidence, life experience, levels of education, and religious practices; or environmental, such as financial position, family or community support (Gorsuch & Miller, 1999; Holahan & Moos, 1987; Koenig et al., 2001; Pargament et al., 1992; Pearlin & Schooler, 1978). Stress and the availability of resources have been linked to issues of mental health and wellbeing (Cronkite & Moos, 1984). Norris and Murrell (1984) found that the availability of resources acted in a protective capacity against stress, while lower levels of resources during times of stress contributed to an increase in depression. Bolger, DeLongis, Kessler and Schilling (1989) found that ongoing episodes of daily stress contribute significantly to poorer levels of mental health, and the emotional impact of marital conflict increases as incidents become extended over a number of days.

In relation to domestic abuse, many victims find themselves without the resources, either personal or environmental, to cope with their situations. From a personal viewpoint, the victim is often emotionally exhausted, worn down from the constant pressure, suffering from depression, and lacking the confidence to make clear and concise decisions. From an environmental perspective, the victim may be socially isolated and/or financially deprived, and thereby limited in her capacity to put into operation any plan she may be able to devise (see chapter 3). For example, Elizabeth reports suffering verbal and physical abuse that 'really broke my spirit', being isolated from her family, and having very little access to finance due to information being withheld from her and also the careless manner in which her husband conducted his business. In a meeting with the bank manager, Elizabeth recollects being told:

> 'You need to sell that business or you will lose your house, and we don't want your house.' And I just sat there in shock. 'He won't listen to a thing we say. We've tried and tried to talk to him and the end result is we're just going to get your house.'

Miriam also lacked resources. She was afraid to seek assistance from her parents as her perpetrator husband had threatened to harm them if she followed this course of action. Miriam openly states, 'I didn't know what he was capable of'. Although Miriam was employed as a nurse, her financial resources were severely limited. Miriam explains how she was forced to use the finance that was available to her, in an effort to survive, when her husband decided to substantially reduce his contribution to the household:

> I used all my wages, you know, to buy a freezer the food and that sort of stuff. And I could only sneak away, you know, 10 or 20 bucks. And it took a while to mount up. My husband sort of spent pretty freely with his hobbies ... but he sort of cut things right back. At one stage he went through a thing of must cut down on the hot water bill. So we were only allowed to turn the hot water on for 30 seconds and soap ourselves and then we had to turn it off until we'd washed ourselves and then we could turn it back on to rinse off. And, I mean it was just so over the top.

In this situation, the perpetrator was not specifically taking the money, but rather monopolising the finance by withholding assistance and forcing Miriam to use her income to meet the needs of the family. For victims of domestic abuse, coping in the absence of basic resources and support systems becomes extremely challenging.

In contrast, Susanna, who also faced major financial issues within her marriage, including bankruptcy and a fraud conviction against her husband, was able to receive both financial and emotional support from her family. This level of support was, in some way, able to sustain Susanna throughout her ordeal and assist her in her decision to divorce her abusive husband.

Sarah, too, although isolated from her family and in possession of only limited finance, was able to obtain enough encouragement and support from her minister to enable her to break away from her situation and return to a safe haven of family and friends located on the mainland. Thus, the availability of resources, either personal or environmental, can play a major role in the options available to victims of domestic abuse, and are therefore of significant importance in relation to the degree of stress experienced and the coping responses of the individual.

Methods of Coping

Coping strategies can involve a problem-focused approach aimed at solving the specific problem, with the result that the problem simply goes away or has its impact lessened. Alternatively, an emotion-focused approach to coping is aimed at managing the emotions associated with the problem. Most coping methods, however, involve a blend of both the problem- and emotion-focused approaches (Carver & Scheier, 1994; Carver, Scheier & Weintraub, 1989; Cole & Pargament, 1999). The following section will consider the process of appraisal and reappraisal, the implementation of problem-focused and/or emotion-focused methods of coping, and the benefits of taking a blended approach to coping.

Appraisal and Reappraisal

Bjorck (1997) presents a cyclic model in which appraisal and reappraisal continues throughout the coping process. Initially, when confronted with a difficulty, the individual assesses the positive and negative potential of the presenting event or situation. Such assessment will include an appraisal of possible threat, loss or damage, and also any potential benefit that may result. The manner in which an individual appraises an event is not only influenced by the event itself, but is also directed strongly by personal characteristics that include the beliefs and values held by the individual (Ganzevoort, 1998). If a situation is viewed as a source of stress, the person then assesses the availability and effectiveness of her own coping resources. For the individual affected, resource appraisal 'determines the gravity of the crisis' (Ganzevoort, p. 270). Stress can result if individual resources are not perceived as being sufficient or appropriate to deal with the presenting difficulty. Upon following a selected course of action, such as a problem-focused response, the individual is then able to reassess the situation in the light of the action taken and, if the problem persists, plan a new course of action.

The cyclic model of appraisal and reappraisal can be applied to domestic abuse. Many of the women (Esther, Joanna, Naomi, Eve) reported either blaming themselves or being blamed by the perpetrator for the abuse occurring within the relationship. As a result, they chose to modify their own behaviour in an effort to maintain some level of peace and harmony in the home. Such behaviour modification could be classified as a form of problem-focused coping, which is then reappraised and perceived to be ineffective, thus causing each one to move onto a different approach. A new approach could include a complete change of strategy or perhaps the modification of a different behaviour. Mary reflects the thoughts of a number of the women when she explains how she questioned her own behaviour: 'I wondered what I did wrong. I wondered what I hadn't given him that he was looking for'.

In relation to behaviour modification and ongoing reappraisal in an effort to solve the problems associated with domestic abuse, Hannah tells how she constantly felt the need to either change her behaviour or change something relating to who she was as a person:

> When it was happening I thought I had to change. I thought, I always thought I had to do something different. I had to learn how to ... If I could do this, if I was prettier ... If I was this. If I was smarter. If I was — you know, whatever. Then you would be ... wouldn't be doing this to me. He would be happy with me. I just thought it was just 'cause I wasn't what I should have been. I wasn't good enough.

Problem-Focused Coping

The concept of problem-focused coping is encapsulated in the very name given to the process. This form of coping focuses specifically on the problem and determining the most effective means by which to deal with it (Bickel et al., 1998; Carver & Scheier, 1994; Cole & Pargament, 1999). Carver et al. (1989) maintain that individuals faced with a difficulty will often adopt a problem-focused approach to coping if they believe there is something that can be achieved. Clements and Sawhney (2000) found a decrease in hopelessness when battered women in their study were able to adopt a problem-focused approach to coping. Frequently, motivation is increased if one is confident in achieving a positive outcome as a result of increased effort (Carver & Scheier).

Closely connected with problem-focused coping is the concept of planning or strategising. At this stage, the individual considers any viable options that might serve to alleviate the difficulties associated with the presenting problem, and develops an appropriate strategy which may later be executed as part of the problem-focused coping process (Carver et al., 1989).

While Eunice does not describe her actions as being distinctly connected with a consciously organised plan for survival, she clearly states that she was constantly reviewing her situation in the light of a cost–benefit analysis and making decisions accordingly. Eunice explains her position:

> I suppose the point I'm making is, I never set up a plan, but I was just doing things. I was becoming more and more independent ... gradually. I visualise a set of scales. And there was a time in my married life when to stay with my husband — that was better than to leave my husband. Because he was earning a good wage and we were being well provided for, even though I was having to suffer some ... abuses. It got to the point when the total balance changed. There was just no point in remaining. I sort of thought — I'm out of here. There's nothing that he was putting in that was a positive experience.

As part of the journey to achieve gradual independence, Eunice methodically addressed each problem as it occurred. Eunice found full-time work, saved enough money to purchase a small vehicle, gained a university degree, wisely orchestrated the purchase and subsequent repair of the marital home, and endeavoured to create a more positive life for herself and her girls. In effect, Eunice employed a problem-focused approach to coping, utilising whatever strategies were available to her in an effort to achieve a reasonable and functional solution.

Emotion-Focused Coping

Emotion-focused coping aims at dealing with the emotions associated with a particular crisis (Bickel et al., 1998). If an individual believes she is able to deal effectively with a crisis at a practical level by adopting a problem-focused approach, then a strong emotional response is less likely. However, if the situation is perceived to be either beyond the control or outside the resources of an individual, it is more likely that she will resort to emotion-focused coping in an effort to adjust to the prevailing set of circumstances (Carver et al., 1989). Not all situations lie within the scope of control of an individual (Cole & Pargament, 1999; Connors et al., 1999). For example, if one perceives that a situation cannot be changed but must be endured, as in the case of chronic or terminal illness, adjustment is necessary, and the person may make a shift from problem-focused coping to emotion-focused coping (Gordon et al., 2002). This principle could also be applied to Christian women who are victims of domestic abuse, and are told emphatically that 'God hates divorce' (Malachi 2:16), or that divorce is spiritually and morally wrong (see chapter 6). As a result of feeling trapped in an untenable situation, the woman may turn to an emotion-focused method of coping as a means of enduring a situation that appears to be outside her own powers of influence.

Benefits of a Blended Approach

In some cases, a particular choice of action could be defined as either a problem-focused or emotion-focused response, depending on the underlying reason for the action. Carver et al. (1989) cite the example of an individual seeking social interaction in relation to a given situation. If such interaction is the result of searching for a solution to the problem, then the action may be considered problem-focused. However, if the interaction is borne of a need for emotional support, then it may be considered emotion-focused. More appropriate to the focus of this book is the example of the use of prayer as a coping strategy. If prayer is targeted at locating a specific solution to a specific problem, it could be classified as a problem-focused approach to coping; in contrast, praying for the purpose of gaining strength and peace, to both accept and endure the situation, may be classified as an emotion-focused approach to coping.

While problem-focused and emotion-focused coping have different aims and may employ a variety of different strategies, each can be utilised as a compliment to the other. Carver and Scheier (1994) explain that by minimising the emotional distress associated with an event, a problem-focused approach to coping may operate more freely. Equally, by removing some of the more threatening aspects of the problem, negative emotions may be diminished. Thus, a blend of both problem- and emotion-focused coping, where possible, may prove to be a more appropriate coping response.

Religion and Coping

While there is no one specific coping strategy that can be considered the most appropriate (Pargament, 1994; Pearlin & Schooler, 1978; Rutter, 1981), and individuals usually need to adopt those strategies that are most useful and meaningful to their personal worldview, value system, lifestyle and environment; religion does serve as a means by which individuals can elect to cope with life's difficulties (Ganzevoort, 1998; Koenig et al., 2001; Pargament, 1997; Pargament & Brant, 1998; Wong-McDonald & Gorsuch, 2000).

Religion can play a major role in the coping process. Depending on the particular beliefs held by an individual, and the degree to which those beliefs and practices are integrated into the life of the person, religion has the capacity to influence both the initial appraisal of an event and the subsequent coping responses (Ganzevoort, 1998; Gordon et al., 2002). Religion can also provide a selection of personal and environmental resources. Krause, Ellison, Shaw, Marcum, and Boardman (2001) found that spiritual support from congregational members in times of difficulty, resulted in an increase in the utilisation of 'positive religious coping responses' (p. 637). It is further suggested that congregational members possess the means by which a selection of religion-based, problem-focused and emotion-focused coping strategies can be developed and implemented. Thus, congregational members can form an empowering support network. Pargament (1997) suggests that 'next to the family, no other institution offers the possibility of such sustained contact throughout the lifespan' (p. 211).

Religion can also provide an increased sense of control for those in crisis (Ganzevoort, 1998; Pargament, 1997; Pargament & Brant, 1998; Pargament et al., 2000). Although a wide range of beliefs can be found within the Christian faith (Gorsuch & Miller, 1999), a God-centred worldview, which places all things within the ultimate control of an omnipotent creator and provides access to that One through prayer, gives the troubled individual the possible means by which to influence the outcome of a situation (Koenig et al., 2001). A belief in the power of such influence can contribute directly to the amelioration of stressful emotional responses, not only by offering a sense of control but also by operating in opposition to overwhelming feelings of hopelessness (Koenig et al.) and providing an increased sense of strength, security and inner peace (Gordon et al., 2002; Van Uden & Pieper, 1994). Within the context of this worldview, religious coping responses can prove particularly advantageous when individuals are confronted with serious situations, such as illness or death, over which there is no apparent means of control (Osborne & Vandenberg, 2003). For example, Tix and Frazier (1998) found that religious coping responses contributed to improved levels of psychological adjustment for patients undergoing transplant surgery, and also to the minimisation of emotional distress experienced by family members.

Individuals who are actively involved in their faith are more likely to engage in religious coping responses. Even then, the degree to which religious coping responses are employed is frequently related to the degree of difficulty presented by the problem. Thus, the more serious the problem, the greater the degree to which religious coping responses are employed. In some cases, individuals are able to use their religious faith to reframe a negative event, thereby viewing it in a more positive light and embracing it as an opportunity to establish a deeper union with God (Pargament, 1997, 2002; Pargament & Brant, 1998; Pargament et al., 2001).

Religious Coping Styles

Within the framework of religious coping, three predominant styles have emerged: self-directing, deferring and collaborative. While each style reflects a belief in God, the manner in which each style is utilised may differ according to the personal belief system of the individual, the nature of the difficulty and the degree of challenge it presents (Maynard, Gorsuch & Bjorck, 2001). For example, in situations where the individual is afforded higher levels of control, a self-directing style of coping may prove an appropriate choice, whereas in circumstances where the ability of the individual to control the outcome is limited, deferring to God can present an acceptable alternative (Pargament & Brant, 1998; Pargament et al., 1992). The following section will provide a brief outline of the three coping styles.

Self-Directing

The individual who employs a self-directed style of coping takes personal responsibility for problem-solving, and deals with life issues by utilising those resources available to her. Such a person actively engages in the problem-solving process and, although a religious commitment may be demonstrated, in this style of coping God is not considered an active participant in the task of problem-solving. God is understood as being present, but is viewed as allowing an individual the opportunity and the right to govern her own life (Bickel et al., 1998; Maynard et al., 2001; Pargament & Brant, 1998; Pargament et al., 1992).

Deferring

In marked contrast to the self-directing style of coping is the choice to totally defer to God in relation to an existing problem. In this style of coping, the person takes no responsibility for solving the problem but waits for God to provide an appropriate answer in His own time (Bickel et al., 1998; Maynard et al., 2001; Pargament & Brant, 1998). Thus, the person adopts a passive role, assuming that God is in control and will make any necessary decisions. As an individual embraces a deferring style of coping, God becomes 'the source of solutions' (Pargament et al., 1998, p. 92). In the extreme situation of suffering abuse, even in the midst of receiving treatment for cancer, Susanna chose to defer to God in relation to the ultimate outcome, expressing confidence in Him to choose the best alternative for her life.

Collaborative

The collaborative style of coping, in which both God and the individual assume an active role in the problem-solving process, presents a balanced alternative between the self-directing and deferring styles of coping. In a sense, the individual who adopts this form of coping views herself as being in partnership with God, actively considering alternatives and acting together upon the chosen solution (Pargament, 1997). Pargament also found the collaborative style of coping to be indicative 'of a more relational form of religion' (p. 182) and an increased sense of control over life events. This form of relationship with God, combined with a collaborative or partnership approach to coping, appears to foster lower levels of anxiety in individuals compared with those individuals who do not engage in an interactive relationship with God and instead elect to embrace a self-directing style of coping (Wong-McDonald & Gorsuch, 2000).

Each coping style reflects an element of trust in God and His providential care. The self-directing style of coping trusts that God has already provided the skills and resources though which the problem might be solved. The deferring style reflects a trust in God as the One who not only knows best but also will provide the most suitable response in all situations. Finally, the collaborative style of coping demonstrates a trust that God will provide the insight, knowledge, understanding and necessary opportunities to deal with the problem as the individual undertakes an equally active role in the process (Pargament, 1997).

Each of the women interviewed favoured a collaborative style of coping. Even when the behaviour of the perpetrator was beyond their control in a physical sense, each one chose to consult God on the issue, thereby making Him an active member of the partnership. Additionally, each of the women endeavoured to undertake whatever action she felt possible, in an effort to alleviate both the physical and emotional stresses brought about by domestic abuse. Sarah, for her own safety and on the advice of her minister, took the practical steps of arranging a protection order and eventually moving to another state. She also attended counselling. Throughout her ordeal, however, Sarah also acknowledges ongoing communication with God, and a high level of awareness regarding His care and provision for her.

Eve also chose an approach that linked her responsibilities for the marriage and her own wellbeing with her relationship to God. In an effort to actively fulfil her marital obligations and thereby minimise the level of abuse, Eve endeavoured to follow the guidelines of the church. When this failed, she then chose to attend counselling with an organisation outside the local church, an experience which she describes as '*very*, very helpful'. Eve speaks of a close relationship with God, emphasising the manner in which she sought His insight and guidance before making a final decision to end the marriage. Eve reflects upon her communication with God at this time:

> I guess once I realised what was happening, I just — I felt that God was saying … God said, 'I'm not part of this marriage any more. I hate what's happening to you, and I don't condone it. I don't like what is happening to you, and I want you to get out'. I felt that God was … He didn't like what was going on. And yeah, I really felt that. And so I felt that — yeah, He didn't like the way I was being treated. And He didn't expect me to stay there and be nice to someone who was doing that.

Religion and Coping: Potential Problems

A number of difficulties can arise as a result of religious involvement. These include a lack of flexibility, a legalistic approach to the application of rules and regulations, and the possible neglect of family in favour of religious practices (Koenig et al., 2001; Pargament, 1997). A negative or distant and uncaring image of God can also inhibit the ability of the individual to relate to God in a positive manner, and thereby inhibit her ability to cope with a stressful life event. Koenig et al. also question the effectiveness of religious practices, such as ceasing necessary medication or refusing blood transfusions, as such actions have the capacity to minimise the level of practical healthcare available to an individual.

Hannah, who attended a very legalistic church that placed a strong emphasis on rules and regulations, explains how she found it easier to deal with life events once she experienced a shift in her thinking in relation to her image of God:

> I think differently about God now. God is more loving and the rules don't matter so much. I always thought God was laws and, you know, you had to behave a certain way and please Him. And now I think — you know, God is graceful and loving and kind and good things ... I still read the Bible and pray, but it's different now. It's like I came to the place where I thought, 'No. Hang on. The God that I've been thinking and serving, the way I thought He is, is cruel and nasty and is too difficult to damn well please'. And the God that I think now of, and pray to now is entirely the opposite.

Upon being asked when this cognitive shift occurred, Hannah replies:

> After I left church ... My idea of God was that I had to please Him and I had to do everything right while I was at church. When I left church, my idea of God became — I can make mistakes. I can stuff up and God will still love me. But I never knew that at church.

Ganzevoort (1998) highlights specific situations, such as divorce or AIDS, in which religious affiliation may not only offer no assistance, but may substantially hinder the progress and wellbeing of the individual as a result of rejection, isolation and condemnation. A number of women (Elizabeth, Anna, Eve, Joanna) reported experiencing a considerable level of condemnation regarding either the state of their marriage or their desire to separate and/or divorce (see chapters 6 and 7). If prescribed religious coping responses do not appear to work effectively, an individual may begin to question her faith, become angry towards God or turn aside from her religion (Ganzevoort). Thus, Pargament (1997) suggests that if any religion is unable to address the difficult areas of life, such as pain and suffering in its many forms, that religion will ultimately prove inadequate for the person in crisis.

The Role of Hope

Like religion, hope contributes significantly to the physical and emotional wellbeing of the individual, and has been linked to increased levels of optimism (Koenig et al., 2001). Vandecreek, Nye, and Herth (1994) report a positive connection between church attendance and increased levels of hopefulness. Hope can be directed towards life goals, events and opportunities; or to the eternal aspects of religion that present a larger context for life and focus on a positive view of life after death (Carson et al., 1988). A hope for the future or for the ultimate eternal reward can provide an anchor for an individual in crisis, allowing her to see beyond the current situation (Yahne & Miller, 1999). Such hope has the capacity to transcend the most devastating of circumstances (Post, 1998). Koenig et al. explain that 'even the threat of death itself cannot easily destroy the confidence of a person who believes in a new and better life in the hereafter' (p. 215).

Susanna illustrates clearly the role of hope in her life, and also draws attention to the peace that is borne of hope, stretches beyond circumstance and 'passeth all understanding' (Philippians 4:7; Fee, 1995; Kent, 1978). As a practising Christian, Susanna exhibits a strong and positive belief in life after death as she tells of her combined experience with both cancer and domestic abuse:

> The cancer started to develop in May. Then I was raced to hospital because they thought I would die. That was December, because I was haemorrhaging so much. And then I was having treatment. And then ... I was having the abuse again because of the treatment and things. I coped with it because I had a religious belief and conviction, and I knew that this life wasn't all that there was. So there were better things. And also with my cancer, the only thing that I could hold on to was that my Heavenly Father would look after me and do what was best ... But I did know that there was an ultimate plan and that things would work out either way. But I was quite prepared to die at that stage, because my life was so difficult and so hard. But also, through everything, after that cancer, I realised there was ... that the things — material things are not important. That the way you feel, your peace inside is what is the most important part of your life. [Interviewer: 'It would appear there was no fear of death'.] No. No. I wasn't scared of that at all. And even today, I know that there are worse things in life than death.

Snyder (2002) likens hope to a 'rainbow of the mind' (p. 269), depicting it as a positive image or experience having the capacity to encourage a person to focus on possibilities and opportunities that lie ahead. Hope, in the context presented by Snyder, can be linked to coping in that it initially enables an individual to set specific goals, and then assists her in determining the most effective route by which to achieve those goals. Those individuals who are high in hope are often able to create contingency plans to reach set goals should the initial route prove ineffective or unavailable. Snyder, Sigmon and Feldman (2002) refer to this process as 'pathways thinking' (p 235). Working in conjunction with pathways thinking is the concept of 'agency thinking' (p. 235), which applies to the individual capacity of the person to follow the prescribed pathways, renegotiate the route if necessary, and ultimately achieve the desired goal. Snyder maintains that successful goal achievement, despite apparent blockages or obstacles encountered throughout the journey, contributes significantly to one's confidence in achieving future goals.

A religious lifestyle is expected to contribute favourably to levels of hope by providing the individual with a positive view of herself (Blaine & Trivedi, 1998; Koenig et al., 2001), together with the encouragement that personal and religious goals can be achieved by selecting the appropriate pathway and maintaining a steady course (Snyder et al., 2002). In stark contrast, however, is the glaring reality that victimisation in any form 'can rob people of their hope' (Snyder, 2002, p. 264). Even individuals high in hope can lose the desire to continue an interactive and goal-oriented lifestyle in the face of severe adversity. For example, 16 of the women (including Ruth, Esther and Elizabeth) noted some negative change in their personality, outlook and ability to cope as a result of their experiences of domestic abuse (see chapter 3); and a number of them described their situations as 'hopeless' (e.g., Eve) as they struggled to manage depleted personal and environmental resources in the midst of emotional turmoil. In this situation, both positive and negative aspects of religious involvement are clearly depicted. Already facing the trauma of being victimised by their husbands who, as professing Christians, were perpetrators of domestic abuse, some of the women (Anna, Elizabeth), found themselves revictimised as a result of their association with the church (see chapter 3). However, those who did receive support and encouragement from their ministers and churches (Mary, Susanna,

Sarah, Miriam, Lydia) were more able to move forward through the difficulties of domestic abuse, separation and subsequent divorce than were their counterparts (Anna, Elizabeth, Eve, Joanna) who experienced substantial levels of opposition, and even condemnation, from their ministers or churches. Some of the women (Hannah, Eve, Leah) were so disillusioned that they lost confidence in the church and its ability to meet their needs. Others (Ruth, Anna) elected a position of compromise by changing their denominational affiliation and endeavouring to rebuild their faith on what they perceived to be a more stable platform. According to Pargament (1997), this response to the inability of the church to offer relevant and adequate means of coping in times of crisis is in no way surprising.

For those who have suffered and are feeling a sense of disillusionment, Yahne and Miller (1999) maintain that the role of the therapist is one of evoking hope by assisting the individual to once again draw upon the wealth of her own resources. The need for professionals to provide positive levels of input and guidance is significant, as 15 of the 20 women interviewed sought the assistance of a counsellor, psychologist or psychiatrist at some time during the course of their experience.

Coping Strategies Reported

The coping strategies employed by the women can be separated into two basic categories: religious and nonreligious. In most cases the women involved did not limit themselves solely to either category, but rather developed a blended strategy by combining the options most suited to their individual needs and situations. The following section will describe both the religious and the nonreligious coping strategies employed by the women interviewed. Religious coping strategies include maintaining a relationship with God, praying, seeking both guidance and comfort from Scripture, and scriptural song. Many of these choices were based on the experiences of a foundational and childhood faith. Nonreligious coping strategies include a primary focus on the children of the marriage, involving oneself in activities, reading for the purpose of information and guidance, and planning a course of action (see Figure 8.1).

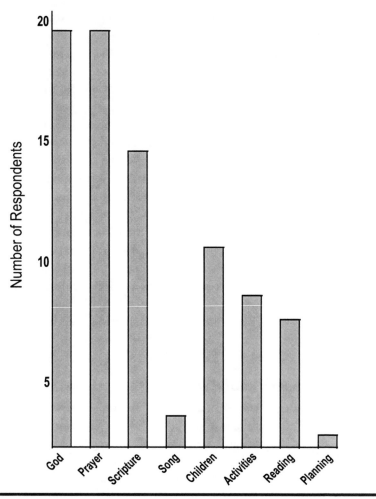

Figure 8.1
Coping strategies.
Note: (*N* = 20).

Religious Coping Strategies

As practising Christians, the women interviewed utilised their faith and employed a number of religion-based strategies in an attempt to cope with the trauma of living in a domestic abuse situation on a daily basis. For women in this situation, religious faith is considered by Nason-Clark (1997) to be a 'vital component of an authentic coping process' (p. 17). The three primary strategies — maintaining a relationship with God, prayer, and reliance upon Scripture — could be classified as forms of both problem-focused and emotion-focused coping, as the strategies can contain an element of either (Carver et al., 1989). Each strategy is utilised in both forms: to either search for an answer to the existing problem, or to endeavour to manage the emotional response generated by the same problem. The fourth response — the use of song as a coping strategy — could be classified as an emotion-focused approach, in that it enables the individual to temporarily step aside from the problem and perhaps find a sense of calm amid the turmoil. It could also be argued, however, that the use of song is aimed at deepening the level of intimacy and communication in the individual's relationship with God in an effort to find a practical solution to the problem, and as such could be classified as a problem-focused approach to coping. Regardless of the manner in which the strategies may be classified, it remains apparent that each of the women employed a blended strategy while relying heavily upon her Christian faith.

Maintaining a Relationship With God

The Christian faith centres around a personal relationship with God, based on the atoning work of Jesus on the cross, in relation to God's ultimate purpose for man (John 3:26; 14:6; Gaines, 1998; Hiebert, 1978; Kostenberger, 2002; Mayfield, 1965; Tenney, 1981a). It is a faith that fosters the image of a loving and caring God whose desire it is to nurture and sustain His people (Psalms 23, 91; Briggs & Briggs, 1906; Kirkpatrick, 1933; Leslie, 1949; Schaefer, 2001). For those who choose to embrace this image of God, it can serve as a buffer to stress and stressful events as individuals continue to feel loved and cared for regardless of the circumstances (Maton, 1989). The sense of security that originates from a positive attachment to God can contribute significantly to the manner in which an individual is inclined to appraise, and eventually respond to, a stressful event (Gall et al., 2005; Koenig et al., 2001; Pargament et al., 2001).

A relationship with God is presented as one of the most effective and necessary religious coping strategies employed by each of the women interviewed. Every one of them stressed the need to maintain a strong personal relationship with God. Throughout the interviews, the women repeatedly referred to their relationship with God as one of friendship (Naomi, Leah), or that of a Father (Mary, Susanna, Eunice, Eve), and fully expected the assistance, guidance and protection deemed to be associated with those roles. They spoke openly and positively of gaining strength, encouragement, peace and comfort as a result of a personal relationship with God (Elizabeth, Rachel, Deborah, Naomi).

Speaking confidently of the benefits of her Christian faith, Mary explains an aspect of her relationship with God, in which He has proven Himself faithful:

> I truly believe that God will look after me. I really, like, deep down, that's a fundamental part of me. It's not just something I've learned. It's a part of me. Because I've found time and time again God has been there for me.

These thoughts are echoed by Naomi as she expresses her expectation for God to look after her, and talks of the manner in which her faith in God assisted her to maintain a reasonable level of stability as she prepared to leave her husband:

> Well, my faith was — yes, I expected God to look after me. And my faith was getting stronger all the time, because I could see little ways that He was working in my life ... Probably not long before I left when I was just in abstract fear [laugh]. Yes. I think that just helped me to get through. Ah ... I think so I didn't go mad [laugh]. It just helped me keep my sanity really. And to know that God wasn't going to let anything really, really, bad happen to me ... or He'd help me through.

Ruth speaks of the reality of God for herself and her children, even amid the trauma of ongoing abuse:

> God has never faulted me. I believe that after I had been violently attacked, and I wasn't allowed to go to church anymore with the children ... we established our own family worship, the children and I. And we became very strong. And God became very real to us. And we practised our faith every day, the kids and I ... and much as we still tried to love Daddy, it became a bond [with God] that's

never been broken, I don't think. I really don't. And that is all I've ever wanted for them. For them to have a faith that could be so, so strong it could overcome any obstacle in life — any struggle. Even if they felt like Job they could they could find God.

While the experience of each of the women is different, they all highlight the benefit of a personal relationship with God as being particularly relevant in times of crisis. The value of such a relationship is expressed clearly by Ruth when she focuses on her desire for her children to both embrace and retain a strong and functional faith in God.

Prayer

Directly related to a relationship with God is the concept of prayer, through which that relationship is fostered (Gall et al., 2005; Lewis, 1975). A belief in the power of prayer carries with it the belief that an individual can perhaps exert some influence over her situation by appealing to an all-powerful God. Such prayer may result either in change or in the assurance that God will provide the individual with the strength required to accept or deal with the presenting problem (Koenig et al., 2001). Gordon et al. (2002) found a positive link between religious beliefs and a commitment to prayer, and the ability of chronically ill women to adapt to their illness. The helpfulness of prayer has also been acknowledged in relation to its perceived benefits for patients dealing with the anxiety attached to cardiac surgery (Saudia, Kinney, Brown & Young-Ward, 1991). Maltby, Lewis and Day (1999) recognise a connection between personal prayer and psychological wellbeing, while McCullough and Larson (1999) list a number of categories of prayer — including quiet meditation; petitioning God for specific needs; and conversational, ritual and intercessory prayer — all of which may be employed throughout the coping process.

The Lord's Prayer (Matthew 6:9–13) provides a model for Christians to follow. Included in this model is the request for the provision for needs, and also for deliverance (Carson, 1984; Earle, 1964). This instruction to make requests of God through prayer is reinforced in the teachings of Paul (Philippians 4:6) when he advises those of the Christian faith to ask for whatever is required. The effectiveness of prayer can be seen throughout the Scriptures, but is particularly apparent in the lives of leading personalities such as Jesus, Moses, Elijah and David (Grounds, 1981).

In light of the acknowledged benefits and effectiveness of prayer, both in Scripture and secular literature, it is not surprising to discover that each one of the women highlighted prayer as a significant means of coping with the problems associated with domestic abuse. However, they did vary in the style of prayer employed. The style of prayer moved from conversational communication with God, to personal petition, and also included a ritual style of prescribed prayer designed to meet a specific need.

Eunice, who grew up imagining God as a kind old man and a father figure, chose to adopt a conversational style of prayer, as opposed to a set structure. Eunice describes the style and aims of her prayer:

> I just mostly talked to God. You know, through prayer. Not just saying Hail Marys and Our Fathers, but — you know — communication would have been more the thing. And talking over the ... looking for answers, or — I think I used to pray for either support to be able to keep going, you know, and get through it or some, you know, resolution ... and sort to sort itself out to give me ... I wanted to be able to get through it. Either solve it or sort it out — that sort of thing.

Mary chose to adopt a different approach to prayer from that of Eunice, and explains how she began creating her own book of prayers by collecting copies of poems and prayers she felt were encouraging and personally meaningful to her, as each prayer could be applied to her own situation in some way:

> I collect it all. That's why I think my prayer book ... it's my personal prayer book. I've written the prayers as I've found them. And I find that God gives you prayers as you need them. Because one of the things I collected during 1980 was this ... and it says, 'Do not worry about what may happen tomorrow. The same loving Father who cares for you today, will care for you tomorrow and every day. Either He will shield you from suffering, or He will give you unfailing strength to bear it. Be at peace then and put aside all anxious thoughts and imaginings'.

Mary was able to read or say this prayer, in addition to numerous others that she had collected over the years, whenever she felt the need for comfort, peace or the assurance that God would meet her physical and/or emotional needs.

Leah, like many of the women, felt quite alone in the turmoil of her experiences. She describes how, at difficult times, she would turn to God in prayer and find comfort:

> When I felt really alone and there was no one to talk to, I felt that God was there — I'd just talk to God. And I really felt like a presence, like a comforting presence. I'd just say, 'God, I don't know what to do, and I feel ... I just don't know what to do'. But I just felt that there was just this presence ... comforting presence there.

Drawing Encouragement from Scripture

If one believes in a personal God who is omniscient, omnipotent and omnipresent, one might expect to be able to trust the integrity of His word, offered within the framework of Scripture. The Scriptures are replete with examples of the honesty and truthfulness of God (Buswell, 1981; Holmes, 1975), stating specifically that 'God is not a man that he should lie' (Numbers 23:19), thus describing the 'immutability of the Lord and the integrity of his word' (Allen, 1990, p. 901). Scripture further presents the character of God as unchanging (Malachi 3:6), declaring that in Him there is 'no variableness, neither shadow of turning' (James 1:17) (Burdick, 1981; Harper, 1967b; Moo, 2002a). Jesus too, as one with God, is depicted as being 'the same yesterday, to day and for ever' (Hebrews 13:8) (Davies, 1967; Morris, 1981; Neil, 1959; Taylor, 1967). For the individual who chooses to embrace these concepts, a belief in the accuracy and relevance of Scriptures that promise protection (Psalms 91:14–16), health and healing (Psalms 103:2–5; Proverbs 3:8) and peace (Isaiah 26:3) can prove an empowering coping strategy (Koenig et al., 2001).

Fifteen of the women reported finding the Scriptures a valuable coping resource, on which they could draw in times of crisis. Many had developed a lifestyle that incorporated both prayer and the reading, recitation and/or memorisation of Scripture. Speaking of the book of

Psalms and the book of Proverbs, Leah provides a simple message regarding the relevance of the Scriptures in her life, when she states:

> Oh they made … just seemed to make sense out of life … used to make me feel inspired and encouraged.

Deborah, who set aside regular times for personal devotion, explains how she was able to draw strength from the Scriptures:

> I can do this. I can move on. I mean, in the Scriptures I had some wonderful examples of people that had had much worse experiences than I have, and have survived. And in doing that, I never felt the Lord left me alone. I never felt isolated. I never felt forgotten. So that was where my strength came.

Lois speaks of the very practical manner in which she was able to relate to God through Scripture, as she sought answers to the difficulties she was facing. Lois expresses the value of Scripture in her life, particularly throughout the recovery stage of her ordeal:

> The word of God just really was my lifeline. Because it was the only thing that I could trust in that was truth and was unchangeable. And you know, I had this relationship with God where He does speak to me through the Scriptures. And I can — I can sort of, you know, have this ongoing dialogue with Him in prayer and ask Him for answers and I can get some answers through the word of God.

During times of fear and stress, Naomi also speaks of how she turned to the Scriptures in search of peace:

> I was reading the Bible. There were a few texts that some friends had sent through to me, that I'd kept close to me. And they were sort of promises that helped me through. It just gave me some hope and helped me through. I couldn't see — it was just like a dark tunnel. I couldn't see a solution. And it was these Scriptures that sort of helped me to think, 'Well, there must be a solution'. But at the time it was just so, you know, I was too afraid to stay, and I was too afraid to leave. Yeah. So … yeah these Scriptures [Philippians 4:6–7; Jeremiah 29:11–13], I think, just gave me that … hope that yes there was [a solution]. And … and that God was there too.

In providing information regarding the assistance offered by the Scriptures, a number of the women were able to either name a specific verse or passage of Scripture that was helpful to them — even so far as providing the actual location of the Scripture within the Bible— or alternatively to quote the specific Scripture they had committed to memory. For example, referring to Philippians 4:6–7, Naomi says:

> There were times when I was just so frightened and stressed
> that … and I'd repeat that verse over and over to myself,
> and I'd start to feel some peace.

Due to the significance of particular passages of Scripture for the women interviewed, and also their relevance to the coping response, a number of Scriptures listed by the women have been included in this section in addition to subsequent explanations. Some of the Scriptures presented may initially appear slightly unusual in relation to domestic abuse, such as the experiences of the nation of Israel during exile as expounded in the book of Jeremiah. However, the central issue is the fact that the women involved looked to God for justice and freedom, and care and provision, in a similar manner to the people of Israel during their search for deliverance from suffering.

Psalms and Proverbs

The book of Psalms and the book of Proverbs proved to be popular sources of Scriptural support for a number of the women (Ruth, Hannah, Eve, Leah). This is possibly due to the fact that both books deal with the reality of life, and frequently address the struggles of humanity with which the reader is able to identify (Harris, 1981b; Hembold, 1975; Schaefer, 2001; Toy, 1899). From an inspirational perspective, the reader is able to draw hope from the experiences of the psalmist (Payne, 1975b; VanGemeren, 1991), and wisdom from the book of Proverbs (Horton, 1891; Ross, 1991; Whybray, 1972; Wolf, 1967).

Among specific references to Scripture were Psalm 23 (Ruth), which has already been addressed (see chapter 6), and Proverbs 3:5–6 (Ruth, Eve), which encourages the reader to 'Trust in the Lord with all thine heart; and lean not unto thine own understanding. In all thy ways acknowledge him, and he shall direct thy paths'. The element of trust highlights a total commitment to God, regardless of apparent circumstance. Such trust reflects the personal assurance that God will direct the life of the individual, and ultimately bring about His own good purpose (Ross, 1991; Toy, 1899; Wolf, 1967).

Isaiah

Hannah turned particularly to the book of Isaiah for comfort, and assurance of continued strength. Isaiah 40:11 employs the imagery of a gentle and caring shepherd, protecting and nurturing his flock, as the prophet writes, 'He shall feed his flock like a shepherd: he shall gather the lambs with his arm, and carry them in his bosom, and shall gently lead those that are with young'. The focus of this verse is on those who, like the young lambs, are weak, defenceless and perhaps unable to continue without substantial assistance from a loving God who seeks to sustain them (Grogan, 1986; Herbert, 1975; Price, 1966; Wade, 1911). As a victim of domestic abuse, Hannah also desired to be upheld and supported as she, like the Israelites, traversed the seeming desert of her own environment.

Also pertaining to Israel's journey through the desert, Isaiah writes of the impartation of supernatural strength to endure the rigours of the journey. Isaiah tells the weary travellers, 'They that wait upon the Lord shall renew their strength; they shall mount up with wings as eagles; they shall run, and not be weary; and they shall walk, and not faint' (Isaiah 40:31). Numerous authors (Grogan, 1986; Price, 1966; Skinner, 1929; Wade, 1911) support the concept that through their relationship with God, the people of Israel would be able to exchange their weariness for the omnipotent, enduring and unfailing strength of their God. Numerous women (Mary, Hannah, Elizabeth, Rachel, Deborah) also expressed their need for ongoing strength to endure the day-to-day struggles associated with domestic abuse.

In her search for peace, Naomi also turned to the book of Isaiah (26:3), which promises 'Thou wilt keep him in perfect peace, whose mind is stayed on thee'. Linked also to the concept of trust, and despite the difficulties that may abound, this verse expresses the presence of a deep and abiding peace for those who choose to place their confidence in God, and make Him the primary focus of their attention. As in many cases throughout Scripture, the actual receipt of strength or peace from God is contingent upon the individual choosing to diligently undertake her part which, in this case, is placing her trust and confidence in God (Grogan, 1986; Price, 1966).

Jeremiah

Naomi found hope for her future wellbeing in the book of Jeremiah (29:11), which declares:

> For I know the thoughts that I think toward you, saith the Lord, thoughts of peace, and not of evil, to give you an expected end.

The New International Version of the Bible expresses this particular verse of Scripture with a greater focus on plans and positive future results, rendering it thus:

> For I know the plans I have for you, declares the Lord, plans to prosper you and not to harm you, plans to give you hope and a future.

The second translation provides greater clarity for the reader, and with it comes an increased level of encouragement regarding future security, as God provides His assurance of ultimate blessing (Bennett, 1895; Cunliffe-Jones, 1960; Feinberg, 1986; Gray, 1966; Nicholson, 1975). Once again, the phrase 'walking on eggshells' (Anna, Hannah, Elizabeth, Leah) depicts the high level of insecurity present within a domestic abuse relationship. Thus, the issues of future personal security and the blessing of God are significant for those suffering as a result of domestic abuse.

Habakkuk

At the suggestion of her minister, Sarah was able to find encouragement in the book of Habakkuk. Although a very short book consisting of only three chapters, in it the prophet openly addresses issues concerning violence and injustice. Like many victims of abuse, Habakkuk expresses his confusion at the fact that the God whom he understands to be righteous, just, and in control appears to have made no response to the violence and injustice prevailing at the hand of the wicked (Habakkuk 1:1–4) (Armerding, 1985; Dunning, 1968; Sweeney, 2000). As the book unfolds, God responds to questions presented by Habakkuk, assuring him that He is in control, He will bring judgment, and those who do evil will ultimately reap what they sow. Smith (1898) parallels the tyrannical behaviour of the wicked to actual suicide, thus highlighting the degree to which the actions of the wicked will contribute to their own demise. At the same time, righteous individuals are encouraged to diligently maintain their faith in God, trusting that He is in control, regardless of any appearance to the contrary (Habakkuk 3:17). The book of Habakkuk could certainly prove encouraging for the victim of domestic abuse who desires justice, and yet feels that God at times is somewhat distant, showing no apparent regard for the circumstances that threaten to overwhelm her. For the Christian woman who has faith and trust in the integrity of the Scriptures, the assurance of God-given strength (Habakkuk 3:19), and ultimate justice, has the potential to offer at least some level of comfort.

The Four Gospels

Turning to the New Testament, the gospels contain a positive message of hope, compassion and protection, in addition to peace and restoration, which is able to provide the reader with an increased sense of personal security through her relationship with God (Jackson, 1975; Tenney, 1981b). Further, the gospels indicate the availability of a deeper level of intimacy with God, highlighted by the use of the term *Abba* in relation to the father role of God (Mark 14:36; Jackson). This terminology also appears in the book of Galatians (4:6), again indicating the closeness of the relationship existing between the believer and God (Boice, 1986; Howard, 1965). Sarah was able to draw encouragement from the positive nature of the concepts contained within the four gospels. For the victim of domestic abuse who lacks a functional support network, or is unable to discuss her predicament with anyone outside the immediate family unit, the option of an intimate relationship with a caring and loving God forms an essential component of her ability to cope.

Philippians

Naomi found the peace she so earnestly desired by applying the principles of Philippians 4:6–7, in which believers are advised to be:

> … careful [anxious] for nothing but in every thing by prayer and supplication with thanksgiving let your requests be made known unto God. And the peace of God, which passeth all understanding, shall keep your hearts and minds through Christ Jesus.

This passage of Scripture not only emphasises the need for continued prayer but also expresses the need for an ongoing trust in God to provide and protect through times of crisis (Bruce, 1989; Fee, 1995; Kent, 1978). The image of peace presented in the passage is one of standing guard around the heart and mind of the individual, offering a constant protection against anxiety, just as the Roman garrison relentlessly guarded the city of Philippi (Knight, 1965; Martin, 1959). Mary and Esther also testified to the peace they found through a personal relationship with God, which effectively combines prayer and the use of Scripture.

Romans

Eve chose to focus on the fact that 'all things work together for good to them that love God, to them who are the called according to his purpose' (Romans 8:28). While some maintain that this Scripture can relate to the present age, other commentators claim that the primary focus of this verse is the ultimate glory of God to be attained throughout eternity (Bruce, 1975; Moo, 2002b). Thus, although one may be unable to determine the actual 'good' in a given situation, one can trust that the ultimate purpose of God is being fulfilled. If God forms the central focus for the life of an individual, then that individual is assured that all things will work for her ultimate good, either in this life or the next (Greathouse, 1968). Harrison (1976) suggests that, in and of themselves, all things may not work for the good of the believer, outside the presence of the sovereign intervention of God. From this perspective, the 'good', be it in the present age or in the age to come, is contingent upon the divine action of God. Thus, the individual who chooses to place her faith in God is able to trust that ultimately something positive will emerge even from the most difficult of circumstances. Although they did not specifically consider this particular verse of Scripture, five of the women reported endeavouring to locate something positive in their situation.

Song

Scriptural song, or singing praises to God, is initially borne of a relationship with God; using music and voice, it combines the characteristics of prayer and the Scriptures. Traditionally, music and song formed a part of community life, featuring in temple worship

(2 Chronicles. 5:12–14), celebrations, rejoicing (Exodus 15:20–21), and even military victories (Joshua 6:4–20) (Best & Huttar, 1975; Madvig, 1992; Olson, 1981; Sawyer, 1965). Four of the women reported using song as part of their coping response.

Joanna, a musician and singer, describes herself as a 'worshipper' and explains that she is able to connect with God through music:

> I love to worship. Obviously, being in music, so I just enjoy just being with God. So I just put my CD on, and off I'd go. And I just, you know like … God would give me a word [insight] — give me something. Give me a verse [of Scripture] — give me something [in the form of encouragement].

Elizabeth also enjoyed the experience of singing, blending it effectively with prayer and Scripture. Elizabeth explains that while her husband created untold difficulties in many areas, and succeeded in stopping her from becoming involved in a variety of activities, this is one area in which he could not control her actions. She recounts her experience:

> Eventually, all I had left was, he couldn't stop me praying, and he couldn't stop me worshipping. I'm a worshipper. So I just found my strength in singing and praying, and I'd just get all my things, my Bible and my concordances and all my bits and pieces of paper. See, I write — God gives me songs. And my daughter is actually a composer. But she's a trained one. I'm a Holy Spirit one. But I just got lots of encouragement from getting that sort of thing.

Foundational Faith

Although the women involved did not specifically mention the fact that a foundational faith from childhood contributed significantly to their ability to cope in times of crisis, a religious upbringing did prove to be a common occurrence as their stories unfolded. Fifteen of them indicated the definite presence of a religious lifestyle forming part of their upbringing.

Ruth, having grown up in the Seventh Day Adventist church, not only continued to maintain her faith throughout the abuse she suffered, but also made a conscious endeavour to pass that same faith on to her children. After an extreme episode of physical abuse, and being forbidden by her husband to any longer attend church, Ruth recounts the details of how she was able to positively direct her energies towards the spiritual growth of her children:

> Believe it or not, out of something that seemed horrific that day … I started to bring the children … when he went to work, very early in the morning, the children and I would have daily devotions and prayers. And believe it or not, I think that would have been the foundation of spirituality. Not really attending church or Sunday school, but the belief that God was there with us … and God was working every day of our life. Protecting us, providing for us, regardless of that environment that we lived in.

Likewise, Sarah, grateful for the spirituality in her upbringing and recognising the value of being raised in the Catholic faith, is also choosing to pass that faith on to her small daughter. Even amid the discussion of trauma and conflict, Sarah exudes joy as she shares briefly the early steps of faith depicted in the interactions between her small child and her omnipotent God:

> Julia and I pray at night. It's kind of gorgeous. Because she's not yet two and it's like, 'Hello God! It's Mummy and Julia'. And then she added, 'How are you?' [laugh] And then we just go through and we go, it's just like thank you for this and thank you for that and then at the end it's 'God blesses Julia. God blesses Daddy. God blesses Mummy. Goodnight God' [laugh]. And it's just so beautiful. Oh it's just so lovely.

Mary relies heavily on her faith during the difficult times of her life. She attributes this to various facets of her upbringing, both in her family of origin and throughout her private education at a Catholic school. After explaining how she has been able to maintain her faith and trust in God, Jesus, the Holy Spirit and the Blessed Virgin for help, protection and guidance on a daily basis, Mary forms a distinct connection between the depth and significance of her faith and the religious experiences of her childhood, when she says:

> I suppose it comes back to my mother and father. They were very religious, very Catholic. And their fundamental thing was, when you're in trouble — I've got a novena which we call, which is a nine-day prayer to Our Lady. And

they said, when you're in trouble take that out and read it, and start reading it and praying it until the crisis is passed, you know. So that's … I suppose I've had that since I was a child. Yes. And I think too, it even goes back, I still remember in Grade 4, we had Irish nuns in those days. Young girls that had come out like … and their faith, they were full of it, you know. And a sister would be writing on the board and she'd say, 'I can't see who's talking, but He can'. And we all knew who He was [laugh]. So like we were getting that reality that God was there for us all the time even when we were little kids.

Successful coping involves the mobilisation of a wide variety of resources, both personal and environmental (Osborne & Vandenberg, 2003; Pearlin & Schooler, 1978). Accordingly, the women interviewed also utilised nonreligious coping strategies.

Nonreligious Coping Strategies

In conjunction with religious coping strategies, the women also employed nonreligious coping strategies. As with religious coping, a number of the nonreligious coping strategies — such as caring for the children, reading books and planning a course of action — could be classified both as problem-focused and emotion-focused approaches to coping, as each strategy addressed the presenting problem while offering an overflow effect into the realm of emotion. For example, the provision of both practical and emotional assistance to the children can help to maintain an harmonious balance for at least some members of the household, and knowing one's children are appropriately cared for can possibly assist in alleviating some of the stress for the victim of abuse. Thus, as suggested by Carver and Scheier (1994), there is both a practical and an emotional outworking of the strategy. The choice to focus on activities is perhaps best classified as an emotion-focused approach to coping, as it provides the individual with the opportunity to emotionally disengage, although temporarily, from the pressures of the presenting problem.

Children

Eleven of the women noted the importance of their children in relation to coping. In some cases, there was a strong realisation of the need to protect the children, either physically or emotionally, from the ongoing abuse. This need was often a contributing factor in any decision to separate from or divorce the perpetrator (Ruth, Miriam, Eunice). Additionally, the women reported a desire to direct their positive energies towards meeting the needs of their children (Mary, Anna, Leah). Such action allowed them to feel some level of worth within the family by providing them with a purpose.

Susanna, favouring death rather than the struggle to continue living, still chose to fight cancer because she believed her children needed her. Susanna says, 'The only thing that kept me going was the family and the prayers and my youngest children that I knew I needed to be around for. That kept me going'. Anna says of her children, 'having my children was the ... absolute paramount ... joy to me', while Joanna states directly, 'I've got four kids, so you just have to keep going'. It is interesting to note that each of the women refers to her children with a singular sense of ownership from which the perpetrator is excluded. This appears to be an established pattern throughout the interviews, and could perhaps be indicative of the sole responsibility and initiative taken by the women for the wellbeing of their children.

Lois speaks of the impact that domestic abuse had on her children, and also of the way in which she continued to function for the sake of the children and their wellbeing:

> I think if I didn't have to [crying] ... if I didn't have to think of their future, I would have been quite happy to lay on my bed and never get up again and just ... go back into that isolation and live in my own little world in this ... It was because I recognised that my isolation which had obviously harmed my marriage as well, was harming my children. And that the isolation, which was really a result of this abuse and this, you know, poor relationship in our marriage — that isolation was as much a part of the children getting to the point where they couldn't maintain eye contact ... much a part of it.

Without hesitation, Mary explains how the simplicity of adhering to a basic routine for the children provided her with a reason to continue:

> I found that what got me through it was I had to look after my children. And the love that I felt that God gave me for my children gave me a purpose in life. And my daughter, who's in between my two sons, well she had major health problems. She's a very, very big girl and, sort of, I had to drive the children to school because at that stage the main road had no lights on it, and I wouldn't let the children cross the busy road to go to school. So I had to get up in the morning, and I had to take the children to school, and I had to be there in the afternoon to pick them up. So that gave me a purpose in life.

The high level of motivation generated by the need to protect one's children is encapsulated in the brief words offered by Miriam when she asserts, 'If anything happened to me, I would dread to think what happened to those two boys'. Thus, concern for the wellbeing of the children acted as a driving and sustaining force for many of the women.

Activities

The use of activities, busyness or an external focus appeared to serve as a positive form of escape from the pervading presence of domestic abuse. This strategy, provided emotional release by allowing the women to momentarily step aside from the pressures associated with daily life, and enjoy the peace afforded by the temporary distraction of activity. Nine women reported engaging in activities as part of their overall coping strategy. This method of coping included keeping busy with the routine activities for the day (Mary, Susanna), focusing on work or voluntary activities (Ruth, Esther, Deborah), undertaking a course of study (Leah, Eunice), or becoming involved in hobbies such as gardening or sewing (Anna). Some women also endeavoured to focus on helping others, such as an elderly relative.

Amid the pressure of her own situation, Mary tells the story of how her brother became ill and was admitted to hospital, where he remained for some time and had no one to care for his two children. This left Mary, who was also unwell at the time, caring for five children, and attempting to disentangle her brother's affairs, while endeavouring to come to terms with her own marriage difficulties. Upon listening to the details of her story, as the interviewer, I acknowledged the intensity of Mary's burden, to which she calmly replied:

> It was [a burden]. But, see, when you're that involved, and
> you're that far down, all you can do — life becomes simple
> in some ways, because — well that's what I've got to do next,
> and that's what I've got to do next, and I've got to get the
> kids to school, and I've got to remember to pick them up,
> and I've got to remember, like ... and I found that if I kept
> the house tidy and in order ... I could keep things in order
> and deal with it as it happened.

Realising that the situation could easily slip from her control, Mary
had out of necessity developed her own step-by-step, no-frills strategy
of coping. She did this by dealing solely with the basic requirements
and establishing a firm routine to which she, and all five children,
adhered. This strategy helped to maintain order in the household, but
also assisted Mary to function adequately until she was able to seek
further assistance from both her minister and her doctor.

Deborah found the sense of validation that was not available
through her marriage by teaching religion at the local school. Deborah
relates her experience:

> You know, one of the reasons I teach my class of religion is
> because I get to study my Scriptures and for that little period
> of time, it's my escape. That's the wrong term. I'm not using
> it as an escape. But to me, that's where I feel validated. That's
> where I feel welcomed. That's where I feel successful.

Eunice describes how planning to do her senior schooling and then
moving on to university helped her to discover more of herself, regain
her autonomy, and build the confidence she needed to move forward
and eventually separate from her husband:

> I always had definite ideas, but I was never ... I know, well,
> if I say I know my strengths, my inner strengths grew when
> I started to go to university and ... oh, it wasn't university
> then, but when I got my degree and started teaching I
> became probably Eunice. Up until then I'd been Eunice,
> wife of [husband]. So, you know, I became me. And then
> — even now, strangely enough, I still think that I'm
> becoming more confident.

Anna, a 'very busy, creative person', explains how she used activity,
and general busyness to help her cope with the stress of living in an

abusive environment. Even now, Anna continues to remain active in an effort to ameliorate the effects of the grief and loss she has suffered. Anna reflects thoughtfully on her experiences:

> I'm a gardener. I sew. I had friends. I had little children to cope with. I was in a mother's group from the church. I had an elderly mother who lived, you know, a few miles away and needed care and that. So I had a very — you know, a lot of young ones today would think that was darned boring, but it wasn't to me and it kept me very busy. So it was the strategy of coping was just doing things really. I guess in a way that is what is still happening to me. I keep extra busy. I … it's in my nature anyway, but I'm getting older and I do get more tired. But it keeps me so occupied that I can't grieve as — you know, I still have a lot of sadness there. But I'm gradually getting stronger. I mean, you have to.

Reading

Reading served as a means by which some of the women were able to glean information regarding the problems they were facing. Many of them had only limited access to support, and so discovered that books had the potential to provide both insight and encouragement. Although they utilised the available literature in a variety of ways, and for a variety of reasons, eight of the women reported benefiting substantially as a result of their access to relevant literature. The use of literature varied from the gathering of information (Elizabeth), to the seeking of encouragement and ongoing strength through reading of the challenges overcome by others (Mary).

While Elizabeth sensed within herself that there was definitely something very wrong with her marital relationship, it was not until she was able to read the relevant literature that she could develop a depth of understanding pertaining to her situation. As the literature confirmed the truth of her experiences, Elizabeth's confidence increased in the knowledge that she was finally able to make some form of progress. As Elizabeth refers to her experiences with books, she conveys a sense of excitement regarding the discoveries that follow:

> It was the beginning of God giving me books into my hands that I can really use to help me. It was really through

books that I had confirmed things that I believe were right, and also it was through books that I learnt, you know, things maybe first off, but mostly it was confirming things that I believed were right.

Lois refers to her books as her 'gold'. After separating from her husband, Lois was deeply concerned for the wellbeing of her children, and desired to make some positive adjustments in her parenting in an effort to help her children cope with their experiences of domestic abuse. Lois says:

I cried out for information to God and I've gotten — there's a Christian boundaries book. There's how to love your children. I've cried out to Him for help and through Christian psychologists that have written books and done teaching, I've got a lot of help and we're actually changing patterns.

Planning

Planning can act as a meaningful problem-focused approach to coping with domestic abuse. Planning affords an individual the opportunity to reflect carefully upon the situation and consider a range of alternatives, prior to taking any decisive action (Carver et al., 1989). Plans can differ depending on the individual and the situation in which she finds herself. For example, Miriam chose to plan her escape from her husband in detail, and gradually moved towards her goal until she was able to execute her plan (see chapter 9). Alternatively, Deborah created a plan that was more suited to the purpose she had for her marriage. While Deborah did express the belief that it was permissible for her to leave the marriage as a result of the abuse, she chose to remain with her husband and do all within her power to maintain the relationship in the hope that he would eventually choose to change (see chapter 3). Regardless of the specific nature of the plan itself, simply devising a feasible plan can help to alleviate emotional stress, as the individual has not only considered the available options but also chosen a specific course of action should the need arise.

Summary

This chapter has considered the coping strategies of Christian women when confronted with domestic abuse. The women are presented as having turned to their Christian faith, actively seeking assistance regarding the difficulties being experienced. A variety of methods of coping are employed by, and also found to be beneficial to, the individuals involved. Such methods include both problem-focused and emotion-focused approaches, which have been shown to operate effectively in both religious and nonreligious domains.

Religious coping strategies appear to have permeated the entire coping response, as Christian women chose to adopt a collaborative approach to problem-solving, thereby seeking wisdom and insight from God in relation to any necessary decisions. The women exhibited a confidence in the ability and desire of God to assist them in solving the problem or to provide them with the strength to endure it.

It is evident that these women, all of whom were active in their Christian faith throughout the course of their marriage and therefore throughout the duration of the domestic abuse, relied heavily upon the tenets of their faith to sustain them, both during times of almost continual abuse and also during the recovery process. They also turned to coping strategies that were both familiar to them and suited the specific situations and the resources available. In numerous cases, some coping strategies, such as prayer, were strongly rooted in the childhood training and experience of the women involved, as a foundational faith proved to be a significantly influential factor regarding the manner in which they chose to deal with the difficulties arising from the abuse.

Reflections for the Counsellor

1. What benefits do you see for the client who practises her Christian faith?

2. Do you see any potential disadvantages for the client who practises her Christian faith? If so, what?

3. What is the importance/significance of the Christian faith for (i) you as an individual and (ii) for your client?

Client Discussion

1. What benefits do you see as a result of your Christian faith? List them.

2. How did/do you cope with stress?
   - What types of things did/do you do?
   - What effect did/do these have on yourself and/or others?

3. What types of resources did you have available to you (e.g. personal, environmental)?
   - Were you able to be inventive in finding ways to cope with the pressure? If so, how?

4. What strategies did you try in an effort to 'fix' the situation (e.g. changing your behaviour)?
   - What sorts of things did you change?
   - Did anything actually work to change the situation?

5. What approaches did you try (e.g. problem-focused, emotion-focused)? Give examples.
   - How did these approaches work for you or in your situation?

6. How did you interact with God?
   - How did/do you see God in your situation?
   - Describe your experience of God.

7. Do you have specific faith-based coping strategies? If so:
   - What are they?
   - How does each one work for you? How would you rate each one?

8. Do you have favourite Scriptures? If so:
   - Which ones are your favourites?
   - How do they help you?

9. What part do you think/feel your Christian faith has played in helping you to come this far?
   - In relation to your faith, what are your expectations for the future?

CHAPTER 9

Listening to the Voice of Experience

> It is not only my task to look after the victims of mad men
> who drive a motor car in a crowded street, but to do all in my
> power to stop their driving at all. (Bonhoeffer, 1959, p. 22)

Firstly, this chapter provides an overview of the continual need for societal intervention in relation to domestic abuse, highlighting the specific need for the Christian church to adopt an active role in the facilitation of ongoing improvements to the current structure. It then identifies some of the key concerns of the women interviewed who, as Christian women and victims of domestic abuse, share the advice they would most like to provide initially to women who like themselves, have fallen victim to domestic abuse, and then to members of the clergy who are often required to provide assistance to members of their congregations.

Advice provided to Christian women currently dealing with issues of domestic abuse includes the necessity of maintaining a strong focus on God and their Christian faith, the importance of seeking professional assistance, the potential advantages of marital separation, and the need to reject abusive behaviour. Victims of domestic abuse are reminded that they are not responsible for the actions of their husbands, nor are they responsible for the abuse they have suffered. However, they are free to choose their own path and make decisions that are both helpful to themselves and relevant to the situation.

Members of the clergy are reminded of the absolute necessity of believing and supporting victims of domestic abuse, without the presence of judgment or condemnation. They are further instructed to listen to victims of domestic abuse, and take responsibility for developing high levels of awareness in relation to the dynamics of domestic abuse. The demonstration of both love and respect are depicted as essential elements of the care-giving process. Finally, members of the clergy are advised to adopt a proactive approach that includes denouncing injustice, developing policies, and networking within the community.

A substantial number of excerpts from the interviews conducted with the women are used in this chapter. This choice was made in keeping with the overall aim of this publication in affording the women the opportunity to speak freely, focusing clearly on the messages they personally wished to convey to both victims of domestic abuse and to members of the clergy.

Overview

Domestic abuse is not a new issue, but has been prevalent throughout history (Hague & Marlos, 2005; Landes et al., 1993; McCue, 2008; Wilson. 1997). While attitudes of both individuals and society have changed considerably over the years (Cooper & Vetere, 2005), there is still need for continual advancement in relation to domestic abuse and the issues facing women who have become victims of it. Klein and Orloff (1999) describe domestic abuse as 'a major societal problem that affects millions of people' (p. 29). As such, domestic abuse must not be ignored, neither by society in general nor by groups or organisations within a society. Accordingly, it is not only necessary to realise that the horror, pain and anguish perpetuated by domestic abuse is present within the Christian churches of the nation, just as it is within the community at large (Victorian Council of Churches' Commission, 1992; White, 1991), it remains imperative that it be addressed in an appropriate manner (JCDVPP, 2002).

Towards the end of every interview, each of the women was asked whether or not she had any advice to offer to victims of domestic abuse or to members of the clergy. Without fail, each one was able to offer something that she, as an individual in possession of substantial firsthand knowledge and experience of domestic abuse, felt was both important and potentially helpful to other Christian women who were suffering, or to members of the clergy who were called upon to assist members of their own congregation or other victims of domestic abuse. While there is no one specific solution that can be presented as a one-size-fits-all response to domestic abuse, it is important to realise that the victims themselves are most frequently in the best possible position to choose which strategies are most appropriate for their individual situation (Department of Communities, 2005b).

The following section will consider the advice offered by the women, dealing first with the advice provided for victims of domestic abuse and then with the advice offered to members of the clergy. Frequently, the key concepts contained within the advice offered by some women were mentioned by different women throughout the course of the interview, being considered relevant within the context of their own story, even though such advice may not have been specifically stated in the final section of the interview. Thus, when considering the recurrent themes contained within the stories of the women interviewed, the number of women indicated as providing a particular form of advice, may in fact, be larger than initially indicated. For example, a total of nine individuals either advised victims of abuse to separate from or leave their abusers, or alternatively stated that leaving was an acceptable option (Esther, Lois). In contrast, 17 of the 20 women did choose the option of separation as the most appropriate course of action.

Advice to Victims of Domestic Abuse

The advice offered by the women to both past and present victims of domestic abuse was often concise and at times reflective of the particular difficulties that were relevant to the individual experience of each one. The advice provided included the need to maintain a strong focus on one's own Christian faith, to seek assistance, and to separate from the perpetrator (see Figure 9.1). In addition to the actual advice offered was the theme of reassurance clearly expressed towards victims (Mary, Leah, Abigail).

Maintaining Faith in God

Walker (1979) found that a belief in God often helped victims of abuse to cope with the suffering they were experiencing. In some ways, it offered a form of peace amid the trauma of abuse. She also found that some victims of domestic abuse turned away from their faith as a result of a conflict between existing theological beliefs that portray a loving

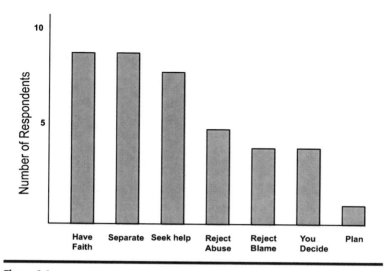

Figure 9.1
Respondent advice to abuse victims.
Note: (*N* = 20).

God, and the fact that the same God had apparently done very little to protect them from the ongoing abuse. For some victims of domestic abuse, turning away from their faith was directly linked to negative encounters with members of the clergy.

Nine women highlighted the necessity of maintaining a strong faith in God both throughout the duration of the abuse and during the recovery period. This advice reflects the fact that each and every woman listed her faith in God, and turning to God in times of adversity, as a key coping strategy in relation to her ultimate survival. Incorporated within the concept of holding God as a central point of focus is the matter of continued prayer (Ruth, Rebekah, Miriam), both in relation to the subject of domestic abuse and the need for wisdom and insight, and also for the purpose of maintaining a balance in one's own life.

Both Naomi and Abigail offer similar thoughts on maintaining a God-centred focus. Naomi says that Christian women dealing with domestic abuse should, 'look to God to give them that strength to get through the situation', while Abigail confidently states, 'I would say, just keep talking to God, and eventually something will happen. But you have to have … patience, I suppose'. Neither of these women advocated remaining with an abusive husband, but rather focused on the need to seek the wisdom and guidance of God regarding the most effective manner in which to deal with the presence of domestic abuse.

Miriam reflects on the importance of prayer in her life:

> Keep your faith and your prayer going, because that gives you a little bit of peace … well, not a little bit of peace, but it gives you a lot of peace. And it seems to — you seem to be able to focus on things better. Not all the time, but just sort of — you know … [Interviewer: When you need to, it's there?] Yes.

Ruth draws a strong connection between trusting God, prayer, and the need to reach out, seek and actually locate assistance, offering a very determined response:

> Seek the right help. Continue to trust and believe God is there with you. Pray. Pray. If it has to be every minute of the day, pray, and God will hear your prayers. But most of all, reach out, don't stay. Reach out to find help, to find a new way or find how you can cope with what you've got at this present time, whatever you're in. But you must reach out. And with the strength that God provides, He will find a way. The best way for you. God is not a God of suffering. God is a God of love.

Seek Assistance

Frequently, victims of domestic abuse do not seek assistance as they are unaware of the options available to them. In many cases, a victim will experience a number of abusive incidents before seeking assistance (Conway, 1998), and often sees herself as the only one who is able to resolve the situation (Walker, 1979). Further, reaching out to others for assistance involves some daunting questions for the victim, relating to the type of response she will receive, issues of confidentiality, the risk of not being believed, and whether or not her situation will improve as a result of the assistance provided (Borkowski et al., 1983; Miles, 2000; Ulrich, 1998).

Eight of the women interviewed echoed Ruth's comments, emphasising the need to reach out and seek assistance. A particularly common theme among the women is the need for victims of abuse to determinedly continue to seek assistance from any number of sources until the necessary support is forthcoming. Both Susanna and Eve stress the need for Christian women who are victims of domestic abuse to be willing to look outside the structure of the church to gain the assistance they require. Eve suggests that victims need professional assistance, describing domestic abuse as 'soul destroying', a comment echoed by Abrahams (2007), who states that 'domestic violence corrodes that fabric of women's emotional and social worlds' (p. 9). Eve further highlights the possibility that with professional help, a victim of domestic abuse is able to work through the trauma and eventually 'get strong and get out of it'. Susanna recommends a number of different organisations saying:

> If you're uncomfortable or unhappy something's not right, so seek help. And if you don't get it from the church, go to the Salvation Army. Go to another counselling group. There's Anglicare, I believe — go to another counselling group and get help, because it's not right and you should never put up with it … You deserve peace of mind. You deserve comfort and calm in your life. So you go and get that help from whereever you need to. If your pastor won't give it to you, go somewhere else, but do not stay and do not let it get worse.

Rachel regularly visited her minister on a weekly basis, but to no avail. Based on her experience, Rachel makes a determined recommendation in favour of the Domestic Violence Telephone Service (now DVConnect), an organisation that was instrumental in providing her with assistance, and ultimately helping her to leave the abusive relationship. Rachel explains the benefits of such a service:

> Well, ring the Domestic Violence Telephone Service. I mean that's the first big thing, is to know that they're there — to know that you can have counselling on the telephone. They can talk to you about the stuff that happens. They've got the knowledge to be able to explain about the cycle and the power of control, and everything. They have got those skills too, and the knowledge to be able to do that even when … as yourself, you might not realise what

to do. And I think it's ... and I think the other thing is trying to keep moving till you find someone who can help you. Don't don't just go, like, I think I went to the minister for too long. I think that I should have, like, in hindsight ... instead of going week by week. After the first couple of weeks and nothing was changed, go to somewhere else. Go and talk to someone else. Tell them your story.

Separation is an Option

Separating oneself from the union of marriage is a choice that often attracts the disapproval of the church (see chapter 6). Thus, it is a decision that is not only affected by numerous situational factors, such as finance, housing and safety, but is further compounded by the belief system of the victim and any negative pressure that is applied by members of the clergy. However, it is essential to realise, first of all, that 'abuse is not of God' and, second, that 'divorce is not the unpardonable sin' (Hegstrom, 2004, p. 121).

While not all the women experienced pressure from their ministers, and some were in fact assisted greatly by members of the clergy, nine of the women felt it necessary to encourage victims of abuse to leave the abusive situation, highlighting the fact that separation is a very real option, and an equally acceptable choice in the case of domestic abuse. Rebekah, while clearly supporting the need for continued prayer, emphasises the need for separation and also stresses the fact that victims of domestic abuse can be in fear of their lives. Rebekah advises:

> It would be to leave. To keep taking it to God and not to allow that person to do that. Because that doesn't bring glory to God. It's not what God wants — just to leave and to really trust that God can change the situation. But if you end up dead, then that — that doesn't glorify God in any way. And that's a very real possibility that ... you can get killed through it.

As an initial step, Hannah suggests a temporary time of separation in an effort to gain a clearer perspective, from which one is then free to make a less pressured and therefore more certain decision.

While Hannah asserts that she does not feel she can tell anyone else what action to undertake, she proposes:

> Get out. Have a break away for a while — like, but if they don't get out and see ... if they stay there they won't see things that they would if they'd gotten out for a little while. It gives you a chance to look a bit differently on things, I think ... So I think that while you're there and while you're listening to everybody else, you can't see it as clearly. If you get away for a little while you seem to be able to get your head around it better.

Deborah, who at this point in time has chosen to remain with her husband, states simply, 'you don't have to stay there', as she reflects upon the decision of her two sisters to leave their marriages and continue life as single parents. Deborah openly acknowledges that while she supported the choices made by her two sisters, she remains hesitant to follow this course of action herself.

Adding a touch of encouragement for the many victims of domestic abuse who are for numerous reasons often hesitant to leave a relationship, Eunice states with assurance:

> There is life after it [laugh] ... that you can ... I suppose, I was able to get through it and create another life. You know, I've re-created myself. The most important thing I believe is that you don't see yourself as a victim. That you see yourself as able to get out of it.

Refuse to Accept Abuse

Numerous high profile organisations such as the Domestic Violence Resource Centre (DVRC, 1998b) and Legal Aid Queensland (1998), in addition to smaller local agencies, are releasing printed material encouraging women to refuse to accept abuse, emphasising the fact that women do have a choice and highlighting the options available to them (DVRC, 1998b). These thoughts are reinforced through the advice provided by the women interviewed. Recommendations by these women were very clear on this issue: abusive behaviour should not be tolerated, and some form of stand should be made in relation to it. Five women chose to make this a distinct message to victims of domestic abuse.

Anna did not advocate an immediate separation, instead expressing the hope of many victims of domestic abuse that the perpetrator would modify his behaviour at least to some degree. However, she recognised that if there was no apparent change, then a decision must be made. At the age of 70, Anna explains her position, highlighting the years of her life that were lost as a result of inaction:

> I'd say to them, firstly, hopefully, they recognise they shouldn't have to accept the behaviour, which I didn't know, 'cause my mother accepted it. Don't accept the behaviour. Try to get counselling, or support and help and for your husband too. And get the courage that if there is no change in his behaviour ... to have the courage to move away from it. Not lose your life in lots of ways that I did. Valuable years I've lost.

Leah echoes these sentiments, listing a variety of forms of abuse, and maintaining that a woman should not be expected to tolerate abusive behaviour regardless of the form in which it is manifested. Leah further emphasises that domestic abuse is not the fault of the victim, and that no victim should ever blame herself for her predicament. She states concisely:

> You don't have to take abuse. You are a special person and you're important and you're worth something and so there is no way that anyone should treat you wrongly by putting you down with words, or putting you down emotionally, or putting you down by quoting Bible verses. I guess ... don't blame yourself if something's happening. It's not your fault. I don't know how to say it, but it's something like that. Stand up for yourself. Don't let them do it.

Abuse is Not Your Fault

Following on from the need to take a stand and not tolerate the presence of abusive behaviour in a relationship, is the point introduced by Leah: that a victim should not accept responsibility for the abuse she is experiencing. Unfortunately, many victims of domestic abuse often do accept responsibility, or blame themselves, for the abuse (Bagshaw & Chung, 2000; Douglas, 1987; Hoff, 1990; Walker, 1994). Clearly, the responsibility for the abusive behaviour of the perpetrator remains solely with the perpetrator (see chapter 4). The advice not to blame oneself or accept responsibility for perpetrator behaviour is significant. While only four of the women mentioned it directly in relation to providing advice for victims of domestic abuse, 16 of the 20 did state that they had, at some time, blamed themselves for the abuse they experienced and also for the associated deficiencies within their marriages.

Without hesitation, Naomi responds to the question regarding advice with the words, 'Oh [slight laugh] to not feel that it's their fault … they're not creating the problem [slight laugh]'. Esther also tells victims of domestic abuse, 'they cannot be responsible for the actions or nonactions of their partner', particularly when their own safety or welfare is in jeopardy.

Miriam expresses concern for the complications that may arise as a result of blaming oneself for the abusive behaviour of the perpetrator, explaining that in an effort to find a solution and remedy the situation, she remained in the marriage far too long. Miriam's current feelings reflect this thought. Her position is clear when she states:

> There's such a thing as cutting your losses. As long as you know in your heart that you have done everything you can. And if it is for a reason like safety or — and that includes physical safety, mental, emotional, the lot, you know. If you're at peace with yourself then you've done everything, then there's no good hanging around and blaming yourself trying to fix something that cannot be fixed.

Freedom to Choose

Walker (1994) stresses the fact that victims of domestic abuse must be permitted the freedom to choose the manner in which they will respond to the abuse. Such decisions include medical and legal issues, reporting options, whether or not to leave a relationship, and the specific timing of that decision. A victim of domestic abuse should not be pressured to take any action with which she is not comfortable, or for which she is not ready (Berry, 1998).

Four women stressed the fact that the freedom to make the final choice regarding any course of action to be taken remains with the individual victim of domestic abuse, as she alone is privy to the details, the extent of the abuse involved, and the manner in which it is affecting both her and her children. The decision to leave or to remain in a relationship, even the timing of a particular action, cannot be made by a concerned parent or a member of the clergy. It remains the sole choice of the individual involved.

Although Abigail reports that her father provided her with very good advice, she continues to believe:

> You still have to ... Christian women who are in that relationship, still have to make a decision. And it has to be their own decision.

Sarah suggests that victims of domestic abuse need to be willing to trust their own judgment of a situation, offering the advice:

> ... that they listen to their inner voice ... that they trust that inner voice.

This can often prove quite difficult for an individual who has endured a lengthy period of domestic abuse, as she can be so demeaned and demoralised as a result of the abuse, she lacks confidence in her own ability to arrive at an acceptable decision.

Develop a Strategy

Developing a plan to leave an abusive situation can be classified as a survival strategy (Keys Young, 1998). Landenburger (1998) highlights the need for a functional safety plan, particularly if the victim is reticent to leave the relationship immediately. If victims of domestic abuse choose to seek assistance from a counsellor or agency, appropriate interventions include the development of safety plans (King, 1998). While only one of the women (Eunice) included developing a plan, or set of life goals, as part of her advice to victims of domestic abuse, at least two others (Naomi, Miriam) did endeavour to develop a plan that would assist in their ultimate escape from their home and their perpetrator husbands.

Eunice explains how the setting and achieving of life goals provided her with a sense of security, and helped her to make progress in fulfilling her desire to separate from her husband and then to continue to move forward after her separation:

> I tend to set goals. I set goals. I knew I set goals to do my
> senior [schooling] at night. That was the first goal. That
> was the first ... that was the starting point of getting out. I
> always set goals and I still set goals. You know, I know
> what's going to happen next and what I'm doing. I plan
> ahead. I'm a long-term planner I suppose.

Over a period of time, Miriam carefully planned the details of her
escape. She endeavoured to save some money, retained information
regarding her sons' medical records in an effort to block any potential
custody issue with her husband, sought legal advice regarding her
planned departure, and was particular in choosing a geographical
location where she believed she would be safe, avoiding any potentially obvious locations such as the home of her parents.

Miriam maintained a high level of secrecy regarding her planned
escape, knowing 'we'd only ever get one chance at it', as both Miriam
and her parents had been threatened on the two previous occasions
she had attempted to flee. Miriam tells of the response of her older
son when she finally advised him that they would be leaving the following morning, and suggested that he collect the few things that he
and his younger brother would like to take with them:

> I got my oldest son the day before and this was just after
> he had been through a very rough time with his father.
> Anyhow, I told him what I had decided to do and why
> and he didn't bat an eyelid and he said, 'Will we be safe?'
> ... So that answered all my questions.

The safety of Miriam and her sons depended heavily on the success
of her strategy. Thus, the details of Miriam's plan even included
precise instructions to the removalist. Miriam recalls:

> I've only got a certain amount of money. So I had to say to
> the removalist — I had to be honest with him and say
> why. I told him I'd labelled the things that I wanted and
> the deal was they would fit in what they could that was
> labelled, but if anyone showed up at the house, they were
> to shut the door on the van and go with whatever they
> had. That was the deal, and I had to go along with that.

Miriam recounts the way in which a well-planned strategy helped her to escape, highlighting the necessity of maintaining a strong focus on the things that needed to be accomplished:

> Even the day we left, I said to the oldest one. I said, 'Now you've got to sit in the front of the car with Mummy'. I said, 'Mummy hasn't been to bed. She slept … she worked all night'. Even though, when I got to work and told the other sister that I was on with. Night duty — you have a dull spot, somewhere between one and three. And she said to me, 'Right'. She said, 'You go into the infirmary, and get on the bed'. 'Cause she knew how far I had to drive [1,680 km]. She said, 'I'll come and dig you up if there's anything I can't handle'. And I think I did go to sleep. But I said to him — I said, 'Now, you've got to keep Mummy awake all day today'. It was 10 o'clock before we'd left town.

Miriam goes on to explain that whenever she needed to stop the vehicle to rest, she was careful to avoid the highway. Instead, knowing that her husband might consider the direction in which she would travel, Miriam wisely chose to pull off the main roads 'three or four kilometres into a town' as a precaution against being caught.

In addition to the need for a detailed strategy, part of the advice offered by Miriam to victims of domestic abuse includes the need to communicate as openly as possible with the children and keep them informed as appropriate. Such a decision must of necessity be governed by the age and maturity of the children involved, and the nature of the situation. This was demonstrated by the way Miriam chose to include her older son in some aspects of the situation, but initially avoided providing her younger son with information due to the risk involved and the potential consequences if the secrecy was broken.

Miriam's situation highlights the need for victims of domestic abuse to not only develop a strategy, but to pay close attention to each detail of that strategy. Miriam's story further stresses the significance of developing a contingency plan that can be put into operation quickly and efficiently should the need arise.

Reassurance

A number of the women included some form of reassurance in the advice they offered to victims of domestic abuse. Victims were reminded that they were special, that God had a plan for each of their lives, and that whatever happened they were ultimately free to make their own decision without fear of condemnation.

One of the most decisive messages for victims of domestic abuse was contained within the advice offered by Mary. When asked what she would most like to say to other Christian women facing situations similar to her own, Mary replied emphatically and without hesitation, 'It's only a bend in the road'. Mary expanded on her very concise message of hope, saying:

> I don't know whether you like Helen Steiner Rice or you don't, but that's one of her things. It's only a bend in the road, and the road goes on and it's smoother.

Abigail also chose a positive focus for her message of reassurance as she described the manner in which even some helpful things can eventually emerge from painful experiences. Abigail reflects on her own experience, saying:

> God has a plan for everyone … God's in charge … sometimes there are things — there's results you can't see. Like I look back now, and over the last even three-and-a-half years, I've been able to help — well, in some way, about three or four women that have come to me because of what I went through.

Susanna describes the Christian woman as 'a daughter of Heavenly Father' who deserves the best, while Leah says, 'You are a special person and you are … you're important and you're worth something'. Both women highlight the fact that victims of domestic abuse need to realise the truth that focuses on their unique value as an individual, as opposed to the destructive lies of worthlessness proffered by the perpetrator as part of his overall method for achieving and maintaining power and control (see chapters 3 and 4).

Advice to Members of the Clergy

The women were very clear in their expectations regarding members of the clergy. Those who reported receiving high levels of support (Mary, Sarah) were able to speak positively from their own experiences, praising members of the clergy for their ongoing efforts in ensuring assistance was both forthcoming and relevant to the prevailing circumstances. Alternatively, those who either did not receive the support and assistance required (Anna, Hannah, Elizabeth), or who experienced judgment or revictimisation by members of the clergy, were equipped to respond from a different perspective, being extremely concise in pinpointing negative actions that should be avoided by those members of the clergy wishing to provide genuine assistance to victims of domestic abuse. Further, these women were able to use their own negative experiences with members of the clergy to contribute positive information regarding the specific needs of Christian women who are suffering as a result of domestic abuse, highlighting the key areas of focus and the relevant action that should be undertaken by those desirous of providing the necessary assistance. The following section will address the advice offered by the women to members of the clergy. Their insight focused on the need for members of the clergy to believe, love, care for and support the victim and her children without judgment, condemnation or allocation of blame. Also evident was the expectation that members of the clergy should make every possible endeavour to become informed regarding the dynamics of domestic abuse and its prevalence within Christian homes, demonstrate complete respect for those women who do present as victims of domestic abuse, avoid issues of male headship, and exhibit a willingness to confront the perpetrator when necessary (see Figure 9.2).

Believe the Victim

One of the key elements in assisting victims of domestic abuse is the need to believe the story presented by the victim and take it seriously (King, 1998; Leehan, 1992; Miles, 2000). Demanding proof of an abusive incident is tantamount to disbelief, and minimises the suffering of the victim (Schlueter, 1994). Linked closely to the importance of believing the victim is the fundamental principle of ensuring her

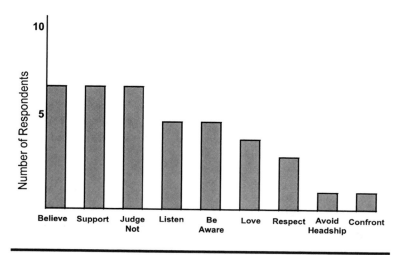

Figure 9.2
Respondent advice to clergy.
Note: (N = 20).

safety, together with that of her children (Douglas, 1987; Fortune & Poling, 1995; Gott, 1995; Walker, 1994). Members of the clergy must turn away from common misconceptions that suggest a victim of domestic abuse may exaggerate the incidents of abuse she has experienced, and instead develop a clear understanding that the victim will far more frequently attempt to understate the level of abuse she has suffered (Browne, 1987; Lemon, 1996; Miles, 1997, 2000).

Seven of the women interviewed wished to remind members of the clergy of the necessity of believing the reports provided by the victim and treating the situation seriously. A number of these women were not believed, and suffered accordingly (Anna, Elizabeth, Hannah, Deborah). Susanna, who was believed by her minister and subsequently referred for professional assistance, chose to highlight the necessity of such action. Susanna says:

> I would say to them, it [domestic abuse] happens and it is happening and if a woman comes to you saying that she's been abused believe her and take her in. Because even if you don't perceive it as abuse, she perceives it as abuse and she is the one that's the most important person here. So

believe her and take it in and help her. If you can't talk to
her yourself get somebody professional that can talk to her
if you can't deal with it. There are people out there that will
help and who are anxious to help, so don't let a woman go
through that hell and that misery. Get her help.

Elizabeth provides a particularly clear example of the manner in
which victims of domestic abuse tend to understate the levels of abuse
present within their relationships, and offers very direct advice to
members of the clergy:

I would like to say, for goodness sake, if a woman comes
to you, believe her. Just believe her. And remember that
she only says one-tenth of what is actually going on. So
whatever she says, multiply it by at least ten and you will
get a small idea of what she's living in. Believe her ... and
do not judge.

Anna eventually had the opportunity to share her story with someone
in authority within her denominational structure. She explains how,
during a woman-to-woman interaction, she finally felt valued and
believed:

Believe the woman. Because when I spoke to the principal
there, several times in my conversations I said, 'I'm telling
you the truth'. And she said, 'I know you are'. I was being
heard and I was being believed.

Be Supportive

Adams (1994) states emphatically that a woman should never be
placed in a position where she has to 'choose between safety and the
support of the church' (p. 11). Members of the clergy should be
capable of providing acceptable levels of support for those in need
(Fortune, 1995b; King, 1999). Schlueter (1994) reports a situation
where the church congregation elected to take responsibility for the
financial needs of the victim, which included the cost of geographical
relocation for the purpose of safety. Parallels may be drawn between
this situation and the parable of the Good Samaritan, as presented by
Jesus in the Gospel of Luke (10:30–37) in response to a discussion
centring around those within the community who should be regarded
as neighbours and toward whom mercy and kindness should be

demonstrated. The Good Samaritan overcame the hostility generally present between the Jews and the Samaritans to offer practical assistance to an individual in need. The relief provided by the Good Samaritan included the use of his own wine and oil for the disinfecting and soothing of the wounds that had been savagely inflicted, transportation in the form of the Samaritan's own donkey, accommodation, the financial assistance of two days' wages together with the promise to supply further finance should the need arise, coupled with a substantial personal commitment of time and effort (Childers, 1964; Liefield, 1984; Strauss, 2002). In effect, the Good Samaritan, whose example is upheld as a model for emulation by the Christian church, did all within his power to assist the victim of abuse.

Much like the Jewish victim in the parable who did not receive any assistance from his own people (Luke 10:31–32), Elizabeth and Rachel made a clear distinction between the help they received from secular seminars or external organisations such as the Domestic Violence Telephone Service, and the assistance available in their own churches, although members of the clergy in both cases were well aware of the prevailing situations. The agencies were able to provide both facts and practical assistance, neither of which was readily available from the churches involved.

Seven of the women advised members of the clergy to not only be responsive and supportive, but to extend such support to the care of both the victim of domestic abuse and her children, who also may be classified as victims. As in the parable of the Good Samaritan, caring for the needs of victims of domestic abuse may involve addressing issues relating to safety, housing, finance or transport, all of which form a portion of the fundamental needs pertaining to daily survival. A variety of suggestions were offered by the women interviewed. Naomi reflects upon the need for practical assistance by advising:

> Be supportive. Be there ... and not just with words, but in
> a practical way as well.

Miriam, although recognising the fact that it must be extremely difficult for members of the clergy to become involved in domestic abuse cases, still stresses the need for aid to be forthcoming, and illustrates one form of practical support:

> As much as you realise they mustn't like getting involved in domestic situations ... and I can understand that. [It would] be the same with the police, you know. I can really understand it. But those women do need support. And by support, it might only be just to be there while they pack up a few things. Just to have someone there. They wouldn't care who it was, as long as it was another bloke or, you know, someone that could intervene or whatever. Just be a buffer zone.

Rebekah extended her comments to include the members of the congregation as well as members of the clergy, highlighting the benefit of building friendships with other members of the church through regular interaction in the form of fellowship groups. Rebekah explains her position:

> It's the cell group's [role]. I guess to a person who comes in off the street and doesn't know God, the minister probably has to deal with it. But it's about their fellowship being connected to each other. Because it's not until you have those close relationships that it can be brought out, because you're not going to tell someone straight away. And it takes time. So they should be looking at their congregation really being open.

Eunice offers pertinent advice that acknowledges not only the shift from being a member of a couple to being a single parent experienced by many victims of domestic abuse who choose to leave a relationship, but also the social adjustment that occurs as a result of that change. Eunice views this as yet another area in which victims of domestic abuse require support, suggesting a policy of inclusion as an appropriate option:

> They need to know, and go to that person and invite them to be — not attending ... special things for ... I suppose the whole thing that really bugged me was not to be pushed off and be a sole parent away there in that group of sole parents. But for me just to be part of the normal group, contributing as though we were a whole family, contributing along with all of the other total, whole families who had husbands and wives. You know — to be included in the whole part, rather than isolated in a separate section.

Do Not Judge

Frequently, victims of domestic abuse are directly blamed for their own victimisation as the suggestion is made that the victim must have in some way provoked the incident (Eilts, 1995; Fortune & Poling, 1995; Scutt, 1990). Even asking a victim of domestic abuse why she did not leave the situation is a subtle form of judging her and blaming her for the manner in which she has been treated (Magen, 1999). Walker (1994) provides insight into the dangers of blaming the victim for her own abuse, explaining that the victim may withdraw, choosing to terminate the counselling relationship and thereby limit her access to further assistance. Hegstrom (2004) reminds his readers that domestic abuse is a crime for which the victim should not be blamed, judged or held accountable.

Seven women were concise in the advice they provided to members of the clergy not to judge victims of domestic abuse. Ruth suggests victims of abuse should be treated and assisted in a 'nonjudg-mental' manner, while Abigail is direct in her instructions to members of the clergy when she states:

> Don't ever say to a woman that she needs to smarten up her act. Always be open.

Elizabeth is emphatic in her initial comment 'do not judge', but then continues to present a different perspective on the concept of judging a victim of domestic abuse. While most of the advice provided by the women in this area was related to the manner in which members of the clergy should treat victims of domestic abuse who sought their counsel, Elizabeth extended the concept to include the overall attitude of members of the clergy to those women who are divorced as a result of domestic abuse, as well as the content of sermons that are regularly delivered from the pulpit. The following comments by Elizabeth reflect the plight of many women in similar situations:

> But if they [ministers] don't start to believe women and look past this big unpardonable sin of divorce, where you wear the big 'D' over you — if they don't start looking and seeing one person has broken the covenant ... the other person who hasn't broken the covenant becomes divorced from that person through their choice, not the spouse's

> choice. Then in the church, they're divorced again, from
> the help that they need. And I believe I have been doubly
> divorced. And that is very, very painful.

Elizabeth continues to explain her position on sermons that have a
tendency to treat women who are divorced as sinners and second-class
citizens, describing her own anger at the arrogant attitude conveyed
by her minister:

> And it's very hard for pastors. They say things from the
> pulpit now ... and I can tell you, I sat and listened to one
> on Sunday night and I almost went up to him and I
> thought, 'No. Not the right time yet'. But he said, like, 'If
> you're divorced, now don't get me wrong, I'll ... we love
> divorced people. We love divorced people. Right. We really
> love divorced people. But before it gets to that stage, why
> don't you go and do something about it? Let's get these
> things fixed up'. And I just felt like I would like to go and
> smash his face in.

The minister's comments on divorce not only adopted a perspective
from which he appeared to look down upon those who had been
divorced, but also made no allowance whatsoever for the reasons for
the divorce. There was no presumption of innocence regarding those
who never wanted the marriage to fail, those who sought constant
assistance, or those who were forced into a divorce through the
actions of their spouse. Elizabeth thoughtfully states:

> But it was like ... that is automatically saying that both
> people don't want the marriage, and in my case that was
> not true. It was never true. It's still not true.

This is a position that holds both partners accountable for the failure
when, in a domestic abuse situation, it is the perpetrator of abuse
who is accountable for the failure of the marriage, not the victim (see
chapter 6).

The insensitivity of the minister in question was further highlighted when Elizabeth recounted her experience as mother of the
bride on the day of her daughter's wedding; the minister, in full
knowledge of Elizabeth's situation, still chose to address the issue of
divorce as part of his words to the congregation during the wedding

ceremony. Elizabeth tells of the pain she felt as a result of the inconsideration of the minister:

> A few days after the wedding I realised I was really distressed. Really distressed ... 'cause that was disgusting. That was absolutely disgusting. That was cruel. It was cruel, and that was our day, and why even mention that word [divorce]. And why do his talk around that ... But, I just thought ... it just brought back a whole lot of old stuff to me and I thought, this is so impossible. And, and you know why he did that? I believe he did that because he has made a judgment on me as a divorced woman.

Esther also complains of the frequent negative references to divorce within weekly sermons, and questions the effect it could have on her own children:

> I've been tempted to actually even send them [the minister] a letter. Because in every circumstance they bring up an example, it's always ... divorce. Every example seems to be brought back to divorce. And I just wanted to write and remind them that when they're saying that, they're also subconsciously telling my children how bad I am as a parent because I am divorced. [Esther is extremely upset at this point.] And I don't think they've realised that. I also want to tell them that it is healthier to go out of some relationships because there can be more damage to remain in them. It's just, everything — every example seems to include divorce. And I think that subconsciously all that negativity is going onto my children.

While many situations do need to be addressed from the pulpit as part of weekly sermon material, members of the clergy are encouraged to develop a keen level of sensitivity to the feelings of members of their congregations, either known or unknown, who may be or have previously been victims of domestic abuse.

Listen

Active listening is also classified as a key element when dealing with victims of domestic abuse (King, 1998), and can be considered a demonstrable form of respect for the victim and the courage she is exhibiting by telling her story and reaching out for assistance (Adams, 1994). Actively listening to a victim of domestic abuse as she recounts her experience aids the listener in understanding the perspective of the victim (Landenburger, 1998), and affords the listener the opportunity of validating the thoughts and feelings of the victim (Walker, 1994). Such acknowledgment and validation can prove empowering for the victim, assisting her to come to terms with her own thoughts and feelings in relation to her experiences, and possibly helping her to gain the strength she requires to leave the relationship (Landenburger).

Five women noted the importance of listening carefully to the reports provided by victims of domestic abuse, accentuating the need to be heard and understood in conjunction with being believed. Numerous others (Hannah, Deborah, Joanna) expressed their difficulty in this area, but Anna reports an extreme case where a church elder not only refused to listen, but instead 'shouted me down and said, "I will not listen to this"'.

Joanna relates her experience with her fundamentalist minister, explaining how she was unable to even tell her story fully, or express her feelings regarding the abuse that was being perpetrated against her, before he began pressuring her on the action she should take. Joanna explains:

> Listen. That's important. Listen to what they're saying and listen to how they're feeling before you start telling them what they should and shouldn't be doing. Like they — like my experience they've come out with guns blazing, 'You've got to do this. You've got to do that'. Rather than just trying to help and just trying to nurture you through what you're going through at that time.

Deborah provides a helpful image for members of the clergy, illustrating for them the potential benefits that can result from a willingness to listen attentively to victims of domestic abuse. Deborah explains:

Believe them. Even if you don't do anything about it, listen. And women like to talk. They can unload. And then sometimes women solve their own problems. And even if they go back, it's like emptying the bucket. You can go back and deal with it and let the bucket fill up again and ... but if you can just empty it on somebody.

Leah also adopts a practical position, advising members of the clergy to:

... think outside your own experiences, of what you've been taught. Be very open to listen to what ladies are saying — to actually hear their experience without colouring it with your opinions and views. Even if [sigh] ... it doesn't fit in with what you think. See them as — don't see yourself as someone who's got the answers and a representative of God. See yourself on the same level as this person.

Be Aware and Informed

To deal appropriately with victims of domestic abuse, it is necessary for members of the clergy to take personal responsibility for increasing their own understanding of the basic operating principles pertaining to domestic abuse. White (1991) suggests such training be mandatory, while Nason-Clark (1997) supports the need for increased awareness in relation to the church as a whole. Adopting a proactive approach can assist members of the clergy in providing effective spiritual support and guidance to the women who require their assistance. A simple understanding of the basic principles of domestic abuse can help to guard against the incorrect treatment of a situation, thus ensuring the continued safety of the victim (Miles, 2000). While Johnson (1995) reports a general absence of specific training in areas of domestic abuse in a number of theological colleges, Dixon (1997), in an Australian study of Anglican male clergy, reports that 80% of the 125 participants indicated an interest in attending further training on domestic abuse. The essential nature of pertinent training for members of the clergy is highlighted by Pellauer (1986), who explains that the minister has the capability to 'make the difference between anguish and health, sometimes between death and life for victims of family violence' (p. 17).

Five women viewed the need for members of the clergy to be informed regarding the issues surrounding domestic abuse as paramount. A further two included, as a significant issue, the willingness of members of the clergy to refer victims of domestic abuse for professional assistance. Both Susanna and Mary benefited substantially as a result of discussing their situations with trained professionals. Additionally, both women consulted professionals who possessed a distinct understanding of the specific Christian faith of their clients, a detail that helped to foster a more wholistic approach to treatment.

Esther focuses on the fact that difficulties can occur if members of the clergy are not aware of domestic abuse and the plethora of issues that arise as a result:

> First of all, I'd need to absolutely ensure that they [ministers] know what domestic violence is. I've been to a minister and he didn't know if and what it incorporated, which made it totally worse. So first of all, they would have to know and understand what domestic violence is.

Rachel expresses a marked level of personal confidence in the services provided by the Domestic Violence Telephone Service (now DVConnect). She recommends this service to members of the clergy, in addition to the training offered at the time by the Joint Churches Domestic Violence Prevention Project:

> I think the best thing that they can do is while the woman's in the office with them, just to ring the telephone service and find out all the options for the woman. Our minister is one of two ministers that attend the Joint Churches Domestic Violence training that's offered in Brisbane. He has gone every year and taken other members of the eldership with him I think the last time. But last year when he went, he was either the only one that went or there were two ministers that went.

Demonstrate Love

In many ways, the concept of demonstrating love to suffering individuals embraces every suggestion that has been offered to members of the clergy by the women interviewed. A description of the expectation of Christian love is provided by the Apostle Paul in 1 Corinthians

13:4–7 (Hiebert, 1981; Funderburk, 1975b). Again, the Greek word used for love in this instance is *agape*, which denotes the form of love expressed by God for His people (Gill, 2002; Mare, 1976). Metz (1968) describes this form of love, not only as 'Christlike', but also as 'the parent of patience and kindness' (p. 440). This form of support, when offered by members of the clergy, in addition to members of their congregation, has the potential to provide substantial levels of reassurance and empowerment to victims of domestic abuse, who are then able to sense 'a compassion that validates their loss and pain as wrong', and also an 'encouragement to resist the dehumanizing effects' (Ramsay, 1999, p. 54) of the abuse they have suffered.

Four women reinforced the need for love and compassion to be demonstrated towards victims of domestic abuse. Ruth links the action of loving and guiding with the attitudes of acceptance and compassion, and explains what she would like to gain from members of the clergy:

> … an acknowledgment of what I've been through, but not to ponder on it — to rise above it and find ways of just dealing with it. Not necessarily physical things. One priest said to me, 'Ruth, if you just find peace within your self, there will come peace around you'. And I have never forgotten that.

Throughout the duration of the interview, Mary frequently mentioned the caring nature of her priest, together with the manner in which he endeavoured to nurture her through the difficulties she was facing. Mary views the demonstration of love as potentially the most significant, single, positive action that can be taken by members of the clergy when dealing with victims of domestic abuse. She elucidates:

> It doesn't matter what it is. It is the love that's within a situation or within a person that will be most help to you. You've got to tell them that they're loved. You've got to show them that they're a very special person — that they are special in their own right and they are loved by God.

Demonstrate Respect

While respect for an individual may be able to exist outside the parameters of demonstrating love, love in the form of agape cannot be truly active without also incorporating the presence of genuine respect for the individual in question. When applying this concept to victims of domestic abuse, if members of the clergy are responding in accordance with the description of love provided in 1 Corinthians 13:4–7, they must also be responding with an attitude of respect for the dignity, autonomy and individuality of the victim and her situation. Metz (1968) explains that love in this context demonstrates a 'proper respect' (p. 441) for those over whom one has authority. Coupled with this is the overall desire to 'seek the well-being of others' (p. 441), a concept which again demands the demonstration of respect towards victims of domestic abuse.

Three of the women mentioned the need for members of the clergy to demonstrate respect for those women who present to them as victims of domestic abuse. Ruth mentioned respect as an integral part of her expectation when seeking assistance from members of the clergy, whereas Joanna placed the concept of demonstrating respect more within the framework of valuing the person as a whole, rather than focusing solely on the situation.

Sarah expresses only praise for the priest who assisted her throughout her ordeal, and explains the varying ways in which he chose to demonstrate respect for her as an individual:

> He listened. He didn't treat it as — I should just get above all this, that I should keep to my — you know, he didn't have a lot of 'shoulds' to it. He dealt with stuff that came up for me, as it came up for me. So he was respectful of what was happening for me. And in hindsight, was probably aware of where it was going from the moment I phoned him ... but didn't necessarily bounce onto that. He didn't have all the answers. And he doesn't, and that's what I love about him. And when I was ready to have a laugh about it, he joined in which was good [laugh].

In this excerpt, Sarah highlights the fact that members of the clergy do not have, and are not expected to have, all the necessary answers for every situation. Frequently, members of the clergy can function only with the skills and information available to them, but this does not lessen the need for respect or the sense of empowerment such respect can provide for the victim of domestic abuse.

Avoid Issues of Male Headship

Buxton (2000) suggests that accentuating the hierarchical nature of female submission to male headship has the potential to 'reinforce the dysfunctional patterns of relating' (p. 57) that already exist in relationships where domestic abuse is present. He further maintains that adopting such a position can excuse the abusive behaviour of an already violent perpetrator (see chapter 7). Leehan (1992) also considers the emphasis on issues of male headship to be detrimental to victims of domestic abuse. Members of the clergy must refrain from delivering to victims of domestic abuse meaningless platitudes relating to wifely submission and duty (Miles, 1997).

While a number of the women reported experiencing difficulties as a result of their church embracing the concept of female submission to male headship (see chapter 7), only one directly mentioned it in specific advice to members of the clergy. Esther's frustration is apparent when she says, 'and don't go on about the ... head of the house issue'. Esther had reported earlier in her interview that she felt her belief in this concept 'made it [her situation] worse'.

Confront the Perpetrator

There are a number of ways in which perpetrators may be confronted regarding their actions. While a direct confrontation may be considered an appropriate option when a member of the clergy is specifically aware of the existence of domestic abuse in a particular family, other options are available. Patterson (1998) refers to preaching as 'nonviolent resistance' (p. 99). Individual members of the clergy who wish to confront issues of domestic abuse in a less direct manner may elect to use weekly sermons to indicate and illustrate the stand of the church; conduct Bible studies centred around relevant topics, such as Jesus' own attitude to women (see chapter 7); or perhaps conduct seminars designed to raise overall congregational awareness of domestic abuse (Leehan, 1992; Miles, 1997). Unfortunately, very few members of the clergy actually choose this option (Miles, 2000; Nason-Clark, 2000a, 2000b).

Deborah advises in favour of members of the clergy confronting the perpetrator directly, and establishes a link between the presence of specific consequences for the perpetrator and a sense of empowerment for the victim of domestic abuse. She clarifies her position:

Confront the perpetrator. Give the victim a validity for life. Give them a reason to live. But I think validating a women is probably one of the most important things that she can have in what she's going though. For some really will endure a lot and I just ... if they [members of the clergy] can call the men in and say, well, look, you know for this ... for this period of time, you won't be able to ... perhaps partake of the sacrament, or you're not going to be able to offer prayers in our meetings. You know, something that's going to wake them up ... But I think too, it would have been helpful to me if my bishop had said, 'Look, he's not allowed to pray in any church meetings'. Then I would have thought, 'Oh. You've heard what I said. You've taken notice of what I've said'. I think ... don't leave the wife, the spouse out in the dark. Let them know. And it's not breaking any confidentiality. It's just saying, 'I've heard what you've said. What you've said is relevant and these are the conditions I've placed on it'.

Final Words of Direction

Many members of the clergy are genuine in their endeavour to assist congregational members to the best of their ability. However, there eventually must come a point of realisation when both victims of domestic abuse and members of the clergy openly acknowledge that there is a limit to the services that can be confidently and effectively provided by clergy members who are not specifically trained to deal with domestic abuse. Such healthy acknowledgment of one's own limitations has the potential to foster the formation of a more acceptable solution for both members of the clergy and the congregational members whom they are attempting to assist.

Speaking first to victims of domestic abuse, Joanna expresses a firm belief in the fact that members of the clergy do not always have an understanding of what is happening for the victim, and accentuates the extremely serious nature of living with domestic abuse:

They [victims of domestic abuse] need to know that God doesn't like this sort of thing going on. And pastors and people in the church don't know everything that goes on, and they don't know ... even you can tell them, but they don't experience it. They can't, they don't know what it's like to ... that you might, gonna die in a second. That to be that frightened. So ... ohhh [sigh] ... it's just so hard, 'cause I know how the church is.

Eve addresses her remarks to members of the clergy, stating:

Admit that you can't help them, that it's out of your league and it is not a spiritual problem. It ... there's emotional issues, psychological issues, issues of abuse. It's got nothing to do with the church, and they [victims of domestic abuse] need professional help. And to acknowledge that, even if they had professional, trained counsellors who had Christian beliefs but ... Christian counselling only confuses the issue. And they need to advise people to go and see professional counsellors.

Choosing a Proactive Approach

In Germany, during World War II, one church chose to make a stand against the influence of the Nazi regime. This was not the established church but a breakaway organisation, referred to as the Confessing church, which recognised the need for strength in the face of an overwhelming move for domination and control that threatened the wellbeing of vast numbers of innocent individuals (Cairns, 1996; Kalland, L.A., 1992). The uncompromising nature of the stand adopted by the Confessing church drew the attention of Albert Einstein who, in his letter to *The New York Times* in December 1940, stated:

As a lover of freedom, when the revolution [Nazism] came to Germany, I looked to the universities to defend it [freedom] ... But no, the universities were immediately silenced. Then I looked to the great editors of the newspapers — they, like the universities, were silenced in a few weeks. Only the church [Confessing church] stood squarely across the path of Hitler's campaign for suppressing truth. I never had any special interest in the church before, but now I feel a great affection and admiration for it. I am forced to confess that what I once despised, I now praise unreservedly. (Ringma, n.d., pp. 225–226)

One may initially question the necessity for such a strong and uncompromising stand to be made by the Christian church of the 21st century. However, as domestic abuse continues to pose an ever-present threat to individuals in society, including those within the Christian church, the need to make a determined stand against a tyrannical desire for domination and control over the lives of other individuals is of paramount importance. Such a stand is possible as a result of choices made by individual members of the clergy, in addition to those made by churches as a whole. The following section will briefly consider some of the issues relevant to developing a proactive approach to overcoming the presence of domestic abuse within the Christian church. These include denouncing injustice, developing church policies, and establishing networks within the church and the community.

Denounce Injustice

A clear and concise message denouncing injustice in all its forms is necessary if members of the clergy desire their congregations to adopt a proactive position regarding domestic abuse. Injustice was commonly denounced by the prophets of the Old Testament (Keener, 1996). The prophet Isaiah calls the people of God to turn away from wickedness and instead 'relieve the oppressed' and 'plead for the widow' (Isaiah 1:16–17). Grogan (1986) considers this a call for a commitment to social justice. Expanding on this concept is the declaration by the prophet that God will not hear the prayers of those individuals who continue religious rituals but choose not to live according to the professions of their faith (Isaiah 58:3–7). Such rituals are 'empty' (Grogan, p. 322) and achieve nothing.

Violence also was clearly labelled as unacceptable. The prophet Malachi (2:16) openly denounces the use of violence (see chapter 6). Other Scriptures declare that God will eventually judge those who embrace violence (Psalms 11:5) (Purkiser, 1967; VanGemeren, 1991), and that perpetrators of violence will be destroyed as a result of their own choices (Proverbs 21:7) (Ross, 1991; Wolf, 1967). Violence is also linked to injustice (Psalms 58:2). VanGemeren describes these individuals as 'evil in the very core of their being' (p. 406). Perpetrators of violence are depicted as liars (Proverbs 10:6), who plot evil (Proverbs 24:2).

In direct contrast to the violence and injustice attributed to the wicked is the image of a loving and just God whose desire it is to protect and nurture the oppressed. Nowhere is this concept so exquisitely illustrated as in Psalm 91, where those who place their trust in God and seek His assistance are depicted as sheltering under His wings, just as young birds would flee for refuge under the feathered wings of their protector (Horne, n.d.; Kirkpatrick, 1933; Leslie, 1949; Schaefer, 2001). This is not an image of a God who approves of violence, but rather of one who condemns it as unrighteous and ungodly behaviour.

This message, focusing succinctly on an unquestionable intolerance of violence and abuse in any form, is one that must be brought to congregations if they are to be expected to recognise the reality of issues surrounding domestic abuse. Herein lies the responsibility of those members of the clergy who nurture a desire to defend and protect the innocent, and call abusers to account (Fortune, 1991).

Develop Policies

Policies must be developed and utilised in an effort to raise congregational awareness, nurture and protect victims, and confront perpetrators (Graham & Fortune, 1993). Beck (1998) advises that churches should adopt a policy permitting them to respond to domestic abuse in the same manner that would be expected of Jesus. This includes the ability to recognise domestic abuse for what it is and the willingness to take action against it, showing compassion for the victim and confronting the perpetrator. Such a position results in the creation of a safe haven in which victims of domestic abuse are able to seek shelter. A policy should never be designed with the intention of covering or excusing the sinful actions of the perpetrator (Graham & Fortune).

Rachel explains the essential nature of a church establishing a policy and a structure for dealing with issues of domestic abuse. The eldership of her church, as well as members of the congregation, are aware of the precise procedure to follow should a member of the church, or perhaps a nonmember, present as a victim of domestic abuse. Rachel provides insight into the benefits of the policy adopted by her church:

> We've got DV [domestic violence] as a structure of the committee. And so if someone turns up at our minister's office with regard to DV, he knows who to call. So they call me or they'll call someone else ... in that ... or like I've had the elders that have received phone calls and they've flipped them over to me. And, you know, with the permission of the person ... Most churches have a foyer with noticeboards and stuff. There's always something there about DV and about help lines and ... I was part of the committee last year that produced a safety card for the north side of Brisbane. So we always, like, there's always some down at the church. And Domestic Violence Week we always have someone do stuff in the church on that week.

Some of the strategies described by Rachel — such as availability of information cards, the utilisation of church noticeboards or the extending of invitations to guest speakers — are neither difficult nor time consuming. However, these simple measures have the capacity to serve as an almost silent indication of the position of the church regarding domestic abuse, thereby encouraging victims of domestic abuse to come forward, knowing that they will receive the assistance they require in an environment that offers love and acceptance.

Network

Networking involves establishing ongoing working relationships with professionals and other community organisations in an effort to ensure that a positive balance of spiritual and professional care is provided for victims of domestic abuse. Such action also ensures the effective utilisation of all available resources (Fortune, 1991; Graham & Fortune, 1993). Ellison and Hewey (1995) support the need for high levels of cooperation between churches and community organisations specifically equipped to deal with situations regarding domestic abuse, viewing it as a necessary focal point for training seminars. As a single entity, the Christian church lacks the skills and resources required to actively confront and deal with the multifaceted nature of domestic abuse. However, working in conjunction with secular organisations — including welfare, police and legal services — it remains possible for the church to become an active force in confronting the injustice of domestic abuse (Fortune & Poling, 1995).

Summary

Based upon the prevalence of domestic abuse both within society as a whole and within the Christian church, this chapter supports the need for positive levels of ongoing intervention by the Christian church in relation to issues of domestic abuse. Advice provided by the women interviewed is utilised in an endeavour to highlight a number of the primary areas for concern, such as the need to demonstrate love and respect towards the victim of domestic abuse by believing, supporting and actively listening to her while refraining from judging her. Coupled with this is the need for pastoral training and awareness regarding the nature of domestic abuse, as victims of domestic abuse are rarely equipped to take a strong stand from an almost totally isolated position, and frequently require the assistance of professional care workers, including members of the clergy. Thus, the wisdom, knowledge and skills available to members of the clergy are considered to be of paramount importance.

Finally, the call for members of the clergy to publicly denounce injustice through the aid of sermons and seminars, while privately working within the structure of church committees to develop relevant policies to assist the church in providing the necessary support and care for victims of domestic abuse, is presented as an essential element in the role of any church wishing to make a formal stand against the presence of domestic abuse within society and within its walls. Networking with welfare, legal, and other aid organisations already operating within the community is highlighted as a practical means by which to ensure the availability of immediate assistance should the need arise.

Reflections for the Counsellor

1. What value can you see in the advice offered by the women in this chapter?
2. How is this advice relevant to clients who uphold the Christian faith?
3. What are the key points of connection for those clients?

Client Discussion

1. How do you currently feel about your Christian faith?
   - What is your present undertaking in this area (e.g. attending church or other meetings; personal devotions)?
2. What forms of assistance have you sought to date?
3. What would you need to do to come to a place where you could trust your own judgment and not second-guess yourself?
4. What sort of choices do you feel you now have?
5. What would you like to do/achieve now?
   - Do you have a strategy in place to achieve this? If so, what?
6. What sort of assistance would you like at this point?
7. What would you most like to say to:
   - victims of domestic abuse and
   - members of the clergy?

CHAPTER 10

Final Words

M uch can be gained by listening to and learning from the experiences of others. This chapter provides a brief review of the material presented, offering a succinct summary of the content of the book and its relevance to the issue of Christian women identifying as victims of domestic abuse. Suggestions made by the women interviewed, to both victims of abuse and to members of the clergy, form the final response to some difficult questions. The wisdom and insight gained by the women provides a guide for those who desire to expand their knowledge regarding domestic abuse and the needs of Christian women (see chapter 9).

Christian Women Dealing with Domestic Abuse

Like many of their nonreligious counterparts, Christian women who experience domestic abuse also experience marked levels of confusion due to the conflicting behaviour of a perpetrator who professes love and yet continues to inflict physical and/or emotional pain through a variety of forms of abuse. The cycle of abuse, with its repetitive pattern of abuse intermingled with periods of seemingly positive and caring behaviour, serves only to increase the confusion experienced by the victims, leaving them unable to clearly and accurately assess the serious nature of the situation (see chapter 3).

Beyond the initial questioning and confusion, most of the women represented turned to members of the clergy for advice and practical assistance in dealing with domestic abuse. Uncertain of how to deal with abuse in any of its forms, these Christian women expected their ministers to be able to provide not only a level of spiritual insight but also much needed compassion and understanding. In some instances (Mary, Susanna, Sarah), this was indeed the case, and the women were able to gain the required assistance. However, in a number of other cases (Elizabeth, Anna, Deborah), the women were met with condemnation and even revictimisation from the very church leaders to whom they turned for assistance.

In cases where the women were able to receive positive communication and encouragement from members of the clergy, they continued to utilise this avenue of support over a period of time (Mary, Sarah), combining it with other aspects of their faith and sometimes with assistance from professional services. In cases where ministerial support was not forthcoming, or was instead supplanted by criticism and condemnation, the women (Elizabeth, Deborah) were forced to rely upon their own personal experience of faith in an endeavour to find the appropriate solution. Additionally, when options of ministerial assistance failed, some women (Rachel, Elizabeth) eventually turned to secular organisations in an effort to learn of the dynamics of domestic abuse and ultimately develop a functional strategy.

While the process of dealing with domestic abuse was in no way linear, the women interviewed appeared to methodically work through each situation, diligently searching for a solution. As part of this process, most individuals turned to members of the clergy, and also to their own personal faith-centred resources, choosing to operate according to the overarching principle of focusing on one day at a time.

The Connection Between Faith and Survival

Physical, as well as emotional, survival are key concerns for victims of domestic abuse. Each day presents a challenge for women who are endeavouring to maintain their relationship and raise their children while ensuring the overall safety of the family (Ruth, Miriam). The unpredictable nature of perpetrator behaviour contributes significantly to the anxiety brought about by constant vigilance, as the victim watches carefully for any sign of conflict, trying to either console the perpetrator or minimise the effect of the outburst (see chapters 3 and 4).

Christian women appear to rely heavily on their faith as part of their survival strategy. The various components of the Christian faith — the belief in an ever-present, all-powerful, all-knowing and loving God, who hears and answers prayers and cares for the wellbeing of His people represents a primary source of strength, courage and hope for Christian women endeavouring to deal with the trauma of domestic abuse. The image of one who cares, listens, guides, and protects provides the Christian woman with somewhere to turn during times of crisis, together with the hope of a more positive future. The belief that God would in some way intervene empowered the women to continue on a daily basis despite the often unrelenting pressure of the environment in which they lived (see chapter 8). A foundational childhood faith was seen as a predominant influence on the lives of those women who had been raised in an environment where religion was actively practised (Mary, Lydia, Susanna, Deborah).

While the role of faith in the lives of Christian women appears to vary slightly according to the specific needs of each individual, it carries with it a confidence and a reassurance that eventually both physical and emotional needs would be met, emphasising that the ultimate plan of God for His people has a positive outcome (Jeremiah 29:11). A number of the women (Miriam, Eunice) reported that on occasions when there appeared to be no possible solution for their situation, circumstances unexpectedly turned in their favour. Others (Elizabeth, Rachel, Deborah) reported gaining strength, peace and hope as a direct result of their Christian faith (see chapter 8). A steadfast trust in both the ability and willingness of God to meet specific needs, or to sustain the individual throughout times of trial, contributes significantly to the ability of Christian women to deal with issues of domestic abuse on a daily basis, and eventually to terminate the relationship should they so choose.

Specific Coping Strategies Employed by Christian Women Faced with Domestic Abuse

All the women represented employed a functional blend of both religious and nonreligious coping strategies. Initially, they primarily turned to their already established relationship with God in an effort to understand, and also to find a solution to, the problems surrounding domestic abuse. Closely associated with maintaining a relationship with God was the strategy of prayer, which again focused on both coping with the presenting situation and seeking a solution. The women interviewed were unanimous in their choice to employ both these strategies as a primary response to dealing with domestic abuse. Flowing from an intimate relationship with God, and the use of prayer, was the expectation that God would fulfil the promises of peace and protection contained within the Scriptures. Drawing inspiration from the Scriptures encouraged the women to focus on the positive assurances of hope and trust (Psalms, Romans 8:28), nurture and protection (Isaiah 40:11), hope for the future (Jeremiah 29:11), peace and restoration (Gospels, Philippians 4:6–7), and ultimate justice (Habakkuk). Finally, some women (Joanna, Elizabeth) found it uplifting to incorporate all of the above strategies in an expression of scriptural song, which provided them with the opportunity to utilise their musical prowess while combining prayer and Scripture in a worshipful relationship with their heavenly Father (see chapter 8).

In a similar manner to religious coping strategies, the nonreligious coping strategies employed by the women shared the common goal of endeavouring to solve the problems of domestic abuse while carefully balancing the emotional repercussions of living in an abusive environment. Those expressing a high level of concern regarding the impact of domestic abuse on their children selectively focused on the physical and emotional wellbeing of those children, endeavouring to meet their needs through whatever means possible. They also focused on a selection of activities, ranging from immersing themselves in the daily routine of the household (Mary, Susanna), to undertaking specific courses or hobbies as a source of distraction (Leah, Eunice, Anna). Reading proved a pertinent source of information for a number of the women (Elizabeth, Mary, Lois), thus increasing their ability to both understand and cope with the dynamics of domestic abuse. Planning also provided individual women with an increased sense of control, thereby assisting them to choose an appropriate course of action (see chapter 8).

While the coping strategies employed by the Christian women represented are a blend of both spiritual and practical resources, each choice is undergirded by the belief and the expectation that God is in control and will direct the steps of those who turn to Him, a concept that is reflected in the words of Psalm 37, which declares, 'The steps of a good man [person] are ordered by the Lord: and he delights in his way. Though he fall, he shall not be utterly cast down: for the Lord upholdeth him with his hand' (Vs. 23–24; Purkiser, 1967; VanGemeren, 1991). A recurring factor influencing the choice of coping strategies of many of the women proved to be a foundational Christian faith upon which their belief system had been established at a very young age.

How Christian Women Comment on Their Experiences

Throughout the course of the interviews, the women were provided with the opportunity to share their stories and express their feelings and beliefs relating to their experiences. The chance to be heard and have their experiences recognised and validated proved beneficial for many of them. Providing pertinent advice for both victims of domestic abuse and for members of the clergy, however, was perhaps the more significant opportunity, as doing so was in keeping with their original motivation to assist others, and it governed the choice of a number of the women to come forward and share their stories (see chapter 2).

The advice offered by the women to both victims of domestic abuse and to members of the clergy is based on the their own personal experience of domestic abuse, and also on the treatment each one received from the members of the clergy to whom they turned for assistance. The women represented chose to highlight the areas of key concern in an effort to raise awareness among victims of domestic abuse and the members of the clergy who are called upon to assist them.

Moving Forward: Harmony of Purpose

The Christian women represented throughout this publication appear to rely heavily on their faith in an effort to cope during times of crisis. Such an awareness of the needs of these Christian women should contribute to an increase in the sensitivity of the church as a whole. Further, the realisation of the deleterious effect of a negative church response — on both the individual and her faith — should act as a catalyst to motivate the church to positive action. Ultimately, it should be ensured that victims of domestic abuse who turn to the church, for either practical or spiritual support, receive a compassionate and caring response that is void of judgment or condemnation.

Pivotal to any congregational change in direction or attitude are the personal choices and attitudes of the individual clergy person who presides over any given congregation. A motivated and caring leader has the opportunity to develop egalitarian and community-based policies conducive to addressing issues of domestic abuse within the local congregation. Thus, the training and overall education of upcoming members of the clergy are crucial in establishing a new generation of clergy who are not only aware of the existing difficulties, but are also willing to address them openly and without conventional bias.

Finally, the depth of insight and the value of this publication is seen in the courage of those women who chose to 'speak up for those who cannot speak for themselves', in an effort to 'ensure justice for those who are perishing' (Proverbs 31:8).

References

Abrahams, H. (2007). *Supporting women after domestic violence: Loss trauma and recovery.* London: Jessica Kingsley.

Adams, C.J. (1994). *Woman-battering.* Minneapolis, MN: Fortress Press.

Adams, D. (1988). Treatment models of men who batter. In K. Yllo & M. Bograd (Eds.), *Feminist perspectives on wife abuse* (pp. 176–199). Newbury Park, CA: Sage.

Alden, R.L. (1985). Malachi. In F.E. Gaebelein (Ed.), *The expositor's Bible commentary* (Vol. 7, pp. 701–725). Grand Rapids, MI: Zondervan Publishing House.

Alexander, R.H. (1986). Ezekiel. In F.E. Gaebelein (Ed.), *The expositor's Bible commentary* (Vol. 6, pp. 735–996). Grand Rapids, MI: Zondervan Publishing House.

Allen, R.B. (1990). Numbers. In F.E. Gaebelein (Ed.), *The expositor's Bible commentary* (Vol. 2, pp. 655–1008). Grand Rapids, MI: Zondervan Publishing House.

Alsdurf, J.M. (1985, Winter). Wife abuse and the church. *Response.*

Alsdurf, J., & Alsdurf, P. (1989). *Battered into submission: The tragedy of wife abuse in the Christian home.* Guildford, UK: Highland Books.

Amnesty International Australia. (2005a). *It's in our hands to stop violence against women.* [Brochure]. Broadway, NSW.

Amnesty International Australia. (2005b). *Stop violence against women.* [Brochure]. Broadway, NSW.

Anderson, K.L. (2002). Perpetrator or victim? Relationships between intimate partner violence and well-being. *Journal of Marriage and Family, 64*(4), 851–863.

Anderson, M.A., Gillig, P.M., Sitaker, M., McCloskey, K., Malloy, K., & Grigsby, N. (2003). 'Why doesn't she just leave?': A descriptive study of victim reported impediments to her safety. *Journal of Family Violence, 18*(3), 151–155.

Armerding, C.E. (1985). Habakkuk. In F.E. Gaebelein (Ed.), *The expositor's Bible commentary* (Vol. 7, pp. 491–534). Grand Rapids, MI: Zondervan Publishing House.

Arnold, C.E. (2002a). Ephesians. In C.E. Arnold (Ed.), *Zondervan illustrated Bible backgrounds commentary* (Vol. 3, pp. 300–341). Grand Rapids, MI: Zondervan Publishing House.

Arnold, C.E. (2002b). Colossians. In C.E. Arnold (Ed.), *Zondervan illustrated Bible backgrounds commentary* (Vol. 3, pp. 370–403). Grand Rapids, MI: Zondervan Publishing House.

Ashur, M.L.C., & Witwer, M.B. (1993). Asking about domestic violence: SAFE. *Journal of the American Medical Association, 269*(18), 2367.

Atkinson, D. (1979). *To have and to hold: The marriage covenant and the discipline of divorce.* Grand Rapids, MI: Eerdmans.

Atkinson, D.J. (1995). Remarriage. In D.J. Atkinson & D.H. Field (Eds.), *New dictionary of Christian ethics and pastoral theology* (pp. 729–730). Leicester, UK: Inter-Varsity Press.

Atkinson, R. (2002). The life story interview. In J.F. Gubrium and J.A. Holstein (Eds.), *Handbook of interview research: Context and method* (pp. 121–140). Thousand Oaks, CA: Sage.

Bagshaw, D., & Chung, D. (2000). *Women, men and domestic violence*. University of South Australia.

Bahr, N. (2007a). Emotional aspects. In N. Bahr & D. Pendergast (Eds.), *The millennial adolescent* (pp. 131–173). Camberwell, Victoria: ACER.

Bahr, N. (2007b). Social beings. In N. Bahr & D. Pendergast (Eds.), *The millennial adolescent* (pp. 174–199). Camberwell, Victoria: ACER.

Baker, L.M. (1998). The role of the church: A political perspective. *Jubilee International Christian College Occasional Papers, 1*(1), 17–21.

Barabas, S. (1981a). Forgiveness. In M.C. Tenney (Ed.), *The Zondervan pictorial Bible dictionary* (pp. 289). Grand Rapids, MI: Zondervan Publishing House.

Barabas, S. (1981b). Bible. In M.C. Tenney (Ed.), *The Zondervan pictorial Bible dictionary* (pp. 115–117). Grand Rapids, MI: Zondervan Publishing House.

Barabas, S. (1981c). Jezebel. In M.C. Tenney (Ed.), *The Zondervan pictorial Bible dictionary* (pp. 431). Grand Rapids, MI: Zondervan Publishing House.

Barnett, O.W. (2001). Why battered women do not leave, part 2: External inhibiting factors, social support, and internal inhibiting factors. *Trauma Violence and Abuse, 2*(1), 3–25.

Barnett, O.W., & LaViolette, A.D. (1993). *It could happen to anyone: Why women stay*. Newbury Park, CA: Sage.

Basham, B., & Lisherness, S. (Eds.). (1997). *Striking terror no more: The church responds to domestic violence*. Louisville, KY: Bridge Resources.

Bass, C.B. (1981). Repentance. In M.C. Tenney (Ed.), *The Zondervan pictorial Bible dictionary* (pp. 711–712). Grand Rapids, MI: Zondervan Publishing House.

Baumeister, R. (Ed.). (1986). *Public self and private self*. New York: Springer-Verlag.

Baumeister, R. (1997). *Evil: Inside human violence and cruelty*. New York: W.H. Freeman and Co.

Baumeister, R., & Boden, J.M. (1998). Aggression and the self: High self-esteem, low self-control, and ego threat. In R.G. Geen & E. Donnerstein (Eds.), *Human aggression: Theories, research, and implications for social policy* (pp. 111–137). San Diego, CA: Academic Press.

Beall, A., & Sternberg, R.J. (Eds.). (1993). *The psychology of gender*. New York: Guilford Press.

Beattie, M. (1989). *Beyond codependency*. Center City, MN: Hazelden.

Beck, J.R. (1998). What can the church do? In C.C. Kroeger & J.R. Beck (Eds.), *Healing the hurting: Giving hope and help to abused women* (pp. 233–237). Grand Rapids, MI: Baker Books.

Beed, C. (1998). *Cultures of secrecy and abuse: A paradox for the church*. Hawthorn, Victoria: Ross Co.

Bennett, W.H. (1895). *The book of Jeremiah: Chapters XXL-LII*. London: Hodder & Stoughton.

Bergant, D. (2001). *The song of songs*. Collegeville, MN: The Liturgical Press.

Bergen, A., & McConatha, J.T. (2000). Religiosity and life satisfaction. *Activities, Adaptation and Aging, 24*(3), 22–23.

Berry, D.B. (1998). *Domestic violence sourcebook*. Los Angeles, CA: Lowell House.

Best, H.M., & Huttar, D.K. (1975). Music: Musical instruments. In M.C. Tenney (Ed.), *The Zondervan pictorial encyclopedia of the Bible* (Vol. 4, pp. 311–324). Grand Rapids, MI: Zondervan Publishing House.

Bickel, C.O., Ciarrocchi, J.W., Sheers, N.J., Estadt, B.K., Powell, D.A., & Pargament, K.I. (1998). Perceived stress, religious coping styles, and depressive affect. *Journal of Psychology and Christianity, 17*(1), 33–42.

Biderman, A., & Zimmer, H. (1961). *The manipulation of human behavior.* New York: John Wiley and Sons.

Bishop, J., & Grunte, M. (1993). *How to forgive when you don't know how.* New York: Station Hill Press.

Bjorck, J.P. (1997). Religiousness and coping: Implications for clinical practice. *Journal of Psychology and Christianity, 16*(1), 73–79.

Black, D.A., Heyman, R.E., & Slep, A.M. (2001). Risk factors for male-to-female partner sexual abuse. *Aggression and Violent Behavior, 6,* 269–280.

Black, D.A., Slep, A.M., & Heyman, R.E. (2001). Risk factors for child psychological abuse. *Aggression and Violent Behavior, 6,* 189–201.

Blaiklock, E.M. (1981). Samaritans. In M.C. Tenney (Ed.), *The Zondervan pictorial Bible dictionary* (pp. 746–747). Grand Rapids, MI: Zondervan Publishing House.

Blaine, B.E., & Trivedi, P. (1998). Religious belief and the self-concept: Evaluating the implications for psychological adjustment. *Personality and Psychology Bulletin, 24*(10), 1040–1052.

Blanchard, A. (1999). *Caring for child victims of domestic violence.* Western Australia: Nandina Press.

Blum, E.A. (1981). 1 Peter. In F.E. Gaebelein (Ed.), *The expositor's Bible commentary* (Vol. 12, pp. 207–254). Grand Rapids, MI: Zondervan Publishing House.

Bograd, M. (1988). Feminist perspecitves on wife abuse: An introduction. In K. Yllo & M. Bograd (Eds.), *Feminist perspectives on wife abuse* (pp. 11–26). Newbury Park, CA: Sage.

Boice, J.M. (1986). Galatians. In F.E. Gaebelein (Ed.), *The expositor's Bible commentary* (Vol. 10, pp. 407–508). Grand Rapids, MI: Zondervan Publishing House.

Bolden, G. (1997). Ministry tools to eliminate violence. *Church and Society, 87,* 38–41.

Bolger, N., DeLongis, A., Kessler, R.C., & Schilling, E. (1989). Effects of daily stress on negative mood. *Journal of Personality and Social Psychology, 57*(5), 808–818.

Bonhoeffer, D. (1959). *The cost of discipleship.* London: SCM Press Ltd.

Borchert, G. (1999, Winter). 1 Corinthians 7:15 and the church's historic misunderstanding of divorce and remarriage. *Review and Expositor, 96,* 125–129.

Borkowski, M., Murch, M., & Walker, V. (1983). *Marital violence: The community response.* London: Tavistock Publications.

Borland, J.A. (1991). Women in the life and teachings of Jesus. In J. Piper & W. Grudem (Eds.), *Recovering biblical manhood and womanhood: A response to feminism* (pp. 113–123). Wheaton, IL: Crossways.

Bowker, L.H. (1993). A battered woman's problems are social, not psychological. In R.J. Gelles & D.R. Loseke (Eds.), *Current controversies on family violence* (pp. 154–165). Newbury Park, CA: Sage.

Bowker, L.H., Arbitell, M., & McFerron, J.R. (1988). On the relationship between wife beating and child abuse. In K. Yllo & M. Bograd (Eds.), *Feminist perspectives on wife abuse* (pp. 158–174). Newbury Park, CA: Sage.

Briggs, C.A., & Briggs, E.G. (1906). *The book of psalms.* Edinburgh: T & T Clark.

Brockmeyer, D.M., & Sheridan, D.J. (1998). Domestic violence: A practical guide to the use of forensic evaluation in clinical examination and documentation of injuries. In J. Campbell (Ed.), *Empowering survivors of abuse: Health care for battered women and their children* (pp. 214–226). London: Sage.

Brown, L.B. (1994). An experimental perspective as a therapeutic resource. In H. Grzymala-Moszczynska & B. Beit-Hallahmi (Eds.), *Religion, psychology and coping* (pp. 159–176). Amsterdam: Rodopi.

Browne, A. (1987). *When battered women kill*. New York: Free Press.

Browne, K., & Herbert, M. (1997). *Preventing family violence*. New York: Wiley and Sons.

Browning, D. (2004a). The problem of men. In D. Blankenhorn, D. Browning & M.S. Van Leeuwen (Eds.), *Does Christianity teach male headship?* (pp. 3–12). Grand Rapids, MI: Eerdmans.

Browning, D. (2004b). Reflections on the debate. In D. Blankenhorn, D. Browning & M.S. Van Leeuwen (Eds.), *Does Christianity teach male headship?* (pp. 126–138). Grand Rapids, MI: Eerdmans.

Browning, J., & Dutton, D. (1986). Assessment of wife assault with the conflict tactics scale: Using couple data to quantify the differential reporting effect. *Journal of Marriage and the Family, 48*(1), 275–379.

Brownmiller, S. (1975). *Against our will: Men, women and rape*. New York: Simon and Schuster.

Brownridge, D.A., & Halli, S.S. (2000). 'Living in sin' and sinful living: Toward filling a gap in the explanation of violence against women. *Aggression and Violent Behavior, 5*(6), 565–583.

Bruce, F.F. (1975). Epistle to the Romans. In M.C. Tenney (Ed.), *The Zondervan pictorial encyclopedia of the Bible* (Vol. 5, pp. 148–161). Grand Rapids, MI: Zondervan Publishing House.

Bruce, F.F. (1989). Philippians. In W.W. Gasque (Ed.), *New international biblical commentary*. Peabody, MA: Hendrickson.

Burdick, D.W. (1981). James. In F.E. Gaebelein (Ed.), *The expositor's Bible commentary* (Vol. 12, pp. 159–205). Grand Rapids, MI: Zondervan Publishing House.

Burke, C. (1999). Redressing the balance: Child protection intervention in the context of domestic violence. In J. Breckenridge & L. Laing (Eds.), *Challenging silence: Innovative responses to sexual and domestic violence* (pp. 256–267). St Leonards, NSW: Allen and Unwin.

Buswell, J.O. (1981). Truth. In M.C. Tenney (Ed.), *The Zondervan pictorial Bible dictionary* (pp. 872–873). Grand Rapids, MI: Zondervan Publishing House.

Buxton, R. (2000). Domestic violence in the church: 'There is an elephant in the sanctuary and no one is talking about it'. *Didaskalia, 12*(1), 51–75.

Caesar, P.L. (1988). Exposure to violence in the families-of-origin among wife-abusers and maritally nonviolent men. *Violence and Victims, 3*(1), 49–63.

Cahill, L.S. (2004). The feminist pope. In D. Blankenhorn, D. Browning & M.S. Van Leeuwen (Eds.), *Does Christianity teach male headship?* (pp. 40–48). Grand Rapids, MI: William B. Eerdmans.

Cairns, E.E. (Ed.). (1996). *Christianity through the centuries* (3rd ed.). Grand Rapids, MI: Zondervan Publishing House.

Campbell, J.C. (1998). Making the health care system an empowerment zone for battered women: Health consequences, policy recommendations, introduction and overview. In J. Campbell (Ed.), *Empowering survivors of abuse: Health care for battered women and their children* (pp. 3–31). London: Sage.

Cansdale, G.S. (1975a). Fox. In M.C. Tenney (Ed.), *The Zondervan pictorial encyclopedia of the Bible* (Vol. 2, pp. 605–606). Grand Rapids, MI: Zondervan Publishing House.

Cansdale, G.S. (1975b). Sheep. In M.C. Tenney (Ed.), *The Zondervan pictorial encyclopedia of the Bible* (Vol. 5, pp. 385–388). Grand Rapids, MI: Zondervan Publishing House.

Carlson, B.E. (1990). Adolescent observers of marital violence. *Journal of Family Violence*, 5(4), 285–299.

Carlson, B.E., McNutt, L.-A., Choi, D.Y., & Rose, I.M. (2002). Intimate partner abuse and mental health: The role of support and other protective factors. *Violence Against Women*, 8(6), 720–745.

Carr, G.L. (1984). *The Song of Solomon*. Leicester, UK: Inter-Varsity Press.

Carson, D.A. (1984). Matthew. In F.E. Gaebelein (Ed.), *The expositor's Bible commentary* (Vol. 8, pp. 3–599). Grand Rapids, MI: Regency.

Carson, V., Soeken, K.L., & Grimm, P.M. (1988). Hope and its relationship to spiritual well-being. *Journal of Psychology and Theology*, 16(2), 159–167.

Carver, C.S., & Scheier, M.F. (1994). Situational coping and coping dispositions in stressful transaction. *Journal of Personality and Social Psychology*, 66(1), 184–195.

Carver, C.S., Scheier, M.F., & Weintraub, J.K. (1989). Assessing coping strategies: A theoretically based approach. *Journal of Personality and Social Psychology*, 56(2), 267–283.

Casey, K.L. (1998). Surviving abuse: Shame, anger, forgiveness. *Pastoral Psychology*, 46(4), 223–231.

Cassiday-Shaw, A. (2002). *Family abuse and the Bible: The scriptural perspective*. New York: Haworth.

Center for Transformational Psychotherapy. (2005). *The Women's Page*. Retrieved January 4, 2005 from http://www.forhealing.org/women.html

CEO Challenge. (2000a). *Domestic violence is a workplace issue*. [Brochure]. Brisbane: CEO Challenge Committee, The Lord Mayor's Women's Advisory Council.

CEO Challenge. (2000b). *Fact sheet: Domestic violence costs*. [Brochure]. Brisbane: CEO Challenge Committee, The Lord Mayor's Women's Advisory Council.

CEO Challenge. (2000c). *Workplace partners against domestic violence*. [Brochure]. Brisbane: CEO Challenge Committee, The Lord Mayor's Women's Advisory Council.

CEO Challenge. (2000d). *Domestic violence: Your business, your bottom line*. [Brochure]. Brisbane: CEO Challenge Committee, The Lord Mayor's Women's Advisory Council.

Childers, C.L. (1964). The gospel according to St Luke. In A.F. Harper, W.M. Greathouse, R. Earle & W.T. Purkiser (Eds.), *Beacon Bible commentary* (Vol. 6, pp. 417–621). Kansas City, MO: Beacon Hill Press.

Churton, H.B.W. (1903). Malachi. In *Commentary on the Old Testament* (Vol. 4). London: Society for promoting Christian knowledge.

Claes, J., & Rosenthal, D.M. (1990). Men who batter women: A study in power. *Journal of Family Violence*, 5(3), 215–224.

Clark, D.B., & Miller, T. (1998). Stress response and adaptation in children: Theoretical models. In T. Miller (Ed.), *Children of trauma: Stressful life events and their effects on children and adolescents* (pp. 3–27). Madison: International Universities Press.

Clements, C.M., & Sawhney, D.K. (2000). Coping with domestic violence: Control, attributions, dysphoria and hopelessness. *Journal of Traumatic Stress*, 13(2), 219–240.

Cole, B.S., & Pargament, K.I. (1999). Spiritual surrender: A paradoxical path to control. In W.R. Miller (Ed.), *Integrating spirituality into treatment: Resources for practitioners* (pp. 179–198). Washington: American Psychological Association.

Collins, G. (1988). *Christian counseling: A comprehensive guide* (Revised ed.). Dallas, TX: Word.

Commonwealth of Australia. (2004). *Violence against women: Australia says no*. [Brochure]. Canberra: PMP Print.

Conner, K., & Malmin, K. (1983). *The Covenants*. Victoria, Australia: KJC Publications.

Connors, G.J., Toscova, R.T., & Tonigan, J.S. (1999). Serenity. In W.R. Miller (Ed.), *Integrating spirituality into treatment: Resources for practitioners* (pp. 235–250). Washington: American Psychological Association.

Connors, P. (1990). The use of psychological and medical reports in marriage nullity cases. In H.F. Doogan (Ed.), *Catholic tribunals: Marriage annulment and dissolution* (pp. 194–209). Sydney, Australia: E.J. Dwyer.

Conrade, G. (1995). *Abuse in families of the Catholic Church community: Gender differences in attitudes and incidence.* Masters dissertation, School of Psychology, University of Queensland, Australia.

Conway, H.L. (1998). *Domestic violence and the church.* Suffolk, UK: Clays Ltd.

Cooper, J., & Vetere, A. (2005). *Domestic violence and family safety: A systemic approach to working with violence in families.* London: Whurr.

Cooper-White, P. (1995). *The cry of Tamar: Violence against women and the church's response.* Minneapolis, MN: Fortress Press.

Coram, M.D. (1990). The psychological assessment. In H.F. Doogan (Ed.), *Catholic tribunals: Marriage annulment and dissolution* (pp. 210–230). Sydney, Australia: E.J. Dwyer.

Cornes, A. (2002). *Divorce and remarriage: Bible principle and pastoral practice.* Ross-shire, UK: Christian Focus Publications.

Cox, L.G. (1969). The book of Exodus. In A.F. Harper, W.M. Greathouse, R. Earle & W.T. Purkiser (Eds.), *Beacon Bible commentary* (Vol. 1, pp. 169–316). Kansas City, MO: Beacon Hill Press.

Cronkite, R.C., & Moos, R.H. (1984). The role of predisposing and moderating factors in the stress-illness relationship. *Journal of Health and Social Behavior, 25*(4), 372–393.

Culver, R.D. (1975). Jezebel. In M.C. Tenney (Ed.), *The Zondervan pictorial encyclopedia of the Bible* (Vol. 3, pp. 589–590). Grand Rapids, MI: Zondervan Publishing House.

Cummings, E.M., Davies, P.T., & Simpson, K.S. (1994). Marital conflict, gender, and children's appraisals and coping efficacy as mediators of child adjustment. *Journal of Family Psychology, 8*(2), 141–149.

Cummings, J.G., Pepler, D.J., & Moore, T.E. (1999). Behavior problems in children exposed to wife abuse: Gender differences. *Journal of Family Violence, 14*(2), 133–156.

Cunliffe-Jones, H. (1960). *The book of Jeremiah: Introduction and commentary.* London: SCM Press.

Cunningham, B.B. (1985). The will to forgive: A pastoral theological view of forgiving. *Journals of Pastoral Care, 34,* 141–149.

Davids, P.H. (2002). 1 Peter. In C.E. Arnold (Ed.), *Zondervan illustrated Bible backgrounds commentary* (Vol. 4, pp. 120–151). Grand Rapids, MI: Zondervan Publishing House.

Davies, J.H. (1967). A letter to the Hebrews. In P.R. Ackroyd, A.R.C. Leaney & J.W. Packer (Eds.), *The Cambridge Bible commentary.* Cambridge: Cambridge University Press.

Deane, W.J. (1995). The book of Malachi. In H.D.M. Spence & J.S. Exell (Eds.), *The pulpit commentary* (Vol. 14, pp. 1–71). Peabody, MA: Hendrickson.

Department of Communities (Queensland Government). (2005a). There's no excuse for abuse. *Community Spirit,* 6.

Department of Communities (Queensland Government). (2005b). Violence prevention rewarded. *Community Spirit,* 7.

Deutsch, R.R. (1987). Calling God's people to obedience: A commentary on the book of Malachi. In G.A.F. Knight & F.C. Holmgren (Eds.), *A promise of hope — a call to obedience* (pp. 61–120). Grand Rapids, MI: Eerdmans.

DeVries, C.E. (1981). Song of Solomon. In M.C. Tenney (Ed.), *The Zondervan pictorial Bible dictionary* (pp. 802–803). Grand Rapids, MI: Zondervan Publishing House.

Diamond, H., & Precin, P. (2003). Disabled and experiencing disaster: Personal and professional accounts. In P. Precin (Ed.), *Surviving 9/11: Impact and experiences of occupational therapy practitioners.* New York: Haworth Press.

Dienemann, J., Boyle, E., Baker, D., Resnick, W., Wiederhorn, N., & Campbell, J. (2000). Intimate partner abuse among women diagnosed with depression. *Issues in Mental Health Nursing, 21*, 499–513.

Dixon, C.K. (1997, Summer). Clergy as carers: A response to the pastoral concern of violence in the family. *Journal of Psychology and Christianity, 6*, 126–131.

Dobash, R.E., & Dobash, R. (1979). *Violence against wives: A case against the patriarchy.* New York: The Free Press.

Domestic Violence Prevention Centre (DVRC) Gold Coast. (2008a). *Domestic and family violence information.* Retrieved November 12, 2008, from http://www.domestic violence.com.au

Domestic Violence Prevention Centre (DVRC) Gold Coast. (2008b). *Domestic violence facts.* Retrieved November 12, 2008, from http://www.domesticviolence.com.au

Domestic Violence Resource Centre (DVRC). (1998a). *Not just another statistic.* [Brochure]. Brisbane, Australia: Author.

Domestic Violence Resource Centre (DVRC). (1998b). *Understanding domestic violence.* [Brochure]. Brisbane, Australia: Author.

Domestic Violence Resource Centre (DVRC). (n.d.). *Domestic violence and children.* [Brochure].Brisbane, Australia: Author.

Douglas, M.A. (1987). The battered woman syndrome. In D.J. Sonkin (Ed.), *Domestic violence on trial* (pp. 39–54). New York: Springer.

Dowrick, S. (1997). *Forgiveness and other acts of love.* Victoria: Penguin.

Drumwright, H.L. (1975). Interpretation. In M.C. Tenney (Ed.), *The Zondervan pictorial encyclopedia of the Bible* (Vol. 3, pp. 297–305). Grand Rapids, MI: Zondervan Publishing House.

Dumbrell, W.J. (1993). *Covenant and creation: A theology of the Old Testament covenants.* Grand Rapids, MI: Baker Book House.

Dunning, H.R. (1968). The book of Habukkuk. In A.F. Harper, W.M. Greathouse, R. Earle & W.T. Purkiser (Eds.), *Beacon Bible commentary* (Vol. 5, pp. 261–290). Kansas City, MO: Beacon Hill Press.

Dutton, D.G. (1994). The origin and structure of the abusive personality. *Journal of Personality Disorders, 8*(3), 181–191.

Dutton, D.G. (1995). *The batterer: A psychological profile.* New York: Basic Books.

Dutton, D.G., & Painter, S. (1993). The battered woman syndrome: Effects of severity and intermittency of abuse. *American Journal of Orthopsychiatry, 63*(4), 614–622.

Dutton, D.G., Saunders, K., Starzomski, A., & Bartholomew, K. (1994). Intimacy-anger and insecure attachment as precursors of abuse in intimate relationships. *Journal of Applied Social Psychology, 24*(25), 1367–1386.

Dutton, M.A., Burghardt, K.J., Perrin, S.G., Chrestman, K.R., & Halle, P.M. (1994). Battered women's cognitive schemata. *Journal of Traumatic Stress, 7*(2), 237–255.

Earle, R. (1964). The gospel according to Matthew. In A.F. Harper, W.M. Greathouse, R. Earle & W.T. Purkiser (Eds.), *Beacon Bible commentary* (Vol. 6, pp. 19–267). Kansas City, MO: Beacon Hill Press.

Eaton, J.H. (1967). *Psalms: Introduction and commentary*. London: SCM Press.

Education Psychology Study Group. (1990). Must a Christian require repentance before forgiving? *Journal of Psychology and Christianity, 9*, 16–19.

Education Queensland. (2000). *The savvy schools kit: Support for students affected by domestic violence*. Brisbane: Author.

Eilts, M.B. (1995). Saving the family: When is the covenant broken? In C.J. Adams & M.M. Fortune (Eds.), *Violence against women and children: A Christian theological sourcebook* (pp. 444–450). New York: Continuum.

Eisikovits, Z., & Buchbinder, E. (1999). Taking control: Metaphors used by battered women. *Violence Against Women, 5*(8).

Eisikovits, Z., Goldblatt, H., & Winstok, Z. (1999). Partner accounts of intimate violence: Towards a theoretical model. *Families in Society: The Journal of Contemporary Human Services, 80*(6), 606–619.

Ellison, M.M., & Hewey, K.B. (1995). Hope lies in 'the struggle against it': Co-teaching a seminary course on domestic violence and theology. In C.J. Adams & M.M. Fortune (Eds.), *Violence against women and children: A Christian theological sourcebook* (pp. 479–501). New York: Continuum.

Enright, R.D., & Zell, R.L. (1989). Problems encountered when we forgive one another. *Journal of Psychology and Christianity, 8*, 52–60.

Ericksen, J.R., & Henderson, A.D. (1998). Diverging realities: abused women and their children. In J. Campbell (Ed.), *Empowering survivors of abuse: Health care for battered women and their children* (pp. 138–155). Thousand Oaks, CA: Sage.

Ess, C. (1995). Reading Adam and Eve: Re-visions of the myth of woman's subordination to man. In C.J. Adams & M.M. Fortune (Eds.), *Violence against women and children: A Christian theological sourcebook* (pp. 92–120). New York: Continuum.

Exline, J.J., & Baumeister, R. (2000). Expressing forgiveness and repentance. In M.E. McCullough, K.I. Pargament & C.E. Thoresen (Eds.), *Forgiveness: Theory, research and practice* (pp. 133–155). New York: Guilford Press.

Ezell, C. (1998). Power, patriarchy, and abusive marriages. In C.C. Kroeger & J.R. Beck (Eds.), *Healing the hurting: Giving hope and help to abused women* (pp. 15–39). Grand Rapids, MI: Baker Books.

Farley, G.E. (1975). Divorce. In M.C. Tenney (Ed.), *The Zondervan pictorial encyclopedia of the Bible* (Vol. 2, pp. 149–151). Grand Rapids, MI: Zondervan Publishing House.

Fawcett, B., Featherstone, B., Hearn, J., & Toft, C. (1996). *Violence and gender relations*. London: Sage.

Feder, L. (1999a). Police handling of domestic violence calls: An overview and further investigation. In L. Feder (Ed.), *Women and domestic violence: An interdisciplinary approach* (pp. 49–68). New York: Haworth Press Inc.

Feder, L. (1999b). Domestic violence: An interdisciplinary approach. In L. Feder (Ed.), *Women and domestic violence: An interdisciplinary approach* (pp. 1–7). New York: Haworth Press Inc.

Fee, G.D. (1995). *Paul's letter to the Philippians*. Grand Rapids, MI: William B. Eerdmans.

Feerick, M.M., & Haugaard, J.J. (1999). Long-term effects of witnessing marital violence for women: The contribution of childhood physical and sexual abuse. *Journal of Family Violence, 14*(4), 377–398.

Feinberg, C.L. (1986). Jeremiah. In F.E. Gaebelein (Ed.), *The expositor's Bible commentary* (Vol. 6, pp. 355–691). Grand Rapids, MI: Zondervan Publishing House.

Feng, D., Giarrusso, R., Bengston, V.L., & Frye, N. (1999). Intergenerational transmission of marital quality and marital instability. *Journal of Marriage and the Family, 61*, 451–463.

Finkelhor, D., & Yllo, K. (1985). *License to rape: Sexual abuse of wives*. New York: Free Press.

Finn, J. (2000). Domestic violence organizations on the web: A new arena for domestic violence services. *Violence Against Women, 6*(1).

Fisher, D. (1999). Preventing childhood trauma resulting from exposure to domestic violence. *Preventing School Failure, 44*(1), 25–30.

Fishwick, N. (1998). Issues in providing care for rural battered women. In J. Campbell (Ed.), *Empowering survivors of abuse: Health care for battered women and their children* (pp. 280–290). London: Sage.

Fleming, S.R. (1996). Competent Christian intervention with men who batter. In C.C. Kroeger & J.R. Beck (Eds.), *Women, abuse, and the Bible: How Scripture can be used to hurt or heal* (pp. 175–192). Grand Rapids, MI: Baker Books.

Fleury, R.E., Sullivan, C.M., & Bybee, D.I. (2000). When ending the relationship does not end the violence. *Violence Against Women, 6*(12), 1363–1383.

Flynn, C.P. (2000). Women's best friend. *Violence Against Women, 6*(2), 162–177.

Fontana, A., & Frey, J.H. (1998). Interviewing: The art of science. In N.K. Denzin & Y.S. Lincoln (Eds.), *Collecting and interpreting qualitative materials*. Thousand Oaks, CA: Sage.

Ford, J., & Deasley, A.R.G. (1969). The book of Deuteronomy. In A.F.Harper, W.M. Greathouse, R. Earle & W.T. Purkiser (Eds.), *Beacon Bible commentary* (Vol. 1, pp. 503–630). Kansas City, MO: Beacon Hill Press.

Forsstrom-Cohen, B., & Rosenbaum, A. (1985). The effects of parental marital violence on young adults: An exploratory investigation. *Journal of Marriage and the Family, 2*, 467–472.

Forster, G. (2000). The changing face of marriage and divorce. *Anvil, 17*(3), 167–175.

Fortune, M.M. (1991). *Violence in the family: A workshop curriculum for clergy and other helpers*. Cleveland, OH: Pilgrim Press.

Fortune, M.M. (1995a). Forgiveness: The last step. In C.J. Adams & M.M. Fortune (Eds.), *Violence against women and children: A Christian theological sourcebook* (pp. 201–206). New York: Continuum.

Fortune, M.M. (1995b, Jan–Feb). Picking up the broken pieces: Responding to domestic violence. *Church and Society, 85*, 36–47.

Fortune, M.M. (1998). Preaching forgiveness? In J.S. McClure & N.J. Ramsay (Eds.), *Telling the truth: Preaching about sexual and domestic violence* (pp. 49–57). Cleveland: United Church Press.

Fortune, M.M., & Poling, J. (1995). Calling to accountability: The church's response to abusers. In C.J. Adams & M.M. Fortune (Eds.), *Violence against women and children: A Christian theological sourcebook* (pp. 451–463). New York: Continuum.

Funderburk, G.B. (1975a). Rod. In M.C. Tenney (Ed.), *The Zondervan pictorial encyclopedia of the Bible* (Vol. 5, pp. 132–133). Grand Rapids, MI: Zondervan Publishing House.

Funderburk, G.B. (1975b). Love. In M.C. Tenney (Ed.), *The Zondervan pictorial encyclopedia of the Bible* (Vol. 3, pp. 989–996). Grand Rapids, MI: Zondervan Publishing House.

Furniss, K.K. (1998). Screening for abuse in the clinical setting. In J. Campbell (Ed.), *Empowering survivors of abuse: Health care for battered women and their children* (pp. 190–194). London: Sage.

Gaines, A.D. (1998). Religion and culture in psychiatry: Christian and secular psychiatric theory and practice in the United States. In H.G. Koenig (Ed.), *Handbook of religion and mental health* (pp. 291–320). San Diego, CA: Academic Press.

Gall, T.L., Charbonneau, C., Clarke, N.H., Grant, K., Joseph, A., & Shouldice, L. (2005). Understanding the nature and role of spirituality in relation to coping and health: A conceptual framework. *Canadian Psychology, 46*(2), 88–104.

Gallagher, M. (2004). Reflections on headship. In D. Blankenhorn, D. Browning & M.S. Van Leeuwen (Eds.), *Does Christianity teach male headship?* (pp. 111–125). Grand Rapids, MI: William B. Eerdmans.

Ganzevoort, R.R. (1998). Religious coping reconsidered, part one: An integrated approach. *Journal of Psychology and Theology, 26*, 260–275.

Garber, J., & Seligman, M.E.P. (1980). *Human helplessness.* New York: Academic Press.

Garland, D.E. (2002). Mark. In C.E. Arnold (Ed.), *Zondervan illustrated Bible backgrounds commentary* (Vol. 1, pp. 204–317). Grand Rapids, MI: Zondervan Publishing House.

Gary, F.A., & Campbell, D.W. (1998). The struggles of runaway youth: Violence and abuse. In J. Campbell (Ed.), *Empowering survivors of abuse: Health care for battered women and their children* (pp. 156–173). Thousand Oaks, CA: Sage.

Geldard, K., & Geldard, D. (2009). *Relationship counselling for children, young people and families.* Los Angeles: SAGE.

Gelles, R.J. (1987). *Family violence.* New York: Sage.

George, L.K., Ellison, C.G., & Larson, D.B. (2002). Explaining the relationships between religious involvement and health. *Psychological Inquiry, 13*(3), 190–200.

Gerard, P.S. (1991). Domestic violence. In S.L. Brown (Ed.), *Counseling victims of violence* (pp. 101–116). Alexandria, VA: American Counseling Association.

Gill, D.W. (1995). Violence. In D.J. Atkinson & D.H. Field (Eds.), *New dictionary of Christian ethics and pastoral theology* (pp. 875–879). Leicester, UK: Inter-Varsity Press.

Gill, D.W.J. (2002). 1 Corinthians. In C.E. Arnold (Ed.), *The Zondervan illustrated Bible backgrounds commentary* (Vol. 3, pp. 100–193). Grand Rapids, MI: Zondervan Publishing House.

Golding, J.M. (1999). Intimate partner violence as a risk for mental disorders: A meta-analysis. *Journal of Family Violence, 14*(2), 99–132.

Gondolf, E.W. (1988). Dealing with the abuser: Issues, options, and procedures. In A. Horton & J. Williamson (Eds.), *Abuse and religion: When praying isn't enough* (pp. 101–111). Massachusetts, USA: Lexington Books.

Gordon, K.C. (1999). *Demystifying forgiveness: A cognitive-behavioral stage model of forgiveness in marital relationships.* Unpublished doctoral dissertation, University of North Carolina, NC.

Gordon, K.C., Baucom, D.H., & Snyder, D.K. (2000). The use of forgiveness in marital therapy. In M.E. McCullough, K.I. Pargament & C.E. Thoresen (Eds.), *Forgivenss: Theory, research, practice* (pp. 203–227). New York: Guilford Press.

Gordon, P.A., Feldman, D., Crose, R., Schoen, E., Griffing, G., & Shankar, J. (2002). The role of religious beliefs in coping with chronic illness. *Counseling and Values, 46*(3), 162–174.

Gore, S., & Colten, M.E. (1991). Gender, stress, and distress: Social-relational influences. In J. Eckenrode (Ed.), *The social context of coping* (pp. 139–161). New York: Plennum.

Gorsuch, R.L., & Miller, W.R. (1999). Assessing spirituality. In W.R. Miller (Ed.), *Integrating spirituality into treatment: Resources for practitioners* (pp. 47–64). Washington: American Psychological Association.

Gott, R. (1995). *Beaten up, beaten down: Violence in Australia*. Melbourne: Cardigan Street Publishers.

Grady, J.L. (2000). *10 Lies the church tells women*. Florida: Charisma House.

Graham, L.K., & Fortune, M.M. (1993). Empowering the congregation to respond to sexual abuse and domestic violence. *Pastoral Psychology, 41,* 337–345.

Graham-Bermann, S.A. (1998). The impact of woman abuse on children's social development: Research and theoretical perspectives. In G.W. Holden, R. Geffner & E.N. Jouriles (Eds.), *Children exposed to marital violence* (pp. 21–54). Washington: American Psychological Association.

Gray, C.P. (1966). The book of the prophet Jeremiah. In A.F. Harper, W.M. Greathouse, R. Earle & W.T. Purkiser (Eds.), *Beacon Bible commentary* (Vol. 5, pp. 301–497). Kansas City, MO: Beacon Hill Press.

Greathouse, W.M. (1966). The book of Malachi. In A.F. Harper, W.M. Greathouse, R. Earle & W.T. Purkiser (Eds.), *Beacon Bible commentary* (Vol. 5, pp. 405–453). Kansas City, MO: Beacon Hill Press.

Greathouse, W.M. (1968). The epistle to the Romans. In A.F. Harper, W.M. Greathouse, R. Earle & W.T. Purkiser (Eds.), *Beacon Bible commentary* (Vol. 8, pp. 17–292). Kansas City, MO: Beacon Hill Press.

Green, H.W. (1984). *Turning fear to hope: Help for marriages troubled by abuse*. Nashville, TN: Thomas Nelson.

Gregory, C., & Erez, E. (2002). The effects of batterer intervention programs: The battered women's perspective. *Violence Against Women, 8*(2), 206–232.

Gregory, L. (2004). *Preventing violence by promoting non-violence*. Fremantle, Western Australia: Fremantle Publishing.

Grenz, S.J., & Kjesbo, D.M. (1995). *Women in the church: A biblical theology of women in ministry*. Downers Grove, IL: InterVarsity Press.

Grider, J.K. (1966). The book of the prophet Ezekiel. In A.F. Harper, W.M. Greathouse, R. Earle & W.T. Purkiser (Eds.), *Beacon Bible commentary* (Vol. 4, pp. 529–616). Kansas City, MO: Beacon Hill Press.

Griffith, M., & Harvey, P. (1998). The SBC resolution: Wifely submission. *Christian Century, 115*(19), 636–638.

Griffith, R.M. (1997). *God's daughters: Evangelical women and the power of submission*. Los Angeles: University of California Press.

Grogan, G.W. (1975). Scripture. In M.C. Tenney (Ed.), *The Zondervan pictorial encyclopedia of the Bible* (Vol. 3, pp. 302–313). Grand Rapids, MI: Zondervan Publishing House.

Grogan, G.W. (1986). Isaiah. In F.E. Gaebelein (Ed.), *The expositor's Bible commentary* (Vol. 6, pp. 3–354). Grand Rapids, MI: Zondervan Publishing House.

Grounds, V.C. (1981). Prayer. In M.C. Tenney (Ed.), *The Zondervan pictorial Bible dictionary* (pp. 679–682). Grand Rapids, MI: Zondervan Publishing House.

Grudem, W. (1991). Wives like Sarah, and the husbands who honor them 1 Peter 3:1–7. In J. Piper & W. Grudem (Eds.), *Recovering biblical manhood and womanhood: A response to feminism* (pp. 194–208). Wheaton, IL: Crossways.

Guthrie, D. (1975). Bible. In M.C. Tenney (Ed.), *The Zondervan pictorial encyclopedia of the Bible* (Vol. 1, pp. 554–566). Grand Rapids, MI: Zondervan Publishing House.

Guthrie, G.H. (2002). Hebrews. In C.E. Arnold (Ed.), *Zondervan illustrated Bible backgrounds commentary* (Vol. 4, pp. 2–85). Grand Rapids, MI: Zondervan Publishing House.

Gwinn, C. (2003). *Moving forward: Changing the world*. Paper presented at the Domestic Violence and Sexual Assault International Conference, Gold Coast, Australia.

Hagner, D.A. (1975). Pharisees. In M.C. Tenney (Ed.), *The Zondervan pictorial encyclopedia of the Bible* (Vol. 4, pp. 745–752). Grand Rapids, MI: Zondervan Publishing House.

Hague, G., & Marlos, E. (2005). *Domestic violence: Action for change* (3rd ed.). Cheltenham, UK: New Clarion Press.

Hague, G., & Wilson, C. (2000). The silenced pain: Domestic violence 1945–1970. *Journal of Gender Studies, 9*(2), 157–169.

Hallowell, E.M. (2004). *Dare to forgive*. Deerfield, FL: Health Communications Inc.

Harman, F. (1990). Incapacity to assume the obligation. In H.F. Doogan (Ed.), *Catholic tribunals: Marriage annulment and dissolution* (pp. 90–103). Newtown, NSW: E.J. Dwyer.

Harper, A.F. (1967a). The Song of Solomon. In A.F. Harper, W.M. Greathouse, R. Earle & W.T. Purkiser (Eds.), *Beacon Bible commentary* (Vol. 3, pp. 599–637). Kansas City, MO: Beacon Hill Press.

Harper, A.F. (1967b). The general epistle of James. In A.F. Harper, W.M. Greathouse, R. Earle & W.T. Purkiser (Eds.), *Beacon Bible commentary* (Vol. 10, pp. 185–252). Kansas City, MO: Beacon Hill Press.

Harris, R.L. (1981a). Canonicity. In M.C. Tenney (Ed.), *The Zondervan pictorial Bible dictionary* (pp. 144–146). Grand Rapids, MI: Zondervan Publishing House.

Harris, R.L. (1981b). Book of Proverbs. In M.C. Tenney (Ed.), *The Zondervan pictorial Bible dictionary* (pp. 692). Grand Rapids, MI: Zondervan Publishing House.

Harris, R.L. (1990). Leviticus. In F.E. Gaebelein (Ed.), *The expositor's Bible commentary* (Vol. 2, pp. 499–654). Grand Rapids, MI: Zondervan Publishing House.

Harrison, E.F. (1976). Romans. In F.E. Gaebelein (Ed.), *The expositor's Bible commentary* (Vol. 10, pp. 1–171). Grand Rapids, MI: Zondervan Publishing House.

Harrison, R.K. (1975). Song of Solomon. In M.C. Tenney (Ed.), *The Zondervan pictorial encyclopedia of the Bible* (Vol. 5, pp. 486–493). Grand Rapids, MI: Zondervan Publishing House.

Hattendorf, J., & Tollerud, T.R. (1997). Domestic violence: Counselling strategies that minimize the impact of secondary victimization. *Perspectives in Psychiatric Care, 33*(1), 14–24.

Heckert, A., & Gondolf, E.W. (2000). Predictors of underreporting of male violence by batterer program participants and their partners. *Journal of Family Violence, 15*(4), 423–443.

Hegstrom, P. (2004). *Angry men and the women who love them: Breaking the cycle of physical and emotional abuse* (Revised ed.). Kansas City, MO: Beacon Hill Press.

Heise, L.L. (1998). Violence against women: An integrated, ecological framework. *Violence Against Women, 4*(3), 262–291.

Hembold, A.K. (1975). Book of Proverbs. In M.C. Tenney (Ed.), *The Zondervan pictorial encyclopedia of the Bible* (Vol. 4, pp. 915–920). Grand Rapids, MI: Zondervan Publishing House.

Henderson, M. (2002). *Forgiveness: Breaking the chain of hate.* London: Grosvenor Books.

Henry, M., & Scott, T. (1979a). The first book of Moses called Genesis. In *Commentary on the Holy Bible* (Vol. 1, pp. 1–127). Nashville, TN: Royal Publishers Inc.

Henry, M., & Scott, T. (1979b). The epistle to the Ephesians. In *Commentary on the Holy Bible* (Vol. 3, pp. 198–222). Nashville, TN: Royal Publishers Inc.

Henry, M., & Scott, T. (1979c). The book of the prophet Malachi. In *Commentary on the Holy Bible* (Vol. 2, pp. 527–536). Nashville, TN: Royal Publishers Inc.

Herbert, A.S. (1975). *The book of the prophet Isaiah: Chapters 40–66.* London: Cambridge University Press.

Herman, J.L. (1997). *Trauma and recovery.* New York: Basic Books.

Hershorn, M., & Rosenbaum, A. (1985). Children of marital violence: A closer look at the unintended victims. *American Journal of Orthopsychiatry, 55*(2), 260–266.

Heth, W. (1995, Spring). Divorce and remarriage: The search for an evangelical hermeneutic. *Trinity Journal, 16,* 65–100.

Hiebert, D.E. (1978). Titus. In F.E. Gaebelein (Ed.), *The expositor's Bible commentary* (Vol. 11, pp. 419–449). Grand Rapids, MI: Zondervan Publishing House.

Hiebert, D.E. (1981). Love. In M.C. Tenney (Ed.), *The Zondervan pictorial Bible dictionary* (pp. 493–494). Grand Rapids, MI: Zondervan Publishing House.

Hill, A.E. (1998). *Malachi: A new translation with introduction and commentary.* New York: Doubleday.

Hill, G. (1987). Hebrews. In G.L. Archer (Ed.), *The discovery bible: New American standard New Testament* (Reference ed., pp. 432–452). Chicago: Moody Press.

Hilton, Z. (1992). Battered women's concerns about their children witnessing wife assault. *Journal of Interpersonal Violence, 7*(1), 77–85.

Hoekstra, W. (1990). Marriage in sacred scripture. In H.F. Doogan (Ed.), *Catholic tribunals: Marriage annulment and dissolution* (pp. 14–24). Sydney, Australia: E.J. Dwyer.

Hofeller, K. (1987). *Battered women, shattered lives.* Saratoga, CA: R & E Publishers.

Hoff, L. (1990). *Battered women as survivors.* London: Routledge.

Holahan, C.J., & Moos, R.H. (1987). Personal and contextual determinants of coping strategies. *Journal of Personality and Social Psychology, 52*(5), 946–955.

Holdridge, H.P. (1981). Occupations and professions. In M.C. Tenney (Ed.), *The Zondervan pictorial Bible dictionary* (pp. 593–601). Grand Rapids, MI: Zondervan Publishing House.

Holmes, A.F. (1975). Truth. In M.C. Tenney (Ed.), *The Zondervan pictorial encyclopedia of the Bible* (Vol. 5, pp. 827–829). Grand Rapids, MI: Zondervan Publishing House.

Hopkins, A., & McGregor, H. (1991). *Working for change: the movement against domestic violence.* Sydney: Allen and Unwin.

Horne, G. (n.d.). *A commentary on the Book of Psalms.* London: Ward, Lock & Co.

Horsfield, P. (1994). Forgiveness and reconciliation in situations of sexual abuse (Occasional Paper No. 7, pp. 1–12). Australia: Uniting Church of Australia, Commission on Women and Men.

Horton, C., Cruise, T.K., Graybill, D., & Cornett, J.Y. (1999). For children's sake: Training students in the treatment of child witnesses of domestic violence. *Professional Psychology: Research and Practice, 30*(1), 88–91.

Horton, R.F. (1891). *The book of Proverbs.* London: Hodder & Stoughton.

Howard, R.E. (1965). The epistle to the Galatians. In A.F. Harper, W.M. Greathouse, R. Earle & W.T. Purkiser (Eds.), *Beacon Bible commentary* (Vol. 9, pp. 17–125). Kansas City, MO: Beacon Hill Press.

Hubbard, M.G. (1996). Depression in abused women. In C.C. Kroeger & J.R. Beck (Eds.), *Women abuse and the Bible: How Scripture can be used to hurt or heal* (pp. 131–147). Grand Rapids, MI: Baker Books.

Huey, F.B.J. (1975). Weights and measures. In M.C. Tenney (Ed.), *The Zondervan pictorial encyclopedia of the Bible* (Vol. 5, pp. 913–922). Grand Rapids, MI: Zondervan Publishing House.

Huey, F.B.J. (1992). Ruth. In F.E. Gaebelein (Ed.), *The expositor's Bible commentary* (Vol. 3, pp. 507–549). Grand Rapids, MI: Zondervan Publishing House.

Hugenberger, G.P. (1994). *Marriage as a covenant: A study of biblical law and ethics governing marriage developed from the perspective of Malachi.* Leiden, the Netherlands: E.J. Brill.

Hughes, H.M. (1988). Psychological and behavioral correlates of family violence in child witnesses and victims. *American Journal of Orthopsychiatry, 58*(1), 77–90.

Hughes, H.M., & Barad, S.J. (1983). Psychological functioning of children in a battered women's shelter: A preliminary investigation. *American Journal of Orthopsychiatry, 53*(3), 525–531.

Hughes, H.M., & Graham-Bermann, S.A. (1998). Children of battered women: Impact of emotional abuse on adjustment and development. *Journal of Emotional Abuse, 1*(2), 23–50.

Humphreys, C., & Thiara, R. (2003). Mental health and domestic violence: 'I call it symptoms of abuse'. *British Journal of Social Work, 33,* 206–226.

Humphreys, J. (1998). Helping battered women take care of their children. In J. Campbell (Ed.), *Empowering survivors of abuse: Health care for battered women and their children* (pp. 121–137). Thousand Oaks, CA: Sage.

Hunter, A.M. (1998). Manna in the wilderness. In J.S. McClure & N. Ramsay (Eds.), *Telling the truth: Preaching about sexual and domestic violence* (pp. 136–140). Cleveland: United Church Press.

Huss, M.T., & Langhinrichsen-Rohling, J. (2000). Identification of the psychopathic batterer: The clinical, legal, and policy implications. *Aggression and Violent Behavior, 5*(4), 403–422.

Huth-Bocks, A.C., Levendosky, A.A., & Semel, M.A. (2001). The direct and indirect effects of domestic violence on young children's intellectual functioning. *Journal of Family Violence, 16*(3), 269–290.

Hynson, L.O. (1998). Sexuality and the Christian character. *Evangelical Journal, 16*(2), 76–88.

Instone-Brewer, D. (2002). *Divorce and remarriage in the Bible: The social and literary context.* Grand Rapids, MI: Eerdmans.

Jackson, D.R. (1975). Gospel (message). In M.C. Tenney (Ed.), *The Zondervan pictorial encyclopedia of the Bible* (pp. 779–784). Grand Rapids, MI: Zondervan Publishing House.

Jaffe, P., Wolfe, D., Wilson, S., & Zak, L. (1986). Similarities in behavioral and social maladjustment among child victims and witnesses to family violence. *American Journal of Orthopsychiatry, 56*(1), 142–146.

Jaffe, P.G., Lemon, N.D.K., Sandler, J., & Wolfe, D.A. (1996). *Working together to end domestic violence.* Tampa Bay, FL: Mancorp.

James, K. (1999). Truth or fiction: Men as victims of domestic violence. In J. Breckenridge & L. Laing (Eds.), *Challenging silence: Innovative responses to sexual and domestic violence* (pp. 153–162). Sydney, Australia: Allen & Unwin.

James, M. (1994). Domestic violence as a form of child abuse: Identification and prevention. Canberra: National Child Protection Clearinghouse.

Jantz, G.L. (2003). *Healing the scars of emotional abuse* (Revised ed.). Grand Rapids, MI: Revell.

Jenkins, J.M. (2000). Marital conflict and children's emotions: The development of an anger organization. *Journal of Marriage and the Family, 62*, 723–736.

Johnson, J.M. (1995). Church response to domestic violence. In C.J. Adams & M.M. Fortune (Eds.), *Violence against women and children: A Christian theological sourcebook* (pp. 412–421). New York: Continuum.

Joint Churches Domestic Violence Prevention Project Queensland (JCDVPP). (2002). *Domestic violence and the churches: Train the trainer manual* (3rd ed.). Brisbane, Australia: Author.

Jones, D.R. (1962). Malachi. In J. Marsh & A. Richardson (Eds.), *Haggai, Zechariah and Malachi: Introduction and commentary* (pp. 181–207). London: SCM Press.

Jouriles, E.N., McDonald, R., Stephens, N., Norwood, W., Spiller, L.C., & Ware, H.S. (1998). Breaking the cycle of violence: Helping families departing from battered women's shelters. In G.W. Holden, R. Geffner & E.N. Jouriles (Eds.), *Children exposed to marital violence* (pp. 337–369). Washington: American Psychological Association.

Kalland, E.S. (1992). Deuteronomy. In F.E. Gaebelein (Ed.), *The expositor's Bible commentary* (Vol. 3, pp. 1–235). Grand Rapids, MI: Zondervan Publishing House.

Kalland, L.A. (1992). Dietrich Bonhoeffer. In J.D. Douglas (Ed.), *Who's who in Christian history* (pp. 90–91). Wheaton, IL: Tyndale House Inc.

Kearney, M. (1999). The role of teachers in helping children of domestic violence (The expandng role of the teacher). *Childhood Education, 75*(5), 290.

Keene, F.W. (1995). Structures of forgiveness in the New Testament. In C.J. Adams & M.M. Fortune (Eds.), *Violence against women and children: A Christian theological sourcebook* (pp. 121–134). New York: Continuum.

Keener, C.S. (1991). *...And marries another: Divorce and remarriage in the teaching of the New Testament*. Peabody, MA: Hendrickson.

Keener, C.S. (1992). *Paul, women, and wives: Marriage and women's ministry in the letters of Paul*. Peabody, MA: Hendrickson.

Keener, C.S. (1996). Some biblical reflections on justice, rape, and an insensitive society. In C.C. Kroeger & J.R. Beck (Eds.), *Women, abuse, and the Bible: How Scripture can be used to hurt or heal* (pp. 117–130). Grand Rapids, MI: Baker Books.

Kelly, L. (1988). How women define their experiences of violence. In K. Yllo & M. Bograd (Eds.), *Feminist perspectives on wife abuse* (pp. 114–132). Newbury Park, CA: Sage.

Kelso, J.L. (1975). Samaritans. In M.C. Tenney (Ed.), *The Zondervan pictorial encyclopedia of the Bible* (Vol. 5, pp. 244–247). Grand Rapids, MI: Zondervan Publishing House.

Kent, H.A. (1978). Philippians. In F.E. Gaebelein (Ed.), *The expositor's Bible commentary* (Vol. 11, pp. 93–159). Grand Rapids, MI: Zondervan Publishing House.

Kernic, M.A., Holt, V.L., Stoner, J.A., Wolf, M.E., & Rivara, F.P. (2003). Resolution of depression among victims of intimate partner violence: Is cessation of violence enough? *Violence and Victims, 18*(2), 115–129.

Kerr, P. (1991). You must forgive: Seventy times seven. *Victims into Victors: Beyond Family Violence*, 44–46.

Keys Young. (1998). *Against the odds: How women survive domestic violence: The needs of women experiencing domestic violence who do not use domestic violence related services.* Sydney, Australia: Office for the Status of Women, Department of the Prime Minister.

Kilpatrick, K.L., Litt, M., & Williams, L.M. (1997). Post-traumatic stress disorder in child witnesses to domestic violence. *American Journal of Orthopsychiatry, 67*(4), 639–644.

King, A.W. (1999). Confronting violence against women: The church's calling? *Church and Society, 89,* 61–65.

King, C.M. (1998). Changing women's lives: The primary prevention of violence against women. In J. Campbell (Ed.), *Empowering survivors of abuse: Health care for battered women and their children* (pp. 177–189). Thousand Oaks, CA: Sage.

Kinlaw, D.F. (1969). The book of Leviticus. In A.F. Harper, W.M. Greathouse, R. Earle & W.T. Purkiser (Eds.), *Beacon Bible commentary* (Vol. 1, pp. 317–395). Kansas City, MO: Beacon Hill Press.

Kinlaw, D.F. (1991). Song of songs. In F.E. Gaebelein (Ed.), *The expositor's Bible commentary* (Vol. 5, pp. 1199–1244). Grand Rapids, MI: Zondervan Publishing House.

Kirkpatrick, A.F. (1933). *The book of psalms.* Cambridge: Cambridge University Press.

Kirkwood, C. (1995). *Leaving abusive partners.* London: Sage.

Klein, C., & Orloff, L. (1999). Protecting battered women: Latest trends in civil legal relief. In L. Feder (Ed.), *Women and domestic violence: An interdisciplinary approach.* New York: Haworth Press Inc.

Knight, G.A.F. (1955). Song of songs. In J. Marsh, A. Richardson & R.G. Smith (Eds.), *Esther, Song of Songs, Lamentations: Introduction and commentary* (pp. 49–93). London: SCM Press.

Knight, G.W. (1991). The family and the church: How should biblical manhood and womanhood work out in practice? In J. Piper & W. Grudem (Eds.), *Recovering biblical manhood and womanhood: A response to feminism* (pp. 345–357). Wheaton, IL: Crossways.

Knight, J. (1965). The epistle to the Philippians. In A.F. Harper, W.M. Greathouse, R. Earle & W.T. Purkiser (Eds.), *Beacon Bible commentary* (Vol. 9, pp. 277–356). Kansas City, MO: Beacon Hill Press.

Koenig, H.G., McCullough, M E., & Larson, D.B. (Eds.). (2001). *Handbook of religion and health.* Oxford: Oxford University Press.

Koss, M.P., Goodman, L.A., Browne, A., Fitzgerald, L.F., Keita, G.P., & Russo, N.F. (1994). *Male violence against women at home, at work, and in the community.* Washington: American Psychological Association.

Kostenberger, A.J. (2002). John. In C.E. Arnold (Ed.), *Zondervan illustrated Bible backgrounds commentary* (Vol. 2, pp. 2–216). Grand Rapids, MI: Zondervan Publishing House.

Krause, N., Ellison, C.G., Shaw, B.A., Marcum, J.P., & Boardman, J.D. (2001). Church-based social support and religious coping. *Journal for the Scientific Study of Religion, 40*(4), 637–656.

Kroeger, C.C. (1995). Let's look again at the biblical concept of submission. In C.J. Adams & M.M. Fortune (Eds.), *Violence against women and children: A Christian theological sourcebook* (pp. 135–140). New York: Continuum.

Kroeger, C.C. (1996). God's purposes in the midst of human sin. In C.C. Kroeger & J.R. Beck (Eds.), *Women, abuse, and the Bible: How Scripture can be used to hurt or heal* (pp. 202–215). Grand Rapids, MI: Baker Books.

Kroeger, C.C., & Nason-Clark, N. (2001). *No place for abuse: Biblical and practical resources to counteract domestic violence*. Downers Grove, IL: InterVarsity Press.

Kroeger, R., & Kroeger, C.C. (1992). *I suffer not a woman: Rethinking 1 Timothy 2:11–15 in the light of ancient evidence*. Grand Rapids, MI: Baker Books.

Kubacka-Jasiecka, D., Dorczac, R., & Opoczynska, M. (1994). The role of religious values in functioning and mental health. In H. Grzymala-Moszczynska & B. Beit-Hallahmi (Eds.), *Religion, psychopathology and coping* (pp. 235–243). Amsterdam: Rodopi.

Lachkar, J. (2000). Emotional abuse of high-functioning professional women: A psychodynamic perspective. *Journal of Emotional Abuse, 2*(1), 73–91.

Lake, D.M. (1975). Woman. In M.C. Tenney (Ed.), *The Zondervan pictorial encyclopedia of the Bible* (Vol. 5, pp. 950–955). Grand Rapids, MI: Zondervan Publishing House.

Lambert, G. (1975). Adultery. In M.C. Tenney (Ed.), *The Zondervan pictorial encyclopedia of the Bible* (Vol. 1, pp. 65–66). Grand Rapids, MI: Zondervan Publishing House.

Landenburger, K.M. (1998). Exploration of women's identity: Clinical approaches with abused women. In J. Campbell (Ed.), *Empowering survivors of abuse: Health care for battered women and their children* (pp. 61–69). Thousand Oaks, CA: Sage.

Landes, A., Siegel, M.A., & Foster, C.D. (1993). *Domestic violence: No longer behind the curtains*. Wylie, TX: Information Plus.

Langhinrichsen-Rohling, J., Shlien-Dellinger, R.K., Huss, M.T., & Kramer, V.L. (2004). Attributions about perpetrators and victims of interpersonal abuse: Results from an analogue study. *Journal of Interpersonal Violence, 19*(4), 484–498.

Leehan, J. (1992, May–June). Domestic violence: A spiritual epidemic. *Christian Ministry, 23*, 15–18.

Legal Aid Queensland. (1998). *Domestic violence: Finding a way out*. [Brochure]. Legal Aid Community Education.

Lemon, N.D.K. (1996). *Domestic violence law: A comprehensive overview of cases and sources*. San Francisco: Austin & Winfield.

Lempert, L.B. (1996). Women's strategies for survival: Developing agency in abusive relationships. *Journal of Family Violence, 11*(3), 269–289.

Lentz, S.A. (1999). Revisiting the rule of thumb: An overview of the history of wife abuse. In L. Feder (Ed.), *Women and domestic violence: An interdisciplinary approach* (pp. 9–27). New York: Haworth Press Inc.

Leslie, E.A. (1949). *Psalms*. Nashville: Abingdon Press.

Levendosky, A., Lynch, S.M., & Graham-Bermann, S.A. (2000). Mothers' perceptions of woman abuse on their parenting. *Violence Against Women, 6*(3), 247–271.

Lewis, G.R. (1975). Prayer. In M.C. Tenney (Ed.), *The Zondervan pictorial encyclopedia of the Bible* (pp. 835–844). Grand Rapids, MI: Zondervan Publishing House.

Liefield, W.L. (1984). Luke. In F.E. Gaebelein (Ed.), *The expositor's Bible commentary* (Vol. 8, pp. 797–1059). Grand Rapids, MI: Regency.

Linafelt, T. (1989). Ruth. In D.W. Cotter (Ed.), *Ruth and Esther* (pp. 1–90). Collegeville, MN: The Liturgical Press.

Lindsell, H. (1975). Inspiration. In M.C. Tenney (Ed.), *The Zondervan pictorial encyclopedia of the Bible* (Vol. 3, pp. 286–293). Grand Rapids, MI: Zondervan Publishing House.

Livingston, G.H. (1969). The Book of Genesis. In A.F. Harper, W.M. Greathouse, R. Earle & W.T. Purkiser (Eds.), *Beacon Bible commentary* (Vol. 1, pp. 31–173). Kansas City, MO: Beacon Hill Press.

Luzzi, M.K. (1998). When right becomes scriptural abuse. In C.C. Kroeger & J.R. Beck (Eds.), *Healing the hurting: Giving hope and help to abused women* (pp. 41–58). Grand Rapids, MI: Baker Books.

Lynch, S.M., & Graham-Bermann, S.A. (2000). Woman abuse and self-affirmation: Influences on women's self-esteem. *Violence Against Women, 6*(2), 178–197.

Mack, C. (1981). Animals of the Bible. In M.C. Tenney (Ed.), *The Zondervan pictorial Bible dictionary* (pp. 40–46). Grand Rapids, MI: Zondervan Publishing House.

Madvig, D.S. (1992). Joshua. In F.E. Gaebelein (Ed.), *The expositor's Bible commentary* (Vol. 3, pp. 237–371). Grand Rapids, MI: Zondervan Publishing House.

Magen, R.H. (1999). In the best interests of battered women: Reconceptualizing allegations of failure to protect. *Child Maltreatment, 4*(2), 127–135.

Malcolm, W.M., & Greenberg, L.S. (2000). Forgiveness as a process of change in individual psychotherapy. In M.E. McCullough, K.I. Pargament & C.E. Thoresen (Eds.), *Forgiveness: Theory, research, and practice* (pp. 179–202). New York: Guilford.

Maltby, J., Lewis, C.A., & Day, L. (1999). Religious orientation and psychological wellbeing: The role of the frequency of personal prayer. *British Journal of Health Psychology, 4,* 363–378.

Mare, W.H. (1976). 1 Corinthians. In F.E. Gaebelein (Ed.), *The expositor's Bible commentary* (Vol. 10, pp. 173–297). Grand Rapids, MI: Zondervan Publishing House.

Margolin, G., & Gordis, E.B. (2000). The effects of family and community violence on children. *Annual Review of Psychology,* 445–479.

Marshall, L.L. (1996). Psychological abuse of women: Six distinct clusters. *Journal of Family Violence, 11*(4), 379–409.

Martin, D. (1976). *Battered wives.* California: Glide Publications.

Martin, L. (2001). *The covenant of marriage.* Retrieved April 16, 2005 from http://www.themarriagebed.com/printer/covenant.shtml

Martin, R.P. (1959). *The epistle of Paul to the Philippians: An introduction and commentary.* London: Tyndale.

Martz, D. (2002). *Christian marriage covenant.* Retrieved April 16, 2005 from http://www.forallnations.com

Mason, R. (1977). Malachi. In P.R. Ackroyd, A.R.C. Leaney & J.W. Packer (Eds.), *The books of Haggai, Zechariah and Malachi: The Cambridge Bible commentary* (pp. 135–162). London: Cambridge University Press.

Mathis, R. (1992, Fall). Submission. *Theological Educator: A Journal of Theology and Ministry, 46,* 71–76.

Maton, K.I. (1989). The stress-buffering role of spiritual support: Cross-sectional and prospective investigations. *Journal for the Scientific Study of Religion, 28*(3), 310–323.

Matthews, K. (1990). Essential elements and essential properties of marriage. In H.F. Doogan (Ed.), *Catholic tribunals: Marriage annulment and dissolution* (pp. 115–137). Newtown, NSW: E.J. Dwyer.

Mayfield, J.H. (1965). The gospel according to John. In A.F. Harper, W.M. Greathouse, R. Earle & W.T. Purkiser (Eds.), *Beacon Bible commentary* (Vol. 7, pp. 17–245). Kansas City, MO: Beacon Hill Press.

Maynard, E.A., Gorsuch, R.L., & Bjorck, J.P. (2001). Religious coping style, concept of God, and personal religious variables in threat, loss, and challenge situations. *Journal for the Scientific Study of Religion, 40*(1), 65–74.

McCloskey, L.A., Southwick, K., Fernandez-Esquer, M.E., & Locke, C. (1995, April). The psychological effects of political and domestic violence on central American and Mexican immigrant mothers and children. *Journal of Community Psychology, 23,* 95–116.

McCord-Adams, M. (1991, July 3). Forgiveness: A Christian model. *Faith and Philosophy, 8,* 277–304.

McCue, M. (2008). *Domestic violence: A reference handbook* (2nd ed.). Santa Barbara, CA: ABC-CLIO.

McCullough, M.E., & Larson, D.B. (1999). Prayer. In W.R. Miller (Ed.), *Integrating spirituality into treatment: Resources for practitioners* (pp. 85–110). Washington: American Psychological Association.

McCullough, M.E., Pargament, K.I., & Thoresen, C.E. (2000). The psychology of forgiveness: History, conceptual issues, and overview. In M.E. McCullough, K.I. Pargament & C.E. Thoresen (Eds.), *Forgiveness: Theory, research, and practice* (pp. 1–14). New York: Guilford.

McDonald, D., & Brown, M. (1996). *Indicators of aggressive behaviour.* Canberra, Australia: Australian Institute of Criminology.

McGrath, A.E. (Ed.). (1995). *The Christian theology reader.* Oxford: Blackwell.

McGuckin, R. (1990). The respondent's rights in a marriage nullity case. In H.F. Doogan (Ed.), *Catholic tribunals: Marriage annulment and dissolution* (pp. 138–147). Sydney, Australia: E.J. Dwyer.

McGuckin, R. (1992). *Can I get an annulment?* Sydney, Australia: E.J. Dwyer.

McMinn, M.R., & Meek, K.R. (1997). Training programs. In R.K. Sanders (Ed.), *Christian counseling ethics* (pp. 57–74). Downers Grove, IL: InterVarsity Press.

Meilaender, G.C. (1995). Sexuality. In D.J. Atkinson & D.H. Field (Eds.), *New dictionary of Christian ethics and pastoral theology* (pp. 71–78). Leicester, UK: Inter-Varsity Press.

Meloy, J.R. (Ed.). (1998). *The psychology of stalking: Clinical and forensic perspectives.* San Diego, CA: Academic Press.

Mertin, P., & Mohr, P.B. (2000). Incidence and correlates of posttraumatic stress disorder in Australian victims of domestic violence. *Journal of Family Violence, 15*(4), 411–422.

Mertin, P., & Mohr, P.B. (2001). A follow-up study of posttraumatic stress disorder, anxiety, and depression in Australian victims of domestic violence. *Violence and Victims, 16*(6), 645–654.

Metz, D.S. (1968). The first epistle of Paul to the Corinthians. In A.F. Harper, W.M. Greathouse, R. Earle & W.T. Purkiser (Eds.), *Beacon Bible commentary* (Vol. 8, pp. 293–486). Kansas City, MO: Beacon Hill Press.

Miles, A. (1997, March–April). Helping victims of domestic violence. *Christian Ministry, 28*, 33–34.

Miles, A. (1999). When faith is used to justify: Helping victims of domestic violence. *American Journal of Nursing, 99*(5), 32–35.

Miles, A. (2000). *Domestic violence: What every pastor needs to know.* Minneapolis, MN: Ausburg Fortress.

Miles, A. (2002). *Violence in families: What every Christian needs to know.* Minneapolis, MN: Augsburg Books.

Millard, S. (1993). Problems of adjustment. In M. McWalters (Ed.), *Understanding psychology* (Revised ed., pp. 51–84). Sydney: McGraw-Hill.

Miller, J., & Knudsen, D. (2007). *Family abuse and violence: A social problems perspective.* Lanham, MD: AltaMira Press.

Miller, L. (1998). Psychotherapy of crime victims: Treating the aftermath of interpersonal violence. *Psychotherapy, 35*(3), 336–345.

Miller, T., Veltkamp, L.J., & Raines, P. (1998). The trauma of family violence. In T. Miller (Ed.), *Children of trauma: Stressful life events and their effects on children and adolescents* (pp. 61–75). Madison: International Universities Press.

Miller, W.R., & Thoresen, C.E. (1999). Spirituality and health. In W.R. Miller (Ed.), *Integrating spirituality into treatment: Resources for practitioners* (pp. 3–18). Washington: American Psychological Association.

Miller-McLemore, B. (2004). A feminist Christian theologian looks (askance) at headship. In D. Blankenhorn, D. Browning & M.S. Van Leeuwen (Eds.), *Does Christianity teach male headship?* (pp. 49–62). Grand Rapids, MI: Willliam B. Eerdmans.

Mills, L. (2008). *Violent partners: A breakthrough plan for ending the cycle of abuse.* New York: Basic Books.

Monsma, P.H. (1975). Forgiveness. In M.C. Tenney (Ed.), *The Zondervan pictorial encyclopedia of the Bible* (Vol. 2, pp. 596–600). Grand Rapids, MI: Zondervan Publishing House.

Monson, C.M., & Langhinrichsen-Rohling, J. (1998). Sexual and nonsexual marital aggression: Legal considerations, epidemiology, and an integrated typology of perpetrators. *Aggression and Violent Behavior, 3*(4), 369–389.

Moo, D. (2002a). James. In C.E. Arnold (Ed.), *Zondervan illustrated Bible backgrounds commentary* (Vol. 4, pp. 86–119). Grand Rapids, MI: Zondervan Publishing House.

Moo, D. (2002b). Romans. In C.E. Arnold (Ed.), *Zondervan illustrated Bible backgrounds commentary* (Vol. 3, pp. 2–99). Grand Rapids, MI: Zondervan Publishing House.

Morris, L. (1981). Hebrews. In F.E. Gaebelein (Ed.), *The expositor's Bible commentary* (Vol. 12, pp. 1–158). Grand Rapids, MI: Zondervan Publishing House.

Morrone, A. (2003). *The right to play safely: A report on violence against women in sport and recreation.* Melbourne: CASA House.

Mulroney, J. (2003). *Australian statistics on domestic violence* (Australian Domestic and Family Violence Clearinghouse Topic Paper, 1–22). Available at http://www.adfvc.unsw.edu.au/PDF%20files/Statistics_final.pdf

Murphy, J.G. (2003). *Getting even.* Oxford: Oxford University Press.

Murray, S. (2002). *More than refuge: Changing responses to domestic violence.* Perth: University of Western Australia Press.

Nabi, R., & Horner, J.R. (2001). Victims with voices: How abused women conceptualize the problem of spousal abuse and implications for intervention and prevention. *Journal of Family Violence, 16*(3), 237–253.

National Association for Prevention of Child Abuse and Neglect. (NAPCAN). (n.d.). *Domestic violence hurts children.* [Brochure].

Nason-Clark, N. (1997). *The battered wife: How Christians confront family violence.* Louisville, KY: John Knox Press.

Nason-Clark, N. (1998). The evangelical family is sacred, but is it safe? In C.C. Kroeger & J.R. Beck (Eds.), *Healing the hurting: Giving hope and help to abused women* (pp. 109–125). Grand Rapids, MI: Baker Books.

Nason-Clark, N. (2000a). Making the sacred safe: Woman abuse and communities of faith. *Sociology of Religion, 61*(4), 349–368.

Nason-Clark, N. (2000b). Has the silence been shattered or does a holy hush still prevail? Defining violence against women within Christian churches. In A. Shupe, W.A. Stacey & S.E. darnell (Eds.), *Bad pastors: Clergy misconduct in modern America* (pp. 69–89). New York: New York University Press.

Neil, W. (1959). *The epistle to the Hebrews: Introduction and commentary.* London: SCM Press.

Nelson, N. (1997). *Dangerous relationships: How to stop domestic violence before it stops you.* New York: Plenum Press.

Nesheim, D.S. (1998). Sexual abuse survivors in the church. In C.C. Kroeger & J.R. Beck (Eds.), *Healing the hurting: Giving hope and help to abused women* (pp. 129–148). Grand Rapids, MI: Baker Books.

Newberg, A.B., d'Aquili, E.G., Newberg, S.K., & deMarici, V. (2000). The neuropsychological correlates of forgiveness. In M.E. McCullough, K.I. Pargament & C.E. Thoresen (Eds.), *Forgiveness: Theory, research, and practice* (pp. 91–110). New York: Guilford Press.

NiCarthy, G. (1986). *Getting free: You can end abuse and take back your life.* Seattle, Washington: Seal Press.

Nicholson, E.W. (1975). *The book of the prophet Jeremiah: Chapters 26–52.* Cambridge: Cambridge University Press.

Nicholson, R.S. (1967). The first epistle of Peter. In A.F. Harper, W.M. Greathouse, R. Earle & W.T. Purkiser (Eds.), *Beacon Bible commentary* (Vol. 10, pp. 253–309). Kansas City, MO: Beacon Hill Press.

Nielson, J.B. (1965). The epistle to the Colossians. In A.F. Harper, W.M. Greathouse, R. Earle & W.T. Purkiser (Eds.), *Beacon Bible commentary* (Vol. 9, pp. 357–430). Kansas City, MO: Beacon Hill Press.

Nolan, C. (1994). *Questions women ask: About domestic violence and Christian beliefs.* Queensland: Joint Churches Domestic Violence Prevention Project.

Norris, F.H., & Murrell, S.A. (1984). Protective function of resources related to life events, global stress, and depression in older adults. *Journal of Health and Social Behavior, 25*(4), 424–437.

Oaklander, V. (1988). *Windows to our children.* New York: Gestalt Journal Press.

O'Donoghue, C. (1990). The dissolution of the marriage bond. In H.F. Doogan (Ed.), *Catholic tribunals: Marriage annulment and dissolution* (pp. 412–433). Newtown, NSW: E.J. Dwyer.

O'Leary, K.D. (1993). Through a psychological lens: Personality traits, personality disorders and levels of violence. In R.J. Gelles & D.R. Loseke (Eds.), *Current controversies on family violence* (pp. 7–30). Newbury Park, CA: Sage.

O'Leary, K.D. (1999). Developmental and affective issues in assessing and treating partner aggression. *Clinical Psychology: Science and Practice, 6*(4), 400–414.

Olender, R.G. (1998). The Pauline privilege: Inference or exegesis? *Faith and Mission, 16*(1), 94–117.

Olson, L.G. (1981). Music and musical instruments of the Bible. In M.C. Tenney (Ed.), *The Zondervan pictorial Bible dictionary* (pp. 562–566). Grand Rapids, MI: Zondervan Publishing House.

Olthuis, J.H. (1995). Marriage. In D.J. Atkinson & D.H. Field (Eds.), *New dictionary of Christian ethics and pastoral theology* (pp. 565–568). Leicester, UK: Inter-Varsity Press.

Ortlund, R.C. (1991). Male–female equality and male headship Genesis 1–3. In J. Piper and W. Grudem (Eds.), *Recovering biblical manhood and womanhood: A response to feminism* (pp. 95–112). Wheaton IL: Crossways.

Osborne, T.L., & Vandenberg, B. (2003). Situational and denominational differences in religious coping. *The International Journal for the Psychology of Religion, 13*(2), 111–122.

Osiek, C. (2004). Did early Christianity teach, or merely assume, male headship? In D. Blankenhorn, D. Browning & M.S. Van Leeuwen (Eds.), *Does Christianity teach male headship?* (pp. 23–27). Grand Rapids, MI: William B. Eerdmans.

Osofsky, J.D. (1995). The effects of exposure to violence on young children. *American Psychologist, 50*(9), 782–788.

O'Toole, M. (Ed.). (1992). *Miller and Keane encyclopedia and dictionary of medicine, nursing and allied health.* Philadelphia, PA: W.D. Saunders & Co.

Owen, M. (1997). Divorce and remarriage: Biblical and theological perspectives. *Colloquium, 29*(1), 37–48.

Page-Adams, D., & Dersch, S. (1998). Assessing physical and nonphysical abuse against women in a hospital setting. In J. Campbell (Ed.), *Empowering survivors of abuse: Health care for battered women and their children* (pp. 204–213). London: Sage.

Pargament, K.I. (1994). Religious contributions to the process of coping with stress. In H. Grzymala-Moszczynska & B. Beit-Hallahmi (Eds.), *Religion, psychopathology and coping* (pp. 177–192). Amsterdam: Rodopi.

Pargament, K.I. (1997). *The psychology of religion and coping.* New York: Guilford Press.

Pargament, K.I. (2002). The bitter and the sweet: an evaluation of the costs and benefits of religiousness. *Psychological Inquiry, 13*(3), 168–181.

Pargament, K.I., & Brant, C.R. (1998). Religion and coping. In H.G. Koenig (Ed.), *Handbook of religion and mental health* (pp. 111–128). San Diego, CA: Academic Press.

Pargament, K.I., Koenig, H.G., & Perez, L.M. (2000). The many methods of religious coping: Development and initial validation of the RCOPE. *Journal of Clinical Psychology, 56*(4), 519–543.

Pargament, K.I., Olsen, H., Reilly, B., Falgout, K., Ensing, D.S., & Van Haitsma, K. (1992). God help me (II): The relationship of religious coping with negative life events. *Journal for the Scientific Study of Religion, 31*(4), 504–513.

Pargament, K.I., Tarakeshaw, N., Ellison, C.G., & Wulff, K.M. (2001). Religious coping among the religious: The relationships between religious coping and well-being in a national sample of Presbyterian clergy, elders and members. *Journal for the Scientific Study of Religion, 40*(3), 497–513.

Paton, D., & Smith, L.M. (1996). Psychological trauma in critical occupations: Methodology and assessment strategies. In D. Paton & J.M. Violanti (Eds.), *Traumatic stress in critical occupations: Recognition, consequences and treatment* (pp. 15–57). Springfield: Charles C. Thomas.

Patterson, B. (1998). Preaching as nonviolent resistance. In J.S. McClure & N. Ramsay (Eds.), *Telling the truth: Preaching about sexual and domestic violence* (pp. 99–109). Cleveland: United Church Press.

Patton, J. (1985). *Is human forgiveness possible?* Nashville: Abingdon Press.

Patton, J. (2000). Forgiveness in pastoral care and counseling. In M.E. McCullough, K.I. Pargament & C.E. Thoresen (Eds.), *Forgiveness: Theory, research, and practice* (pp. 281–295). New York: Guilford Press.

Payne, J.B. (1962). *The theology of the older testament.* Grand Rapids, MI: Zondervan Publishing House.

Payne, J.B. (1975a). Covenant. In M.C. Tenney (Ed.), *The Zondervan pictorial encyclopedia of the Bible* (Vol. 1, pp. 995–1010). Grand Rapids, MI: Zondervan Publishing House.

Payne, J.B. (1975b). Book of psalms. In M.C. Tenney (Ed.), *The Zondervan pictorial encyclopedia of the Bible* (Vol. 4, pp. 924–947). Grand Rapids, MI: Zondervan Publishing House.

Payne, J.B. (1981). Covenant. In M.C. Tenney (Ed.), *The Zondervan pictorial Bible dictionary* (pp. 186). Grand Rapids, MI: Zondervan Publishing House Corporation.

Pearlin, L.L., & Schooler, C. (1978). The structure of coping. *Journal of Health and Social Behavior, 19*(1), 2–21.

Pearson, E. (1998). Battered Christian women. In C.C. Kroeger & J.R. Beck (Eds.), *Healing the hurting: Giving hope to abused women* (pp. 59–69). Grand Rapids, MI: Baker Books.

Pease, B. (1996, November). Naming violence as a gender issue: Victimisation, blame and responsibility. *Women Against Violence: An Australian Feminist Journal, 33*–39.

Peled, E. (1998). The experience of living with violence for preadolescent children of battered women. *Youth and Society, 29*(4), 395–430.

Pellauer, M. (1986). Counseling victims of family violence. *Lutheran Partners*, July/August.

Perriman, A.C. (1998). Disputing the excuse for abuse. In C.C. Kroeger & J.R. Beck (Eds.), *Healing the hurting: Giving hope and help to abused women* (pp. 213–231). Grand Rapids, MI: Baker Books.

Petersen, L.M. (1981a). Money. In M.C. Tenney (Ed.), *The Zondervan pictorial Bible dictionary* (pp. 551–555). Grand Rapids, MI: Zondervan Publishing House.

Petersen, L.M. (1981b). Pharisees. In M.C. Tenney (Ed.), *The Zondervan pictorial Bible dictionary* (pp. 647–648). Grand Rapids, MI: Zondervan Publishing House.

Peterson, C., Maier, S.F., & Seligman, M. (1993). *Learned helplessness*. New York: Oxford University Press.

Piper, J., & Grudem, W. (1991). An overview of central concerns: Questions and answers. In J. Piper & W. Grudem (Eds.), *Recovering biblical manhood and womanhood: A response to feminism* (pp. 60–92). Wheaton, IL.: Crossways.

Pizzey, E. (1974). *Scream quietly or the neighbours will hear*. London: IF Books.

Plath, L.C. (2001). *Domestic violence survivors: The effects of a week of safe shelter on mood and cognition*. PhD dissertation, Southern Illinois University, IL.

Pope, M.H. (1977). *Song of songs: A new translation with introduction and commentary*. New York: Doubleday.

Post, S.G. (1998). Ethics, religion, and mental health. In H.G. Koenig (Ed.), *Handbook of religion and mental health* (pp. 21–29). San Diego, CA: Academic Press.

Power, P. (1990). Pastoral role of the tribunal. In H.F. Doogan (Ed.), *Catholic tribunals: Marriage annulment and dissolution* (pp. 1–6). Newtown, NSW: E.J. Dwyer.

Price, D. (1990). The acceptance and monitoring of a case. In H.F. Doogan (Ed.), *Catholic tribunals: Marriage annulment and dissolution* (pp. 148–154). Newtown, NSW: E.J. Dwyer.

Price, R.E. (1966). The book of the prophet Isaiah. In A.F. Harper, W.M. Greathouse, R. Earle & W.T. Purkiser (Eds.), *Beacon Bible commentary* (Vol. 4, pp. 17–300). Kansas City, MO: Beacon Hill Press.

Ptacek, J. (1988). Why do men batter their wives? In K. Yllo & M. Bograd (Eds.), *Feminist perspectives on wife abuse* (pp. 133–157). Newbury Park, CA: Sage.

Purkiser, W.T. (1965). The book of Samuel. In A.F. Harper, W.M. Greathouse, R. Earle & W.T. Purkiser (Eds.), *Beacon Bible commentary* (Vol. 2, pp. 205–334). Kansas City, MO: Beacon Hill Press.

Purkiser, W.T. (1967). The book of psalms. In A.F. Harper, W.M. Greathouse, R. Earle & W.T. Purkiser (Eds.), *Beacon Bible commentary* (Vol. 3, pp. 125–452). Kansas City, MO: Beacon Hill Press.

Queensland Domestic Violence Task Force. (1988). *Beyond these walls*. Brisbane, Australia: Author.

Queensland Government: Department of Communities. (2008a). *Increasing your safety: Information for people who experience abuse and/or violence in relationships*. [Brochure]. . Brisbane, Australia: Queensland Government.

Queensland Government: Department of Communities. (2008b). *A Queensland Government strategy to target domestic and family violence 2009–2013.* Retrieved November 12, 2008 from http://ww.communities.qld.gov.au

Queensland Government: Department of Communities. (2008c). *Stopping abuse and violence: Information for people who use abusive and violent behaviour in relationships.* [Brochure]. Brisbane, Australia: Author.

Queensland Government: Department of Communities. (2008d). *Legislation: The domestic and family violence protection act 1989.* [Brochure]. Brisbane, Australia: Author.

Queensland Police Service. (2008a). *A message from commissioner of police, Bob Atkinson.* Retrieved November 12, 2008 from http://www.police.qld.gov.au

Queensland Police Service. (2008b). *Australasian policing strategy on family violence.* Retrieved November 12, 2008 from http://www.police.qld.gov.au

Ramsay, N. (1999). Confronting family violence and its spiritual damage. *Family Ministry, 13*, 46–59.

Randall, M. (1991). The politics of woman abuse. In M.M. Fortune (Ed.), *Violence in the family: A workshop curriculum for clergy and other helpers* (pp. 261–278). Cleveland, OH: Pilgrim Press.

Reid, W.S. (1992). John Knox. In J.D. Douglas (Ed.), *Who's who in Christian history* (pp. 402–404). Wheaton, IL: Tyndale House Inc.

Reynolds, G. (1990). Tribunal interviews — Theory and practice. In H.F. Doogan (Ed.), *Catholic tribunals* (pp. 155–165). Newtown, NSW: E.J. Dwyer.

Reynolds, M.W., Wallace, J., Hill, T.F., Weist, M.D., & Nabors, L.A. (2001). The relationship between gender, depression, and self-esteem in children who have witnessed domestic violence. *Child Abuse and Neglect, 25*, 1201–1206.

Richards, S., & Richards, L. (1999). *Every woman in the Bible.* Nashville, TN: Thomas Nelson.

Riessman, C.K. (1989). From victim to survivor: A woman's narrative reconstruction of marital sexual abuse. *Smith College Studies in Social Work, 59*(3), 232–251.

Rinck, M.J. (1990). *Christian men who hate women: Healing hurting relationships.* Grand Rapids, MI: Zondervan Publishing House.

Rinck, M.J. (1998). Christian men who hate women. In C.C. Kroeger & J.R. Beck (Eds.), *Healing the hurting: Giving hope and help to abused women* (pp. 83–98). Grand Rapids, MI: Baker Books.

Ringma, C. (n.d.). *Life in full stride.* Manila, Philippines: OMF Literature Inc.

Roberts, B. (2002). *Biblical issues for abused Christian women.* Ballarat, Australia: Christian Research and Development Association.

Robinson, G. (1984). *Marriage divorce and annulment: A guide to the annulment process in the Catholic Church.* Melbourne: Dove Communications.

Robinson, G. (1990). Unresolved questions in the theology of marriage. In H.F. Doogan (Ed.), *Catholic tribunals: Marriage annulment and dissolution* (pp. 25–57). Newtown, NSW: E.J. Dwyer.

Rosenbaum, A., & Leisring, P.A. (2003). Beyond power and control: Towards an understanding of partner abusive men. *Journal of Comparative Family Studies, 34*(1), 7–22.

Rosenbaum, A., & O'Leary, K.D. (1981). Children: The unintended victims of marital violence. *American Journal of Orthopsychiatry, 51*(4), 692–699.

Ross, A.P. (1991). Proverbs. In F.E. Gaebelein (Ed.), *The expositor's Bible commentary* (Vol. 6, pp. 881–1134). Grand Rapids, MI: Zondervan Publishing House.

Royal Society for the Prevention of Cruelty to Animals Queensland. [RSPCA] (2008). *Pets in crisis.* Retrieved October 9, 2008 from http://www.rspcaqld.org.au

Russell, E. (1981a). Adultery. In M.C. Tenney (Ed.), *The Zondervan pictorial Bible dictionary* (pp. 17). Grand Rapids, MI: Zondervan Publishing House.

Russell, E. (1981b). Woman. In M.C. Tenney (Ed.), *The Zondervan pictorial Bible dictionary* (pp. 898). Grand Rapids, MI: Zondervan Publishing House.

Rutter, M. (1981). Stress, coping and development: Some issues and some questions. *Journal of Child Psychology and Psychiatry, 22*(4), 323–356.

Rye, M.S., Pargament, K.I., Ali, M.A., Beck, G.L., Dorff, E.N., Hallisay, C., et al. (2000). Religious perspectives on forgiveness. In M.E. McCullough, K.I. Pargament & C.E. Thoresen (Eds.), *Forgiveness: Theory, research, and practice* (pp. 17–40). New York: Guilford Press.

Sackett, L.A., & Saunders, D. (1999). The impact of different forms of psychological abuse on battered women. *Violence and Victims, 14*(1), 105–117.

Safer, J. (1999). *Forgiving and not forgiving: A new approach to resolving intimate betrayal.* New York: Avon.

Sandage, S.J., & Worthington, E.L.J. (1997). Ethics in marital therapy and premarital counseling. In R.K. Sanders (Ed.), *Christian counseling ethics: A handbook for therapists, pastors and counselors* (pp. 119–138). Downers Grove, IL: InterVarsity Press.

Sanner, A.E. (1964). The gospel according to Mark. In A.F. Harper, W.M. Greathouse, R. Earle & W.T. Purkiser (Eds.), *Beacon Bible commentary* (Vol. 6, pp. 261–416). Kansas City, MO: Beacon Hill Press.

Saudia, T.L., Kinney, M.R., Brown, K.C., & Young-Ward, L. (1991). Health locus of control and helpfulness of prayer. *Heart and Lung, 10*(1), 60–65.

Saunders, D. (1994). Posttraumatic stress symptom profiles of battered women: A comparison of survivors in two settings. *Violence and Victims, 9*(1), 31–44.

Sawyer, R.L. (1965). The book of chronicles. In A.F. Harper, W.M. Greathouse, R. Earle & W.T. Purkiser (Eds.), *Beacon Bible commentary* (Vol. 2, pp. 509–598). Kansas City, MO: Beacon Hill Press.

Schaefer, K. (2001). *Psalms.* Collegeville, MN: The Liturgical Press.

Schissel, B. (2000). Boys against girls. *Violence Against Women, 6*(9), 960–986.

Schlueter, C. (1994). Valiant women: Survivors of domestic violence. *Consensus, 20,* 91–106.

Scholer, D.M. (1996). The evangelical debate over biblical 'headship'. In C.C. Kroeger & J.R. Beck (Eds.), *Women, abuse, and the Bible: How Scripture can be used to hurt or heal* (pp. 28–57). Grand Rapids, MI: Baker Books.

Schreiner, T.R. (1991). Head coverings, prophecies and the Trinity 1 Corinthians 11:12–16. In J. Piper & W. Grudem (Eds.), *Recovering biblical manhood and womanhood: A response to feminism* (pp. 124–139). Wheaton, IL: Crossways.

Schumacher, J.A., Smith Slep, A.M., & Heyman, R.E. (2001). Risk factors for male-to-female partner psychological abuse. *Aggression and Violent Behavior, 6,* 255–268.

Schwarz, E.D., McNally, R.J., & Yeh, L.C. (1998). The trauma response of children and adolescents: Future directions in research. *Child and Adolescent Psychiatric Clinics of North America, 7*(1), 229–239.

Scott, J.B. (1975). Shepherd. In M.C. Tenney (Ed.), *The Zondervan pictorial encyclopedia of the Bible* (Vol. 5, pp. 397–398). Grand Rapids, MI: Zondervan Publishing House.

Scutt, J.A. (1990). *Women and the law.* London: Sweet & Maxwell Ltd.

Scutt, J.A. (1991). Criminal assault at home: Policy directions and implications for the future. In R. Batten, W. Weeks & J. Wilson (Eds.), *Issues facing Australian families: Human services respond* (pp. 183–193). Melbourne: Longman Cheshire.

Seddon, N. (1993). *Domestic violence in Australia: The legal response* (2nd ed.). Leichhardt, NSW: Federation Press.

Seim, T.K. (1995). A superior minority: The problem of men's headship in Ephesians 5. In D. Hellholm, H. Moxnes & T.K. Seim (Eds.), *Mighty minorities: Minorities in early Christianity* (pp. 167–181). Oslo: Scandinavian University Press.

Shackelford, J.F., & Sanders, R.K. (1997). Sexual misconduct and the abuse of power. In R.K. Sanders (Ed.), *Christian counseling ethics: A handbook for therapists, pastors and counselors* (pp. 86–102). Downers Grove, IL: Intervarsity Press.

Shaw, E., Bouris, A., & Pye, S. (1999). A comprehensive approach: The family safety model with domestic violence. In J. Breckenridge & L. Laing (Eds.), *Challenging silence: Innovative responses to sexual and domestic violence* (pp. 238–255). St Leonards, NSW: Allen and Unwin.

Sheehy, C. (1990). The advocate. In H.F. Doogan (Ed.), *Catholic tribunals: Marriage annulment and dissolution* (pp. 181–193). Newtown, NSW: E.J. Dwyer.

Sherwood, S. (2002). *Leviticus, Numbers, Deuteronomy* (Vol. 3). Collegeville, MN: The Liturgical Press.

Short, L.M., McMahon, P.M., Chervin, D.D., Shelley, G.A., Lezin, N., Sloop, K.S., et al. (2000). Survivors identification of protective factors and early warning signs for intimate partner violence. *Violence Against Women, 6*(3).

Silvern, L., & Kaersvang, L. (1989). The traumatized children of violent marriages. *Child Welfare, 68*(4), 425–436.

Silvern, L., Karyl, J., Waelde, L., Hodges, W.F., Starek, J., Heidt, E., et al. (1995). Retrospective reports of parental partner abuse: Relationships to depression, trauma symptoms and self-esteem among college students. *Journal of Family Violence, 10*(2), 177–202.

Skinner, J. (1929). *The book of the prophet Isaiah: Chapters XL–LXVI.* London: Cambridge University Press.

Slaughter, J.R. (1996). Submission of wives (1 Pet. 3:1a) in the context of 1 Peter. *Bibliotheca Sacra, 153,* 63–74.

Sly, D. (1992). Christian roots of wife abuse. *Guidance and Counselling, 8*(1), 26–34.

Small, D.H. (1981). Marriage. In M.C. Tenney (Ed.), *The Zondervan pictorial Bible dictionary* (pp. 511–513). Grand Rapids, MI: Zondervan Publishing House Corporation.

Smedes, L.B. (1984). *Forgive and forget: Healing the hurts we don't deserve.* San Francisco: Harper.

Smedes, L.B. (1996). *The art of forgiving: When you need to forgive and don't know how.* Nashville, TN: Moorings.

Smith, A. (1995). Born again, free from sin? Sexual violence in evangelical communities. In C.J. Adams & M.M. Fortune (Eds.), *Violence against women and children: A Christian theological sourcebook (pp. 339–350).* New York: Continuum.

Smith, G.A. (1898). *The book of the twelve prophets.* London: Hodder & Stoughton.

Snyder, C.R. (2002). Hope theory: Rainbows in the mind. *Psychological Inquiry, 13*(4), 249–275.

Snyder, C.R., Sigmon, D.R., & Feldman, D. (2002). Hope for the sacred and vice versa: Positive goal-directed thinking and religion. *Psychological Inquiry, 13,* 234–238.

Soeken, K.L., McFarlane, J., Parker, B., & Lominack, M.C. (1998). A clinical instrument to measure frequency, severity and perpetrator of abuse against women. In J. Campbell (Ed.), *Empowering survivors of abuse: Health care for battered women and their children* (pp. 195–203). London: Sage.

Sohn, S.T. (1999). I will be your God and you will be my people: The origin and background of the covenant formula. In *Ki baruch hu* (pp. 355–372). Warsaw, IN: Eisenbrauns.

Somer, E., & Braunstein, A. (1999). Are children exposed to interpersonal violence being psychologically maltreated? *Aggression and Violent Behavior, 4*(4), 449–456.

Sprenkle, D.H. (1994). Wife abuse through the lens of systems theory. *The Counseling Psychologist, 22*(4), 598–602.

Sprinkle, J. (1997). Old Testament perspectives on divorce and remarriage. *Journal of the Evangelical Theological Society, 40*(4), 529–550.

Spurgeon, C.C.H. (n.d.). Psalm the twenty-third. In *The treasury of David* (pp. 353–373). Peabody, MA: Hendrickson.

Sternberg, K.J., Lamb, M.E., Greenbaum, C., Dawud, S., Cortes, R.M., & Lorey, F. (1994). The effects of domestic violence on children's perceptions of their perpetrating parents. *International Journal of Behavioral Development, 17*(4), 779–795.

Stewart, D. (2004). *Refuge: A pathway out of domestic violence and abuse.* Birmingham, AL: New Hope Publishers.

Stiles, W.B. (1993). Quality control in qualitative research. *Clinical Psychology Review, 13,* 593–618.

Stoop, D., & Masteller, J. (1991). *Forgiving our parents, forgiving ourselves: Healing adult children of dysfunctional families.* Ann Arbor, MI: Servant Publications.

Stotland, N.L. (2000). Tug-of-war: Domestic abuse and the misuse of religion. *The American Journal of Psychiatry, 157*(5), 696–702.

Strauss, M. (2002). Luke. In C.E. Arnold (Ed.), *Zondervan illustrated Bible backgrounds commentary* (Vol. 1, pp. 318–515). Grand Rapids, MI: Zondervan Publishing House.

Strawbridge, W.J., Sherma, S.J., Cohen, R.S., & Kaplan, G.A. (2001). Religious attendance increases survival by improving and maintaining good health behaviors, mental health and social relationships. *Annals of Behavioral Medicine, 23*(1), 68–74.

Stuart, E.F. (1994). *Dissolution and annulment.* Sydney: Federation Press.

Sullivan, B. (2003). *Compassionate collaborative confrontation: Group processes with male perpetrators of domestic violence.* Paper presented at the Domestic Violence and Sexual Assault International Conference, Gold Coast, Australia.

Sullivan, C.M., Basta, J., Tan, C., & Davidson, W.S. (1992). After the crisis: A needs assessment of women leaving a domestic violence shelter. *Violence and Victims, 7*(3), 267–275.

Sweeney, M. (2000). The twelve prophets volume 2: Habakkuk. In D.W. Cotter (Ed.), *Berit olam: Studies in Hebrew narrative and poetry* (pp. 450–490). Collegeville, MN: The Liturgical Press.

Taylor, B. (2003). *Domestic violence: Safety and risk assessment.* Paper presented at the Domestic Violence and Sexual Assault International Conference, Gold Coast, Australia.

Taylor, R.S. (1967). The epistle to the Hebrews. In A.F. Harper, W.M. Greathouse, R. Earle & W.T. Purkiser (Eds.), *Beacon Bible commentary* (Vol. 10, pp. 17–183). Kansas City, MO: Beacon Hill Press.

Taylor, W.H. (1965). The epistle to the Ephesians. In A.F. Harper, W.M. Greathouse, R. Earle & W.T. Purkiser (Eds.), *Beacon Bible commentary* (Vol. 9, pp. 129–276). Kansas City, MO: Beacon Hill Press.

Tenney, M.C. (1981a). The gospel of John. In F.E. Gaebelein (Ed.), *The expositor's Bible commentary* (Vol. 9, pp. 3–203). Grand Rapids, MI: Zondervan Publishing House.

Tenney, M.C. (1981b). Gospels. In M.C. Tenney (Ed.), *The Zondervan pictorial Bible dictionary* (pp. 318–322). Grand Rapids, MI: Zondervan Publishing House.

Tenney, M.C. (1988). *John the gospel of belief: An analytic study of the text.* Grand Rapids, MI: William B. Eerdmans.

Thayer, J.H. (1996). *Thayer's Greek-English lexicon of the New Testament.* Peabody, MA: Hendrickson.

Thoresen, C.E., Harris, A.H.S., & Luskin, F. (2000). Forgiveness and health: An unanswered question. In M.E. McCullough, K.I. Pargament & C.E. Thoresen (Eds.), *Forgiveness: Theory, research, and practice* (pp. 254–280). New York: Guilford Press.

Thorne-Finch, R. (1992). *Ending the silence.* Toronto: University of Toronto Press.

Tidball, D.J. (1995). Practical and pastoral theology. In D.J. Atkinson & D.H. Field (Eds.), *New dictionary of Christian ethics and pastoral theology* (pp. 42–48). Leicester, UK: Inter-Varsity Press.

Tifft, L.L. (1993). *Battering of women: The failure of intervention and the case for prevention.* Oxford, UK: Westview Press.

Tix, A.P., & Frazier, P.A. (1998). The use of religious coping during stressful life events: Main effects, moderation, and mediation. *Journal of Counseling and Clinical Psychology, 66*(2), 411–422.

Toon, P. (1996). A sin which can be forgiven: Toward a biblical perspective on divorce and remarriage in the churches today. *Touchstone: A Journal of Ecumenical Orthodoxy, 9*(Fall), 17–20.

Towns, A., & Adams, P. (2000). If I really loved him enough, he would be okay. *Violence Against Women, 6*(6), 558–585.

Toy, C. (1899). *A critical and exegetical commentary on the book of Proverbs.* Edinburgh, UK: T & T Clark.

Tracy, S. (1999). Sexual abuse and forgiveness. *Journal of Psychology and Theology, 27*(3), 219–229.

Trumbull, H.C. (1896). *The threshold covenant.* Edinburgh, UK: T & T Clark.

Trumbull, H.C. (1975). *The blood covenant.* Kirkwood, MO: Impact Books Inc.

Trumbull, H.C. (1999). *The salt covenant.* Kirkwood, MO: Impact books Inc.

Trutza, P. (1975). Marriage. In M.C. Tenney (Ed.), *The Zondervan pictorial encyclopedia of the Bible* (pp. 92–102). Grand Rapids, MI: Zondervan Publishing House.

Turner, G.A. (1975). Repentance. In M.C. Tenney (Ed.), *The Zondervan pictorial encyclopedia of the Bible* (Vol. 5, pp. 62–64). Grand Rapids, MI: Zondervan Publishing House.

Twelve Tribes. (n.d.). *Marriage covenant.* Retrieved April 16, 2005 from http://www.twelve tribes.com//publications/marriagecovenant.html

Ulrich, Y.C. (1998). What helped most in leaving spouse abuse: Implications for interventions. In J. Campbell (Ed.), *Empowering survivors of abuse: Health care for battered women and their children* (pp. 70–80). Thousand Oaks, CA: Sage.

VanGemeren, W.A. (1991). Psalms. In F.E. Gaebelein (Ed.), *The expositor's Bible commentary* (Vol. 5, pp. 1–880). Grand Rapids, MI: Zondervan Publishing House.

Van Hook, M.P. (2000). Help seeking for violence: Views of survivors. *Journal of Women and Social Work, 15*(3), 390–419.

Van Leeuwen, M.S. (2004). Is equal regard in the Bible? In D. Blankenhorn, D. Browning & M.S. Van Leeuwen (Eds.), *Does Christianity teach male headship?* (pp. 13–22). Grand Rapids, MI: William B. Eerdmans.

Van Uden, M.H.F., & Pieper, J.Z.T. (1994). Mental health and religion: A theoretical survey. In H. Grzymala-Moszczynska & B. Beit-Hallahmi (Eds.), *Religion, psychopathology and coping* (pp. 35–55). Amsterdam: Rodopi.

Vandercreek, L., Nye, C., & Herth, K. (1994). Where there's life, there's hope, and where there is hope, there is... *Journal of Religion and Health, 33*(1), 51–59.

Vaughan, C. (1978). Colossians. In F.E. Gaebelein (Ed.), *The expositor's Bible commentary* (Vol. 11, pp. 161–226). Grand Rapids, MI: Zondervan Publishing House.

Vernon, A. (2004). Applications of rational-emotive behavior therapy with children and adolescents. In A. Vernon (Ed.), *Counseling children and adolescents* (3rd ed., pp. 163–187). Denver: Love Publishing Company.

VicHealth. (2004). *The health costs of violence: Measuring the burden of disease caused by intimate partner violence.* Carlton South: Victorian Health Promotion Foundation.

Victorian Council of Churches' Commission: Churches in Solidarity with Women. (1992). *Naming violence against women in our church communities.* Melbourne: CASA House.

Von Steen, P.G. (1997). Adults with witnessing histories: The overlooked victims of domestic violence. *Psychotherapy, 34*(4), 478–484.

Vondenberger, V. (2004). *Catholics, marriage and divorce: Real people, real questions.* Cincinnati, OH: St Anthony Messenger Press.

Vos, H.F. (1999). *Nelson's new illustrated Bible manners and customs.* Nashville, TN: Thomas Nelson.

Wade, C., & Tavris, C. (1996). *Psychology* (4th ed.). New York: Harper Collins.

Wade, G.W. (1911). *The book of the prophet Isaiah.* London: Methuen & Co.

Walker, L. (1979). *The battered woman.* New York: Harper Row.

Walker, L. (1984). *The battered woman syndrome.* New York: Springer Publishing.

Walker, L. (1993). The battered woman syndrome is a psychological consequence of abuse. In R.J. Gelles & D.R. Loseke (Eds.), *Current controversies on family violence* (pp. 133–153). Newbury Park, CA: Sage.

Walker, L. (1994). *Abused women and survivor therapy: A practical guide for the psychotherapist.* Washington: American Psychological Association.

Walker, L. (1995). Understanding battered woman syndrome. *Trial, 31*(2), 30–37.

Walker, L.E., & Meloy, J.R. (1998). Stalking and domestic violence. In J.R. Meloy (Ed.), *The psychology of stalking: Clinical and forensic perspectives* (pp. 140–161). San Diego, CA: Academic Press.

Walker, P., Bratton, T.E., & Acquaviva, D. (1998). Abuse and forgiveness. *The Other Side, 34*(1), 30–33.

Ward, D. (2000). Domestic violence as a cultic system. *Cultic Studies Journal, 17,* 42–55.

Warden, D. (1997). The words of Jesus on divorce. *Restoration Quarterly, 39*(3), 141–153.

Weaver, A.J. (1998). Mental health professionals working with religious leaders. In H.G. Koenig (Ed.), *Handbook of religion and mental health* (pp. 349–364). San Diego, CA: Academic Press.

Wenham, G.J. (1995). Divorce. In D.J. Atkinson & D.H. Field (Eds.), *New dictionary of Christian ethics and pastoral theology* (pp. 315–317). Leicester, UK: Inter-Varsity Press.

Werner-Wilson, R.J., Schindler-Zimmerman, T., & Whalen, D. (2000). Resilient response to battering. *Contemporary Family Therapy, 22*(2), 161–188.

Wessel, W.W. (1984). Mark. In F.E. Gaebelein (Ed.), *The expositor's Bible commentary* (Vol. 8, pp. 601–793). Grand Rapids, MI: Zondervan Publishing House.

White, A.W. (1998). The silent killer of Christian marriages. In C.C. Kroeger & J.R. Beck (Eds.), *Healing the hurting: Giving hope and help to abused women* (pp. 99–107). Grand Rapids, MI: Baker Books.

White, D.S. (1991). *Family violence in the Greater Darwin area: A call to Christian and community response*. Darwin: Uniting Church Australia Northern Synod Mission & Parish Services.

White, W. (1975). Staff. In M.C. Tenney (Ed.), *The Zondervan pictorial encyclopedia of the Bible* (Vol. 5, pp. 510–511). Grand Rapids, MI: Zondervan Publishing House.

Whybray, R.N. (1972). *The book of Proverbs*. Cambridge: Cambridge University Press.

Wiest, W.E., & Smith, E.A. (1990). *Ethics in ministry: A guide for the professional*. Minneapolis, MN: Fortress.

Wilkins, M.J. (2002). Matthew. In C.E. Arnold (Ed.), *Zondervan illustrated Bible backgrounds commentary* (Vol. 1, pp. 2–203). Grand Rapids, MI: Zondervan Publishing House.

Wilson, D. (1995). *Reforming marriage*. Moscow, ID: Canon Press.

Wilson, D. (1999a). *Federal husband*. Moscow, ID: Canon Press.

Wilson, D. (1999b). *Fidelity: What it means to be a one-woman man*. Moscow, ID: Canon Press.

Wilson, J. (1988). Why forgiveness requires repentance. *Philosophy, 63*, 534–535.

Wilson, K.J. (1997). *When violence begins at home: A comprehensive guide to understanding and ending domestic violence*. Alameda, CA: Hunter House.

Wilson, W.P. (1998). Religion and psychoses. In H.G. Koenig (Ed.), *Handbook of religion and mental health* (pp. 161–173). San Diego, CA: Academic Press.

Witkowski, T., & Stiensmeier-Pelster, J. (1998). Performance deficits following failure: Learned helplessness or self-esteem protection. *The British Journal of Social Psychology, 37*(1), 59–71.

Wittwer, T. (Ed.). (1995). *Domestic violence: Handbook for clergy and pastoral workers*. Adelaide, South Australia: Joint Churches Domestic Violence Prevention Programme.

Wolf, E.C. (1967). The book of Proverbs. In A.F. Harper, W.M. Greathouse, R. Earle & W.T. Purkiser (Eds.), *Beacon Bible commentary* (Vol. 3, pp. 453–544). Kansas City, MO: Beacon Hill Press.

Wolfe, D.A., Zak, L., Wilson, S., & Jaffe, P. (1986). Child witnesses to violence between parents: Critical issues in behavioral and social adjustment. *Journal of Abnormal Child Psychology, 14*(1), 95–104.

Wong-McDonald, A., & Gorsuch, R.L. (2000). Surrender to God: An additional coping style? *Journal of Psychology and Theology, 8*(2), 149–162.

Wood, A.S. (1978). Ephesians. In F.E. Gaebelein (Ed.), *The expositor's Bible commentary* (Vol. 11, pp. 3–92). Grand Rapids, MI: Zondervan Publishing House.

Wood, L.J. (1975). Rabbi. In M.C. Tenney (Ed.), *The Zondervan pictorial encyclopedia of the Bible* (Vol. 5, pp. 16). Grand Rapids, MI: Zondervan Publishing House.

Woodbridge, P.D. (1995). Repentance. In D.J. Atkinson & D.H. Field (Eds.), *New dictionary of Christian ethics and pastoral theology* (pp. 730–731). Leicester, UK: Inter-Varsity Press.

Worthington, E.L.J., Sandage, S.J., & Berry, J.W. (2000). Group interventions to promote forgiveness: What researchers and clinicians ought to know. In M.E. McCullough, K.I. Pargament & C.E. Thoresen (Eds.), *Forgiveness: Theory, research, and practice* (pp. 228–253). New York: Guilford Press.

Wortmann, S.L. (2003). *Sacred solace? Faith community responses to domestic violence*. Unpublished doctoral dissertation, University of Nebraska, Lincoln, USA.

Yahne, C.E., & Miller, W.R. (1999). Evoking hope. In W.R. Miller (Ed.), *Integrating spirituality into treatment: Resources for practitioners* (pp. 217–234). Washington: American Psychological Association.

Yllo, K. (1999). Wife rape: A social problem for the 21st century. *Violence Against Women, 59.*

Yoshihama, M., & Horrocks, J. (2002). Posttraumatic stress symptoms and victimization among Japanese American women. *Journal of Consulting and Clinical Psychology, 70*(1), 205–215.

Yost, B. (2003). *Factors influencing battered women's intentions to reject partner violence.* Chestnut Hill College.

Young, P.V. (1966). *Scientific social surveys and research* (4th ed.). New Jersey: Prentice Hall.

Youngblood, R.F. (1992). 1, 2 Samuel. In F.E. Gaebelein (Ed.), *The expositor's Bible commentary* (Vol. 3, pp. 551–1104). Grand Rapids, MI: Zondervan Publishing House.

Yule, W. (1998). Posttraumatic stress disorder in children and its treatment. In T. Miller (Ed.), *Children of trauma: Stressful life events and their effects on children and adolescents* (pp. 219–243). Madison, CT: International Universities Press.

Zodhiates, S. (1984a). *What about divorce?* Chattanooga, TN: AMG publishers.

Zodhiates, S. (1984b). *May I divorce and remarry?* Chattanooga, TN: AMG Publishers.

Zodhiates, S. (Ed.). (1991). *The complete word study New Testament.* Iowa, USA: World Bible Publishers.

Zodhiates, S. (Ed.). (1992). *The complete word study dictionary: New Testament.* Chattanooga: AMG International Inc.

CPSIA information can be obtained at www.ICGtesting.com
Printed in the USA
LVOW111432150512

281812LV00001B/160/P